AMERICAN ROMANTICISM

Volume 2
From Melville to James

AMERICAN ROMANTICISM

Volume 2

FROM MELVILLE TO JAMES

The Enduring Excessive

David Morse

BARNES & NOBLE BOOKS
TOTOWA, NEW JERSEY

© David Morse 1987

All rights reserved.

First published in the USA 1987 by
BARNES & NOBLE BOOKS
81 ADAMS DRIVE
TOTOWA, NEW JERSEY 07512

ISBN 0–389–20586–9, vol. 1
ISBN 0–389–20587–7, vol. 2

Printed in Hong Kong

Library of Congress Cataloging-in-Publication Data
Morse, David.
American Romanticism.
Contents: 1. From Cooper to Hawthorne – excessive America – 2. From Melville to James – the enduring excessive.
   1. American literature – History and criticism.
2. Romanticism – United States.   I. Title.
PS169.R6M67 1985   810'.9'145   85–13424
ISBN 0–389–20586–9 (vol. 1)
ISBN 0–389–20587–7 (vol. 2)

'Beware the pine-tree's withered branch!'
'Beware the awful avalanche!'
This was the peasant's last Goodnight.
A voice replied, far up the height,
'Excelsior!'
                              (Longfellow)

Contents

List of Plates   viii

Preface   ix

1   Introduction: After the Civil War   1

2   Herman Melville: 'Scaffoldings Scaling Heaven'   11

3   Mark Twain: the Torture of Excess   80

4   Henry James: Refusing the Limit   115

Notes   184

Index   188

List of Plates

1 Frederic Edwin Church's *Rainy Season in the Tropics* (The Fine Arts Museum of San Francisco)
2 *The Republican Party Going to the Right House*: from a contemporary campaign cartoon published by Currier & Ives
3a Matthew Brady's *Lincoln in Washington, 1862* (from the Ostendorf Collection)
3b The seated Lincoln in Grant Park, Chicago (by kind permission of the Chicago Historical Society, photograph by Kaufman and Labry, 1929)
4 The frontispiece to Mark Twain's *A Tramp Abroad* (1880)

Preface

These studies in American Romanticism draw on the general analysis of Romanticism presented in my *Perspectives on Romanticism* and *Romanticism: A Structural Analysis* and develop it in another cultural context. Although America's classic literature has not invariably been termed 'Romantic' there are not only strong grounds for doing so, as I hope to show, but equally for thinking that, of all societies, the United States is the one that has been most deeply marked by the impact of Romanticism. I should like to thank Bob Gross, Peter Nicholls, Angus Ross, Douglas Tallack and John Whitley for their helpfulness in reading and responding to sections of the manuscript. I am conscious of a particular debt to Bob Gross for the stimulus of his presence at Sussex in 1982–3 and especially for the fascinating seminars he gave as part of the 'Literature and Democracy' course. The texts I have used are specified in the notes at the end, but for clarity and convenience page references to the most copiously cited works are given immediately after the appropriate quotation.

D.M.

1 Introduction: After the Civil War

The Civil War changed America irrevocably. Formerly it had seemed as if the United States could accommodate an infinity of warring sects and tendencies, as if an expanding America could have no limits either spatial or spiritual, as if the saturnalia of the spirit announced by Emerson would have no end. Now the Union itself had been placed in mortal jeopardy. With immediate retrospective hindsight it seemed that this crisis had always been looming up menacingly on the horizon as an inevitable consequence of the extremism of the age. Henceforth, despite lip-service to a pluralist ideal, diversity would always be laden with implications of division. As the Star-Spangled Banner was called upon to envelop a body in rags and tatters, Americans would be the more censorious about possible infamies beneath. The Civil War also put in question the cherished assumption that the United States as a democratic society was destined to occupy a uniquely privileged place amongst nations, since it would therefore be spared the violence generated by the monarchies and hierarchies of Europe. The model of a confident, progressive America symbolically pitted against the Old World had the effect of symbolically unifying the United States itself. Now it had to be faced that the nation was deeply divided, that it had *not* been spared the ravages of war, that faith in the United States as a source of unequivocal, unimpeachable values was imperilled, that the land of democracy could itself be unjust. The erection of the Statue of Liberty in 1884 was something more than a simple reaffirmation of America; it was an attempt to put back all that the Civil War had taken away. After the Civil War, America faced the future in a sober and chastened mood, beneath which many bitternesses and resentments still rankled.

A suggestive instance of the many ways in which American identity came to be rethought in the post-war decades is William

Dean Howells's novel *A Foregone Conclusion*, published in 1882. The novel, set in Venice at the outbreak of the Civil War, centres on the experience of Ferris, the American consul – a post that Howells himself held during the war years. So the novel is a backward glance to the mood of the pre-war era that can at the same time embrace the war itself as agent and architect of change. To Howells, as to Twain or James, the earlier 'innocent' America now seemed impossibly remote – to have become almost another place altogether. What now defined the United States was its capacity for rapid technological and industrial change. Its representative figure was no longer the general on horseback or the poet in his shirt sleeves, but the inventor in his workshop. *A Foregone Conclusion* was written in the wake of an impressive series of American scientific discoveries, all with immense practical consequences – the Bell telephone in 1876, Edison's invention of the phonograph in 1878 and of the electric light bulb the following year. Howells looked back to the pre-war era through the eyes of the wizard of Menlo Park.

In *A Foregone Conclusion* Ferris, as American consul, finds himself besieged by an eager horde of European adventurers, mostly army officers, who fondly imagine that they have only to present themselves in order to be offered the most exalted positions of command in the Union armed forces. The most improbable of these supplicants is a mournful looking priest, called Don Ippolito, who understands so little of the war that he believes it is being fought against South Americans and who brings with him a beautifully constructed model of his own contribution to the war effort: a breech-loading cannon, which can be blown up via explosive placed in a secret chamber, if there is any danger of it falling into enemy hands. Though Don Ippolito is thus strikingly set apart from his confrères in the Italian Church by this pronounced mechanical bent, Ferris nevertheless sees him as a dreamy and impractical idealist, who understands all too little of the real world. This view is confirmed when, on a visit to Don Ippolito's lodgings, he is shown such things as an unsuccessful attempt at a new type of steam propulsion, a perpetual-motion experiment and a flying-machine, of which Don Ippolito says, 'Fantastic researches in the impossible. I never expected results from these experiments, with which I nevertheless once pleased myself.'[1]

Yet his other inventions seem scarcely more practical or

commercially viable: portable furniture, a movable bridge, a submarine boat, a camera for self-portraiture. To Ferris, Don Ippolito is an innocent hoping to make his way in an American world far more ruthless and hard-headed than he can possibly envisage, so that, even if any of his inventions *were* any good, he would still flounder amidst patent laws and start-up costs, certain to be outwitted by businessmen more astute and resourceful than he. But Ferris has been asked by Mrs Vervain, a scatterbrained but wealthy American widow, to find a suitable tutor for her beautiful daughter, Florida, one who can be relied upon not to make any advances to her. Since Don Ippolito is debarred from such forward behaviour by his vocation and since he also speaks English, albeit with a strong Irish accent, he seems the logical solution to the problem. Ferris himself falls in love with Florida, but he is so irritated by her haughty manner and disturbed by her unpredictable temper that, instead of revealing his feelings to her, he responds by being distant and by treating her mother in an off-hand, patronising manner. Don Ippolito is also powerfully attracted to Florida, and in consequence his priestly vocation, which he has already begun to doubt, is placed under even more of a strain. He is eventually encouraged to lay bare his soul and confess his crisis of religious faith to her. Although Florida is confused and disturbed by this, she nevertheless feels sorry for him and wishes to help him. It is agreed between her mother and herself that Don Ippolito will accompany them on their return to America and they will help to establish him there as an inventor. Don Ippolito now tells Florida he loves her – a feeling which she cannot reciprocate. The Vervains leave Venice abruptly, and as Don Ippolito watches their gondola depart he is astonishingly and ironically stabbed by a madman, who exclaims to him, 'Dog of a priest!'[2] Ferris returns to the United States and enlists in the army as a second lieutenant. He is wounded in the arm and nearly loses it. Ferris's first loyalty is to painting, his original vocation. He has continued to paint whilst in Venice, and after the war he is encouraged to put on show some of the pictures he painted there, including one of Don Ippolito. His exhibition is visited by the Vervains and this time Ferris is finally able to tell Florida that he loves her and to make a proposal of marriage to her, which she accepts. It is as if Don Ippolito has brought them together.

Clearly *A Foregone Conclusion* is designed to develop a contrast between the Old World and the New, and so to foreground the virtues of the latter. Don Ippolito's life is mapped out for him by his family at an early age, and he is entered for the priesthood even though he is clearly unsuited to it for a multitude of reasons. His misdirected attempts at invention nevertheless suggest that he possesses a creative potential that can never come to fruition in the discouraging environment of Europe, but which might be able to find both a stimulus and an outlet in the context of the United States. There he could not but be brought into a relation with the future. Had Don Ippolito never met Florida Vervain, he might well have continued in a path at variance with his own deepest instincts, content to live out a lie to the bitter end without much concern for truth or consequences. The encounter with Florida jolts him out of his accustomed routine and forces him to question the most basic assumptions of his existence. Within the hidebound and constricted persona of an Italian priest the free and spontaneous soul of a potential American is struggling to get out, like a brilliant butterfly from the chrysalis. Yet it is probably already too late for Don Ippolito. His education into unworldliness has already been such as to disable him for life. He would not be equipped to face the vigorous but equal struggle of the New World. He would scarcely be able to make a go of it. Yet in some oblique way the tragic fate of Don Ippolito seems to cast a shadow over the future of the United States also: it is as if the land that once held out a bright promise to everyone who would cross the Atlantic has now become the scene of a ruthless battle for existence, in which the prospects may still be brilliant, but only for the indomitable, inexorable few. Forced to sink or swim, the eccentric priest would, equally inexorably, drift to the bottom.

The experience of war alters Ferris's perception of his own role in the affair. At the end of the Civil War he comes north 'sick and maimed and poor'.[3] He is now conscious of how much time he had wasted in Venice – time that he could have put to good use in developing and practising his skills as a painter. He recognises that his behaviour towards both Florida and Don Ippolito was lacking both in frankness and generosity of spirit. At the time he had no conception of the desperate urgency of life. It is the hardship and suffering of war itself that has brought him to face it. When one of Ferris's friends, concerned at his plight, expresses an interest in seeing some of his sketches, Ferris responds, 'I brought back a lot of sketches and studies. I'm sorry to say that I loafed a good deal there; I used to feel that I had eternity before me; and I was a purist and an idiot generally.'⁴ It is as if he has been a secret sharer in the dreamy, impractical mood epitomised by Don Ippolito, as if he too has been tentative and nebulous in his aims, where he should have been forceful and direct. Don Ippolito is Ferris's unlooked-for double, and Ferris's picture of him serves as an ambiguous reminder of a Venice which may have often been truly idyllic, but which was dangerously remote from the realities of the strenuous American world. If Ferris and his wife feel the need to return to Venice, it is because they are compelled to purge themselves of all retrospection and nostalgia for a way of life which they know has vanished for ever. At bottom, what Don Ippolito represents is not only feudal Europe, but equally the naïvety and innocence of young America, when vast and unrealisable schemes could be optimistically promoted with no thought for the conflict looming.

Whether a man such as Don Ippolito, whose whole being is so much at odds with the institutional structures within which he must live out his life in Europe, could ever actually be at home in the USA is not just an academic question about Don Ippolito. It is one that necessarily raises further questions about the American future. From the point of view of 1861 the priest's hopes seem simultaneously understandable and misplaced:

> Heaven only knows what kind of inventor's Utopia our poor, patent-ridden country appeared to him in these dreams of his, and I can but dimly figure it to myself. But he might very naturally desire to come to a land where the spirit of invention is recognised and fostered, and where he could hope to find that comfort of incentive and companionship which our artists find in Italy.⁵

So at the back of the narrative lies a figure of exchange: as Ferris is to Italy so should Don Ippolito be to the United States. But in the dreary aftermath of war the very idea of such a man as Don Ippolito coming to seek his destiny there seems so improbable and so absurd that Ferris is incredulous that Florida could have entertained the idea even for one moment: '"It's amazing, Florida," he would say, "it's perfectly amazing that you should have been willing to undertake the job of importing into America that poor fellow with his whole stock of helplessness and unpracticality. What *were* you about?"'⁶

It is the Civil War itself which produces this sharpened sense of impossibility. In the pre-war decades, when America was awash with innumerable schemes, nostrums and projects for reform, Don Ippolito might have blended into the background – if he was impractical he would not have been a lot more impractical than anybody else. After the war this distinctive combination of idealism, fervour and vagueness was no longer acceptable. Don Ippolito might stand as representative of the type of person who would have embarked on some Utopian experiment, at Brook Farm or elsewhere, with all kinds of hopeful ideas in his head, only to find the experience more daunting than he had expected. Even Octavius Brooks Frothingham, one of the most stalwart survivors of the Transcendental years, author of that definitive retrospect *Transcendentalism in New England*, felt in duty bound to concede that 'Transcendentalism certainly did produce its share of idle, dreamy, useless people', though he went on immediately to add, 'its legitimate fruit was earnestness, aspiration and enthusiastic energy'.[7]

We may note that this admission occurs in a chapter entitled 'Practical Tendencies', which seems to have been included precisely to rebut the universal assumption that with such a movement as Transcendentalism there could, on principle, have been none. Like Transcendentalism, Don Ippolito is a vivid yet transitory phenomenon who seems to have left no visible trace on the world, save some appealing, slightly disconcerting memories. That which once was so palpably, inescapably present has suddenly been consigned to the past. Ferris and Florida are no longer the same people, and nor, for that matter, are Octavius Brooks Frothingham and William Dean Howells. At times Frothingham can be startlingly censorious. He concludes the chapter 'Practical Tendencies' by saying,

> The Transcendentalist was satisfied with nothing so long as it did not correspond to the ideal in the enlightened soul; and in the soul recognized the power to make all things new. Nothing will content him short of the absolute right, the eternally true, the unconditioned excellence. He prays for the kingdom of Heaven, lives in expectation of it; would not be surprised at its coming any day. . . . Hence his boundless enthusiasm and hope; hence the ardor of his feeling, the glow of his language. Hence his disposition to exaggerate the force of tendencies that

point in his direction; to take the brightest view of events, and to put the happiest construction on the signs of the times. In the anti-slavery period the Transcendentalist glorified the negro beyond all warrant of fact, seeing in him an imprisoned soul struggling to be free. The same soul he sees in women oppressed by limitations; the same in the drunkard, the gambler, the libertine. His eye is ever fixed on the future.[8]

Frothingham is writing in 1876, only ten years after the end of the Civil War and the emancipation of black people, the consummation for which so many Transcendentalists had longed, yet he is able to take it completely for granted – so much so that he does not even bother to argue a case – that the black man is an entirely lost cause. Transcendental hopes were doubtless all very fine and noble in their day, but now they can be packed away in the old oak chest on the landing, like dresses too grand for everyday wear. The Gilded Age prides itself on being realistic and down-to-earth. People have too many pressing problems of a mundane nature to concern themselves overmuch with the fanciful reveries of a bygone idealism. America doubtless still has a future and an imposing future at that, but no one seriously imagines that it is to be the arena where the prophecies of Emerson and Whitman will finally be realised, where spirit and steamboat will be one. As Oliver Wendell Holmes tersely put it, 'Extravagances of opinion cure themselves. Time wore off the effects of the harmless debauch, and restored the giddy revellers to the regimen of sober thought, as reformed spiritual inebriates.'[9] Now that it was abundantly clear that reality would *not* tend toward the idea, it was up to the idea to cope with this new dispensation as best it could.

The clearest evidence of this more sober national mood is to be found in the image of Lincoln as cultural hero. As Richard Hofstadter has pointed out in *The American Political Tradition*,

> The Lincoln legend has come to have a hold on the American imagination that defies comparison with anything else in political mythology. Here is a drama in which a great man shoulders the torment and moral burdens of a blundering and sinful people, suffers for them, and redeems them with hallowed Christian virtues – 'malice toward none and charity for all' – and is destroyed at the pitch of his success. The worldly-wise

John Hay, who knew him about as well as he permitted himself to be known, called him 'the greatest character since Christ', a comparison one cannot imagine being made of any other political figure of modern times.[10]

What needs to be stressed in not simply the ease with which Lincoln is made to eclipse such illustrious predecessors in the American pantheon as Washington and Jackson, but the way in which this symbolic representation of Lincoln marks a radical departure from the values of the pre-war era. In his biography of Lincoln, Herndon writes, 'He was not impulsive, fanciful, or imaginative; but cold, calm and precise.'[11]

Whatever Lincoln may have been, he was certainly not a Transcendentalist. While in former times the hero would have been, almost by definition, a man proud, even overbearing, a charismatic figure utterly convinced of his own righteousness, absolutely intransigent, never prone to doubt – a Jackson, or a John Brown – Lincoln was never this. Where they pressed on unrelentingly, Lincoln hesitated; where they sought to intensify conflict, he strove to moderate it; where they were convinced of their mission, he doubted his; where they were arrogant and flamboyant, he was unpretentious and humble, even shabbily dressed. For Herndon it was Lincoln's slow, torpid disposition in an era of fiery, volcanic personalities that actually saved the day:

> Had it not been for his conservative statesmanship, his supreme confidence in the wisdom of the people, his extreme care in groping his way among facts and before ideas, this nation might have been two governments today. The low and feeble circulation of his blood; his healthful irritability, which responded so slowly to the effect of stimuli; the strength of his herculean frame; his peculiar organism, conserving its force; his sublime patience; his wonderful endurance; his great hand and heart, saved this country from division, when division meant its irreparable ruin.[12]

Lincoln's greatness lay in his ability to work against the grain, to be patient at a time when dramatic cries had a more obvious appeal, and in the immense care he took to avoid an irreparable step or any action that might make a difficult situation worse. The tradition of artistic representation that has grown up around

Lincoln is at pains to moderate anything in him that might seem excessive – especially, of course, his great height, which, in pre-war days made him an especially apt subject for caricature. With his brooding, saturnine countenance and towering stature Lincoln cannot fail to be prepossessing, yet the artists who have depicted him have deliberately striven to avoid presenting him in this light. If Lincoln is to be a Titan he will be an unexpectedly humanised one, devoid of the grandiose or theatrical gesture, and thus it is that he is invariably presented in an undemonstrative pose with his head reflectively bent forward. In the most famous images of him, whether the photograph by Matthew Brady, or the sculptures by Saint-Gaudens and Warren Chester French, he is seated. In this way Lincoln is made more intimate and more familiar, which also becomes a way of suggesting how little he needs to impress. He is, as it were, impressive of himself. In his seated, calm, essentially reasonable posture, Lincoln shows himself to be more the thinker than the man of action. In the sculpture of Warren Chester French he seems, from his judgement seat, to reproach a nation that has so imperfectly followed his example. His is not the greatness of egoistical self-assertion but the moral greatness that sees more than one point of view, that strives both to encompass and overcome division. Under the brooding, sorrowful gaze of Lincoln an excessive America is chastened and finally learns restraint.

But, while Lincoln might be taken to represent unequivocally all that was best in American culture, the redefinition, or, more properly, renewed definition, in terms of technological progress and a business civilisation aroused greater unease. Of the American writers discussed in this volume, Melville, Twain and James, only Melville was a survivor of the Transcendental era and a writer closely associated with the 'young America' period, yet all three sense a hollowness and aridity at the heart of American culture, expressed in texts as diverse as *The Confidence-Man, A Connecticut Yankee in King Arthur's Court* and *The Golden Bowl*. *The Confidence-Man* in particular signals a collapse in the old faith in the essential virtuousness of democratic man, which had been fuelled not only by the American sense of mission but also by English Romantic poetry. Melville still wanted to believe in this himself, as *Billy Budd* demonstrates, but symptomatic of his scepticism in *The Confidence-Man* is the poem discovered on a small handbill entitled:

ODE
ON THE INTIMATIONS
OF
DISTRUST IN MAN
UNWILLINGLY INFERRED FROM REPEATED REPULSES,
IN DISINTERESTED ENDEAVOURS
TO PROCURE HIS
CONFIDENCE[13]

In *A Connecticut Yankee* the old chivalry, loyalty and faith of English culture, though presented as irrational and absurd, nevertheless suggest by implication that something is missing from Hank Morgan's vision of things, whilst the American city of *The Golden Bowl* is scarcely to be conceived of as a city on a hill. What is also noticeable, after the Civil War, is that it becomes more difficult for writers to present characters who can be seen as truly representative. *The Confidence-Man* is notoriously decentred – unlike *Pierre*, for example, which does offer a clear protagonist – whilst in *Israel Potter* the hero can only be an impossible anachronism, a Rip Van Winkle figure. In designating Hank Morgan as a 'Connecticut' Yankee Twain also manages to suggest that the word 'Yankee' itself cannot now be used with much confidence that anyone will have a clear idea what is meant, or whether it is being used positively or derogatorily. In *The Golden Bowl* the more positive and more negative aspects of American life seem to be split between the Ververs: Adam represents the new powerful business civilisation, Maggie the old America of innocence and trust.

Nevertheless Melville, Twain and James endeavour to maintain the high Transcendental claims for the soul, the refusal of all arbitrary limits in an era that is infinitely less receptive to them. They employ modes of writing that are themselves hyperbolic and excessive. So, just where rupture might have been expected, a tradition becomes established that continues into the twentieth century, a tradition whose ramifications are too complex to examine here but whose visibility can be acknowledged simply by referring to such texts as *The Great Gatsby*, *On the Road* and *Catch 22*. This excessive writing is the most enduring legacy of young America.

2 Herman Melville: 'Scaffoldings Scaling Heaven'

Of all American writers none is more defiantly and persistently excessive than Melville. From the very outset Melville, almost as a matter of course, arrogated to himself a quite extraordinary freedom. He is one of the very first writers to grasp that the newly opened-up intellectual and imaginative space of literature permits the writer to assume any role he pleases, and that part of his implicit contract with the unwitting reader is that he may play the pied piper and lead his followers a merry dance along a route that is both unpredictable and potentially destructive. Melville never defers to the expectations of the reader but consistently imposes upon him, trying his patience, his credulity and his tolerance to the very limit. Yet Melville's excessiveness is not simply an imaginative bravado; it is importantly bound up with his claims to speak the truth. What makes Melville outrageous is that he always insists on the truthfulness of his most shameless and whimsical fabrications, like an inebriated anecdotalist who thumps the bar and dares anyone to contradict him. Yet Melville is always deadly serious, and the frantic counterbidding that results between imaginative licence on the one hand and veracity on the other produces endlessly spiralling structures that defy all limits, that are truly 'scaffoldings scaling heaven' (*Mardi*, p. 600). What makes Melville's novels genuinely deceptive and therefore provocative is that their apparent stability of viewpoint, 'guaranteed' by an assertive and confiding narrator, invariably dissolves into a complex and many-sided dialogue that Melville carries on with himself, so that the reader is gradually transformed into a puzzled voyeur.

The riddling and Byzantine nature of Melvillean narrative was apparent from the very outset with Melville's broadly autobiographical tale of adventures in the South Seas, *Typee*. *Typee* was written with unlooked-for virtuosity for a tyro author. Its style, at once allusive, discursive and self-confidently elaborate, adroitly shifting between the registers of genial humour, poetic description and moral outrage, was hardly that to be expected from the common seaman that Melville presented himself as being. On the other hand, by a cunningly placed parenthetical reference early on to his shipmate Toby – 'Toby, like myself, had evidently moved in a different sphere of life' (p. 32) – he made it abundantly clear that he was in fact a gentleman and thus not unjustified in his literary and moral pretensions. This joint ascription is especially well calculated because it precedes their decision to jump ship. Under other circumstances a 'rover' and a deserter would be amongst the least trusted of men. But a young gentleman of refined background might reasonably be expected to baulk at the rigours and injustices of the naval life. But it is symptomatic of Melville's desire to be believed that he is careful to avoid presenting himself as a rover, although he made no bones about it at all in *Omoo* by indicating this in the very title. Yet on the other hand his presentation of himself as a bluff sailor so inured to marvels as scarcely to need to exaggerate them is undermined by the reader's clear deduction that he is in fact nothing of the sort but rather a genteel novice, who might have every reason to embroider and exaggerate his experiences with a view to furthering a literary career. Which, of course, was exactly what Melville did. The credibility of *Typee* is effectively underpinned by Melville's belief that he could get his readers to think of him as being *both* bluff sailor and responsible gentleman, without worrying too much about any possible contradiction between them.

Melville stretched his experiences among the Typees of the Marquesas by exaggerating the length of his stay there, by artfully deploying knowledge of the islanders gleaned from other books and by deliberately idealising their mode of life. Given his desire to turn this episode in his life into a readable narrative, it was a feasible strategy. But for a first-hand report from remote parts it is a curiously literary performance, not simply in style but in the way it becomes a conscious evocation of the simple uncorrupted life as dreamed by Dr Johnson and Rousseau. Melville under the palm trees recalls an Emerson insisting that the individual consult no oracle other than his own genius while laboriously transcribing chunks of wisdom from the great minds of the past. But, of course, stereotyping becomes an important way of enhancing Melville's own credibility, since the conformity of his narrative to certain given notions of the savage life will tend to make it seem more authoritative. From the reader's point of view, much of the delight of *Typee* is that the exotic agenda adumbrated at the beginning –

> Hurra, my lads! It's a settled thing; next week we shape our course to the Marquesas! The Marquesas! What strange visions of outlandish things does the very name spirit up! Naked houris – cannibal banquets – groves of cocoa-nut – coral reefs – tattooed chiefs – and bamboo temples; sunny valleys planted with bread-fruit-trees – carved canoes dancing on the flashing blue waters – savage woodlands guarded by horrible idols – *heathenish rites and human sacrifices*   (p. 5)

– is fully confirmed in the pages that follow, through descriptions that live up to the myth, though all the while Melville is earnestly disclaiming any such intention. The excessive has its own weird plausibility – if only it is excessive enough!

Typee initiates a protracted struggle in Melville's writing between sober fact and exuberant fiction that is most sharply focused in *Moby-Dick* but which echoes and resounds through every work that he wrote. On the one hand Melville tirelessly insists on the veracity of what he sets before the reader, and when caught straying from the paths of righteousness returns to his task in chastened and abstemious mood, yet at the same time he delights in the imaginative freedom that the fictive offers him and secretly exults in his transgressions. In *Typee* Melville is categorical that his narration is entirely literal – 'He has stated matters just as they occurred, and leaves every one to form his own opinion concerning them; trusting that his anxious desire to speak the unvarnished truth will gain for him the confidence of his readers' (p. xiv) – yet he freely admits that the incidents he describes have aroused a lively interest at sea when 'spun as a yarn' (p. xiii). So *Typee* is truth and yarn at one and the same time and Melville's ingenious presentation of his case encourages his auditors to make every allowance for a certain poetic licence without doubting that the basic facts are indeed as he narrates them – the unvarnished truth indeed, but with a layer of varnish over the top. So that the distinction Melville makes between style and content offers a full and definitive resolution of every conundrum that his narrative poses. The reader need feel no guilt when yielding to delight in the undoubted excesses that he encounters, for they are simply an aesthetic frisson induced by a particular mode of presentation. The Utopia of the South Seas that Melville offers can be experienced through a willing suspension of disbelief that can be yielded the more freely if only because it is grounded in genuine circumstance. Melville, alas, makes it all too apparent that the delight of travel books is that they allow the boundary between fact and fiction to be deliciously blurred.

It was scarcely surprising that Melville's early reviewers should have been puzzled and provoked by his style of address in *Typee* or that they should have been forced to speculate about the character and class of the man who wrote it. Even the reviewer for the *Spectator*, who was probably amongst the more credulous, if only because he was willing to believe that it was the product of 'a reading sailor spinning a yarn',[1] despite Melville's abundant attempts to prove otherwise, stated, 'Yet we should like to have the story of the book; to have known the motives of its publication',[2] thus indicating that the book really required another narrative to set it in its proper context – a 'Story of Toby' perhaps, but one written by Toby himself and supported by authentic affidavits. As it was he felt bound to guard against any possibility of deception, by conceding that 'Much of the book is not beyond the range of invention'[3] – though such a *caveat* was virtually valueless, since it tended to suggest that the travel narrative, like the story of Christ, was most plausible where most impossible. Other critics, flatteringly, were less inclined to believe that Melville was quite what he claimed to be – in the Preface at least. Detecting Melville's precocious mastery of style, the London reviewers of *John Bull* and the *Critic* were inclined to suspect a joint venture between sailor and man of letters. The former suggested,

> Like Robinson Crusoe, however, we cannot help suspecting that if there be really such a person as Herman Melville, he has either employed a Daniel Defoe to describe his adventures, or is himself both a Defoe and an Alexander Selkirk.[4]

But the critic in *The Times* was so impressed by Melville's literacy as to question the veracity of his narrative altogether:

We have been somewhat prolix in the narration of this history; first because the book of Mr Melville is really a very clever production; and, secondly, because it is introduced to the English public as authentic, which we by no means think it to be. We have called Mr Melville a common sailor; but he is a very uncommon common sailor, even for America, whose mariners are better educated than our own. In his own province, the voyages of Cook, Carteret, Byron, Kotzebue, and Vancouver are familiar to him; he can talk glibly of Count Buffon and Baron Cuvier, and critically, when he likes, of Teniers. His descriptions of scenery are lifelike and vigorous, sometimes masterly, and his style throughout is rather that of an educated literary man than of a poor outcast working seaman on board of a South Sea whaler.[5]

Yet, sceptic that he was, even the *Times* critic was not led to distrust Melville's motives, but evidently regarded *Typee* as a worthy, if fictional, attempt to present a case for the South Sea islanders and to plead for a less drastic mode of Christianisation. So we must conclude that, in the final analysis, Melville was saved by his moralising. Had he simply described the erotic charms of the lovely Fayaway and the delights of a life without toil he might well have been dismissed as an irresponsible hedonist, but by urgently proselytising the cause of the primitive he could appear as the eloquent advocate of the people without a voice. So, if behind the common sailor we glimpse the gentleman, we can perceive him in turn as only a mouthpiece through which the authentic voice of nature speaks.

But, despite Melville's worthy moral purpose, his reviewers nevertheless found his style excessive. The *Critic* observed, 'The incidents, no doubt, are sometimes exaggerated, and the colouring is often overcharged'[6], while the *Examiner* found 'a little colouring . . . here and there'[7]. *Graham's Magazine*, though giving Melville the benefit of the doubt, wryly invoked his 'strength in drawing the long bow of travellers',[8] while for the *United States Magazine and Democratic Review* it was such as to 'task the credulity of most plain matter of fact people'.[9] The New York *Evangelist*, with an axe to grind, did not mince matters: 'If this be not sheer romance (which there is reason to suspect) it is the extremely exaggerated, but racily-written narrative of a forecastle-runaway.'[10]

But, apart from the missionaries and their support organisations, there was no one who had a special interest in whether or not Melville was telling the truth. Thus they were not disposed to indulge in any irritable searching after fact but were happy just to sit back and be, in the most literal sense, transported. For those who cared, there was always the provenance provided by Murray's Home and Colonial Library, which had featured such illustrious precursors as Borrow's *The Bible in Spain*, not to mention Wiley and Putnam's Library of American Books. Further, the dedication to Lemuel Shaw, Chief Justice of the Commonwealth of Massachusetts, strongly suggested that Melville was, more or less, upon oath. But Margaret Fuller, perhaps the wisest as well as amongst the most indulgent of Melville's readers, suggested that the facticity of Melville's tale was neither here nor there. Very likely part of it was well grounded, but it should be perceived as 'the record of imaginary adventures by someone who has visited those regions'.[11] *Typee* should simply be enjoyed, and should be placed within the frankly fictional context of Johnson's *Rasselas* or Othello's tales that so bewitched Desdemona. It is entertainment and enchantment that matters – not truth.

Melville was greatly irked by the fact that so many of his reviewers – the American ones especially – were determined not to be taken in by his romance of real life. Receiving an abridged account of his adventures in *Chambers's Edinburgh Journal*, he

> could not but feel heartily vexed, that while the intelligent Editors of a publication like that should thus endorse the genuineness of the narrative – so many numbskulls on this side of the water should heroically avow their determination not to be 'gulled by it'. The fact is, those who do not believe it are the greatest 'gulls' – fully fledged ones too.[12]

Yet, from another point of view, Melville's reviewers were quite surprisingly indulgent, since scarcely any questioned that his tale was substantially true, and the real puzzle is why they should have found it so generally believable. The obvious answer would be to say that *Typee* itself bears the stamp of truth, that it conveys an authenticity and circumstantiality of detail of the sort that cannot be feigned. But it might be equally pertinent to suggest that Melville's peculiar achievement was to provide a picture which synthesised imaginative projections about the nature of the primitive life with the more documentary records of discovery and exploration – not that, in any event, a very hard and fast distinction could be made between them, since all who encountered the primitive would be disposed to interpret it in terms of their preconstruction of it as 'happy', 'savage', or both. Everyone from Melville to his readers interpreted the Typee against some kind of background, and it is in the relation of *Typee* to this background that its 'truth' largely consists. The idyllic nature of life amongst the Typees is oddly supported by the difficulty of reaching them through mountainous country and extensive thickets, which symbolically can explain how such a peculiarly fortunate mode of life came to be preserved. Milton's Garden of Eden, after all, had 'hairy sides' and Johnson's Happy Valley was similarly cut off from the world. Moreover, within the frame provided by literary tradition Melville's eagerness to leave the Typees would not have seemed so improbable, even leaving the vexed question of cannibalism aside, since Rasselas rapidly tired of the Happy Valley and sought every means of escape since

> I can discover within me no power of perception which is not glutted with its proper pleasure, yet I do not find myself delighted. Man has surely some latent sense for which this place affords no gratification, or he has some desires distinct from sense which must be satisfied before he can be happy.[13]

One of the things that can make Paradise plausible is to find it not straightforward and uniform but multi-faceted and beset by contradictions. In this sense Melville's *Typee* becomes *denser* the more contradictory it is.

Melville's idyllic presentation of the Typees is as carefully set up as Scott's introduction of his picturesque Highlanders in *Waverley*. For what characterises his early experiences with Toby is an uncertainty about absolutely everything, from the nature of the terrain to the nature of the Typees. The reader hurtles along an emotional switchback in which anxiety and relief are subject to rapid, even frantic, alteration. These changes of mood are so theatrical that their imaginative construction can hardly be ignored. The narrator and Toby first encounter a spectacle that is both alarming and sublime:

> Five foaming streams, rushing through as many gorges, and swelled and turbid by the recent rains, united in one mad plunge of nearly eighty feet, and fell with wild uproar into a deep black pool scooped out of the gloomy-looking rocks that lay piled around, and thence in one collected body dashed down a narrow sloping channel which seemed to penetrate into the very bowels of the earth.   (*Typee*, p. 45)

They build a temporary hut at the foot of a cataract and in consequence get completely drenched: 'In vain did I try to elude the incessant streams that poured upon me' (p. 46). After sleepless nights, extreme discomfort, lack of food, burning fever and an acute swelling in the leg he awakens to see a matchless prospect:

> Had a glimpse of the gardens of Paradise been revealed to me, I could scarcely have been more ravished with the sight.
> From the spot where I lay transfixed with surprise and delight, I looked straight down into the bosom of a valley, which swept away in long wavy undulations to the blue waters in the distance. Midway towards the sea, and peering here and there amidst the foliage, might be seen the palmetto-thatched houses of the inhabitants glistening in the sun that had bleached them to a dazzling whiteness. The vale was more than three leagues in length, and about a mile across at its greatest width. . . . But perhaps there was nothing about the scenery I beheld more impressive than those silent cascades, whose slender threads of water, after leaping down the steep cliffs, were lost amidst the rich herbage of the valley.   (p. 49)

In an instant the threatening, menacing, demoralising streams have become aestheticised and turned into pure objects of contemplation and wonder. All the travellers' struggles and difficulties are 'resolved' by a delightful view – as indeed they are at the end of the next chapter. My point is not that such a switch is psychologically implausible but rather that it is precisely through such carefully judged switches of tone and style that Melville makes his narrative more engrossing and more convincing. The succeeding chapter provides an equally compelling instance:

> In a few minutes we reached the foot of the gorge, and kneeling upon a small ledge of dripping rocks, I bent over to the stream.

What a delicious sensation was I now to experience! I paused for a second to concentrate all my capabilities of enjoyment, and then immersed my lips in the clear element before me. Had the apples of Sodom turned to ashes in my mouth I could not have felt a more startling revulsion. A single drop of the cold fluid seemed to freeze every drop of blood in my body; the fever that had been burning in my veins gave place on the instant to death-like chills, which shook me one after another like so many shocks of electricity, while the perspiration produced by my late violent exertions congealed in icy beads upon my forehead. My thirst was gone, and I fairly loathed the water. Starting to my feet, the sight of those dank rocks, oozing forth moisture at every crevice, and the dark stream shooting along its dismal channel, sent fresh chills through my shivering frame, and I felt as uncontrollable a desire to climb up towards the genial sunlight as I before had to descend the ravine.   (pp. 53–4)

Melville is thirsty but finds the water too cold. The supercharged description does not simply aim to communicate his state of mind but situates the whole episode on a symbolic level. The experience is one of profound disillusionment. Dead Sea fruit turn to ashes. The presumed elixir of life is found to be polluted and poisoned. In true puritan spirit the traveller finds that it is wise to distrust fair appearances, that things which appear attractive may be fraught with destructive potential. The reader is led to believe that he is in the hands of a narrator who may initially have been gullible, but who as the result of his experiences and disillusionments will not readily be fooled again. For this reason his assessment of the Typees can be relied upon. Melville, we feel, is a man who will know a true Bower of Bliss when he sees one. Nobody will be gulled.

But is the valley of the Typees a true Bower of Bliss? Obviously there can be no simple answer to this question even within the terms that Melville provides. *Typee* is a kind of cancelled idyll where we may feel either that the idyll is truly defaced, or that it can be glimpsed the more purely through the cancellation marks, like a tropical postage stamp glimmering with cocoa-nut palms. The very skill with which Melville covers his tracks and endeavours to make the illusion more complete is always in peril because salient features of the Typee way of life will keep breaking through, and Melville's obvious desire to remain in control of them often makes him appear like a ringmaster who is anxious to hurry out of the ring an act that has overstayed its welcome. Some of the most notorious of Melville's 'sea freedoms' occur in chapter 24. Here Melville offers a categorical refutation of charges that the Typees practise human sacrifice by stating,

> Now, all I can say is, that in all my excursions through the valley of the Typees, I never saw any of these alleged enormities. If any of them are practised upon the Marquesas islands they must have come to my knowledge while living for months with a tribe of savages, wholly unchanged from their original primitive condition, and reputed the most ferocious in the South Seas. (p. 170)

Yet Melville sees no reason to modify this statement, despite the fact that he admits subsequently that they may practise cannibalism on the slain bodies of their enemies, and that it is the alleged sight of a human skeleton in a carved wooden vessel that makes his departure a matter of urgency. Granted the sacrificial use of a human corpse is not the same as slaying a man for that specific purpose, but Melville's authoritative tone and note of moral indignation (essential to his own credibility) can scarcely be sustained if he seems merely to be quibbling as to how human sacrifice is to be defined. Melville excoriates the humbuggery of scientific men, whom he alleges simply retail the exaggerated yarns of South-Sea Rovers (among whom Melville, at this time, is not to be numbered) as if they were irrefutable facts. By contrast Melville seeks to be believed by his frank confession that he knows very little about the religion of the Typees and understands it not at all. Unfortunately Melville tries to suggest that the reason why he is unable to do this is that the beliefs of the islanders are ridiculous and nonsensical rather than because his command of the language is so limited as to be totally inadequate to grapple with such complex issues. Thus, Melville, while pretending empathy, reinforces the most patronising stereotypes. Melville with the Typees right before him will nevertheless view them in any way he likes, and no one can gainsay his impressions. Although Melville, for example, elsewhere admits that the system of taboo is extremely intricate and rigorous –

> Situated as I was in the Typee valley, I perceived every hour the effects of this all-controlling power, without in the least

comprehending it. Those effects were, indeed, wide-spread and universal, pervading the most important as well as the minutest transactions of life. The savage, in short, lives in the continual observance of its dictates, which guide and control every action of his being   (p. 221)

– he tries to pretend that the Typees are lackadaisical, partly because this fits in better with his stereotype of savage life and partly because it will make his waterborne erotic fantasies of Fayaway the more credible. So Melville wrote,

> In truth, I regard the Typees as a back-slidden generation. They are sunk in religious sloth, and require a spiritual revival. A long prosperity of bread-fruit and cocoa-nuts has rendered them remiss in the performance of their highest obligations. The wood-rot malady is spreading among the idols – the fruit upon their altars is becoming offensive – the temples themselves need rethatching – the tattooed clergy are altogether too light-hearted and lazy – and their flocks are going astray
> (p. 179)

A further convenience of such a belief is that Melville is the better able to believe that religion is something artificial and unnatural that must necessarily wilt and wither in the precivilised paradises of tropical islands. The idyll of the carefree and unconstrained life is undermined if the Typees are clearly seen to be subjected to a rigorous discipline.

In the exuberant moment when he wrote *Typee* Melville discovered the masterful, irresistible power of style. He could take his experience amongst the Typees and reshape it into almost anything he wished. For, if the truth of his experience was how he chose to view it, both at the time and in retrospect, then it could be just as idyllic as he chose to make it. Like Frederick Edwin Church in such paintings as *Rainy Season in the Tropics* and *Sunrise over Cotopaxi*, Melville found that the sublime had still greater potential if it was located on distant shores. Yet Melville did not merely indulge in the excessive: he also offset it by a comic relief that only served to throw it more distinctively into prominence as the truly sublime. If through the ridiculous Kory-Kory with his gibberish and gesticulations Typee society becomes quaintly familiar, it never loses its poetry or glamour, because of the way in which Melville treats the noble Mehevi and the lovely Fayaway. The facial and corporeal tattooing practised among the Typees shows how the same phenomenon can be presented in an entirely different light. Kory-Kory's appearance borders on the farcical:

> His countenance thus triply hooped as it were, with tattooing, always reminded me of those unhappy wretches whom I have sometimes observed gazing out sentimentally from behind the grated bars of a prison window; whilst the entire body of my savage valet, covered all over with representations of birds and fishes, and a variety of most unaccountable-looking creatures, suggested to me the idea of a pictorial museum of natural history, or an illustrated copy of Goldsmith's Animated Nature'. (p. 83)

Melville at this point almost repents at his 'heartless' (ibid.) portrayal of Kory-Kory, and it is certainly in marked contrast with his introduction of the chief Mehevi, whose tattoos form the climax of a lengthy and reverent description:

> But what was most remarkable in the appearance of this splendid islander was the elaborate tattooing displayed on every noble limb. All imaginable lines and curves and figures were delineated over his whole body, and in their grotesque variety and infinite profusion I could only compare them to the crowded groupings of quaint patterns we sometimes see in costly pieces of lacework. The most simple and remarkable of all these ornaments was that which decorated the countenance of the chief. Two broad stripes of tattooing, diverging from the centre of his shaven crown, obliquely crossed both eyes – staining the lids – to a little below each ear, where they united with another stripe which swept in a straight line along the lips and formed the base of the triangle. The warrior, from the excellence of his physical proportions, might certainly have been regarded as one of Nature's noblemen, and the lines drawn upon his face may possibly have denoted his exalted rank. (p. 78)

Under a frankly uncomprehending Western eye the salient features of the island way of life become almost infinitely malleable. It may indeed be that vertical lines possess a nobility that horizontal ones do not, but we are equally conscious that what is involved is two different stylistic registers that can be deployed at will, one which stresses the alienness and dignity of the noble savage and one which ironically diminishes through the use of familiar comparisons. It is all a question of which gear is chosen. Melville's confident switching between the two seems to show an ability to situate the object he describes and therefore the possibility of offering a lucid and balanced perspective upon it. Indeed at times Melville's ability to relish the spontaneity of the Typee way of life in a spirit of true detachment seems to border on the superhuman. The angry rejection by Mehevi and his people of Marnoo's eloquent plea that Melville–Tommo be allowed to leave becomes a moment when the directness and purity of savage emotion can be fully appreciated:

> The lively countenances of these people are wonderfully indicative of the emotions of the soul, and the imperfections of their oral language [a language, note, which Melville barely understood] are more than compensated for by the nervous eloquence of their looks and gestures. I could plainly trace, in every varying expression of their faces, all those passions which had been thus unexpectedly aroused in their bosoms. (p. 142)

But such dissolves from participant to narrating armchair anthropologist are part and parcel of the style of the whole book.

With the ground so carefully prepared, Melville is free to give way to the excessive. The Feast of the Calabashes is as much a fiesta of language as it is a banquet in fact. Melville finds everything immoderate:

> Within the building itself was presented a most extraordinary scene. The immense lounge of mats lying between the parallel rows of the trunks of cocoa-nut trees, and extending the entire length of the house, at least two hundred feet, was covered by the reclining forms of a host of chiefs and warriors who were eating at a great rate, or soothing the cares of Polynesian life in the sedative fumes of tobacco. The smoke was inhaled from large pipes, the bowls of which, made out of small cocoa-nut shells, were curiously carved in strange heathenish devices. These were passed from mouth to mouth by the recumbent smokers, each of whom, taking two or three prodigious whiffs,

> handed the pipe to his neighbour; sometimes for that purpose stretching indolently across the body of some dozing individual whose exertions at the dinner-table had already induced sleep   (p. 164)

This orgy of somnolence seems all the more outrageous to the Western reader because he knows very well, or at least Melville has so instructed him, that Polynesian life has no cares. So to recuperate from an utterly unstressful life seems paradise indeed. But even this pales before the image Melville conjures up of almost indescribable plenitude:

> Within the spacious quadrangle, the whole population of the valley seemed to be assembled, and the sight presented was truly remarkable. Beneath the sheds of bamboo which opened towards the interior of the square, reclined the principal chiefs and warriors, while a miscellaneous throng lay at their ease under the enormous trees which spread a majestic canopy overhead. Upon the terraces of the gigantic altars, at each end, were deposited green bread-fruit in baskets of cocoa-nut leaves, large rolls of tappa, bunches of ripe bananas, clusters of mammee-apples, the golden-hued fruit of the artu-tree, and baked hogs laid out in large wooden trenchers, fancifully decorated with freshly plucked leaves, whilst a variety of rude implements of war were piled in confused heaps before the ranks of hideous idols. Fruits of various kinds were likewise suspended in leafen baskets, from the tops of poles planted uprightly, and at regular intervals, along the lower terraces of both altars. At their base were arranged two parallel rows of cumbersome drums standing at least fifteen feet in height, and formed from the hollow trunks of large trees. Their heads were covered with shark skins, and their barrels were elaborately carved with various quaint figures and devices. At regular intervals they were bound round by a species of sinnate of various colours, and strips of native cloth flattened upon them here and there. Behind these instruments were built slight platforms upon which stood a number of young men who, beating violently with the palms of their hands upon the drum-heads, produced those outrageous sounds which had awakened me in the morning. Every few minutes these musical performers hopped down from their elevation into the crowd

below, and their places were immediately supplied by fresh recruits. Thus an incessant din was kept up that might have startled Pandemonium. (p. 167)

The effect of the sublime is created by the sensory overload which the description induces. Melville appears to stress the geometry and symmetry of the arrangement of food between the gigantic altars, but it is difficult to grasp because of the way in which Melville switches perspective and zooms in on particular objects. Precise descriptions keep giving way to those that are vague and indistinct, such as 'confused heaps', 'Fruits of various kinds', 'various quaint figures', 'of various colours', as if the mind itself reels before the sheer scale and density of the spectacle. This is reinforced by synaesthesia, since the chaos and confusion of the drumming seems simply an imaginative extension of the culinary excess that is displayed.

The delight of *Typee* – and there is no work of faction more delightful than this – is that it presents a world that is apparently entirely free of all the vices and afflictions that beset Western societies. As Melville points out, 'The penalty of the Fall presses very lightly upon the valley of Typee' (p. 195). In this happy and timeless world there is no friction, strife or envy and even warfare assumes such a desultory character that loss of life is the exception rather than the rule. Typee is without money and the anxieties that go with it – it has neither beggars, servants nor debtors. It is a world without work, without care, without scarcity or sexual repression. The body is displayed without inhibition or shame. It is a world that seems to lack the constraints imposed by religion and the law. It is a world that is natural. Melville chooses to concentrate its unconstrained delights in a series of tableaux of the delectable Fayaway: fanning the author with a fan woven from the leaves of a cocoa-nut palm; smoking a pipe in the stern of a canoe; holding her tappa garment above her naked body like a sail; delicately eating a raw fish – in such moments innocence, indolence and eroticism are exquisitely combined. It all has an uncanny credibility. And why? As the later Melville would certainly have remarked, it's simply a matter of *confidence*.

After the almost visionary intensity with which Melville imbues the antithesis between savagery and civilisation in *Typee*, *Omoo*, the sequel, published in the following year, comes as a distinct anticlimax. Certainly nothing important hangs upon it. *Omoo* is a leisurely ramble through cultural ruins, a casual rummaging through exotic bric-à-brac on the market stall. The picturesque in *Omoo* precludes the sublime and the excessive alike. In depicting himself waiting Melville is simultaneously treading literary water, a wider sea before him.

As a published author, with two books under his belt, Melville was beginning to chafe at the level of aggravation that he was still expected to endure. For John Murray, his publisher, was not merely pestering him for documentary proofs but was actually demanding evidence that Melville was a real person. With *Mardi*, therefore, Melville determined to be bounded by no restrictions whatever, to be as excessive as he pleased:

> To be blunt: the work I shall next publish will be in downright earnest a 'Romance of Polynesian Adventure' – But why this? The truth is, Sir, that the reiterated imputation of being a romancer in disguise has at last pricked me into a resolution to show those who may take any interest in the matter, that a *real* romance of mine is no Typee or Omoo, & is made of different stuff altogether . . . proceeding in my narrative of *facts* I began to feel a incurable distate for the same & a longing to plume my pinions for a flight & felt irked, cramped & fettered by plodding along with dull common places.[14]

Mardi, instead of being offered to the reader as an actual journey of discovery, would be a romance and a work of speculative anthropology that would subject to a sceptical and satirical analysis the incalculably diverse and curious forms of human society. Moreover, Melville's project was a radical one, since it would not privilege civilised customs over the 'irrational' behaviour of tribal society but subject all of them to the same whimsical scrutiny. In *Mardi* the narrator's companion, the old Viking Jarl, is somewhat perplexed on the isle of Willamilla when he finds set before him at table 'the empty hemisphere of a small nut, the purpose of which was a problem' (p. 246). He commits a *faux pas* by placing a piece of Arva-root in it and for this action is criticised by the philosophical sage Babbalanja:

> He assured him, that it argued but little brains to evince a desire to be familiar with all things; that however desirable as incidental attainments, conventionalities, in themselves, were

the least arbitrary of trifles; the knowledge of them, innate with no man. 'Moreover, Jarl,' he added, 'in essence, conventionalities are but mimickings, at which monkeys succeed best. Hence, when you find youself at a loss in these matters, wait patiently, and mark what the other monkeys do: and then follow suit and by so doing you will gain a vast reputation as an accomplished ape.' (Ibid.)

In his observation of social behaviour Melville is struck by the degree to which the everyday conduct of life is completely automatic and unreflective, even though to an intruder from another culture it may appear inexplicably bizarre. Political authority and religious belief raise fundamental questions about the place of the individual in society and the meaning of the universe, yet they are articulated through practices that are both arbitrary and unquestioned and thereby, through their very existence, implicate the subject in complex structures of deference. Melville draws the moral when he describes how the chiefs on the island of Valapee withdraw from the presence of royalty with their heads between their thighs: 'All objects look well through an arch' (p. 203).[15] Social and religious institutions are precisely arches in this sense – they construct an illusion of importance and meaning around themselves, while at the same time providing a shelter from cosmic doubt. Melville's humour in *Mardi* always teeters on the edge of a metaphysical anguish; for to unmask and expose a variety of cultural deceptions necessarily raises the question as to what, if anything, lies beyond and behind them.

Such questions, of course, have not always been felt to fall within the province of the novel. Certainly anyone who tried to read *Mardi* for the plot would hang himself, since there was no way that Melville could have cabined, cribbed and confined his wide-ranging intellectual speculations just at the very moment that he was launching himself on a personal voyage of discovery. Melville has often been criticised for his apparent inability to develop a plot satisfactorily, but the ironic truth is that Melville regarded plots with just as much wariness as his critics regarded his travellers' tales. For one thing plots have endings, and for Melville endings are unwarrantable limits that snuff out and extinguish a range of intellectual possibilities. Just as the spectator's delight in the work of a pavement artist stems from an almost primitive fascination with the way in which figures emerge out of nothing and not from the completed picture, so for Melville writing is a speculative game with everything to play for and which loses its excitement and risk if it is not kept open. The ending of *Mardi* is no ending at all. Melville seeks to keep his work in a dynamic relation with the world and the reader and he therefore refuses to allow it to be pigeonholed. He recognises that writing that is wholly wedded to the representational abdicates its right to question, while writing that remains circumscribed within the fictional abdicates its responsibilities. Melville's spiritual forefathers are not Richardson and Fielding but such speculative intellects as Montaigne, Rabelais and Bayle, and he writes at a time before the shutters and partitions of the three-volume and serialised novel had descended completely. *Mardi* and *Moby-Dick* defy classification. For Arthur Hobson Quinn, Melville's fault was that he could not tell the difference between fact and fiction[16] and certainly Melville was forced by his very literary career to grasp that what appears as an absolute distinction is in practice quite amazingly serpentine and quixotic. In *Mardi* Babbalanja says,

> Truth is in things, and not in words: truth is voiceless; so at least saith old Bardianna. And I, Babbalanja, assert, that what are vulgarly called fictions are as much realities as the gross mattock of Dididi, the digger of trenches; for things visible are but conceits of the eye: things imaginative, conceits of the fancy. If duped by one, we are equally duped by the other.
>
> (pp. 283–4)

Truth, in this provocative formulation, is defined in terms of deception. But from another point of view truth is also to be construed in terms of the destruction of illusions. It is thus in vain to seek in Melville a stable and unproblematic world as much as a stable and unproblematic novel.

When he writes, Melville sees himself as embarked upon a demonic mission in which he becomes compelled to utter what nobody wants to hear:

> My cheek blanches white while I write; I start at the scratch of my pen; my own mad brood of eagles devours me; fain would I unsay this audacity; but an iron-mailed hand clenches mine in a

vice, and prints down every letter in my spite. Fain would I hurl off this Dionysius that rides me; my thoughts crush me down till I groan; in far fields I hear the song of the reaper, while I slave and faint in this cell. The fever runs through me like lava; my hot brain burns like a coal; and like many a monarch, I am less to be envied, than the veriest hind in the land.   (p. 368)

Writing is paradigmatically excessive. Melville's admission that such is the case, together with his attempt to vindicate his own rambling procedures, occurs in chapter 180 of *Mardi*, where Babbalanja becomes advocate for the poet Lombardo, whose grand Koztanza he claims to know by heart. When King Media asks Babbalanja 'What was it that originally impelled Lombardo to the undertaking', he replies, 'Primus and forever, a full heart: – brimful, bubbling, sparkling; and running over like the flagon in your hand, my lord' (p. 592).

The validation of Melville–Lombardo is twofold. On the one hand *Mardi*–Koztanza is an exploratory work in which the writer does not know where he is going and does not know what he is looking for until he finds it:

> When Lombardo set about his work, he knew not what it would become. He did not build himself in with plans; he wrote right on; and in so doing, got deeper and deeper into himself; and life a resolute traveller, plunging through baffling woods, at last was rewarded for his toils.   (p. 595)

The implication also is that the reader must expect to experience a similar frustration, for a quest that has the goal always in sight is no quest at all. On the other hand, if *Mardi*–Koztanza seems disorganised and chaotic this is because the world itself is diverse and multifarious. Literature must not refuse this complexity but acknowledge it in all its fullness. King Abrazza reproaches Babbalanja by saying, 'The Koztanza lacks cohesion; it is wild, unconnected, all episode' – to which Babbalanja replies,

> And so is Mardi itself: – nothing but episodes; valleys and hills; rivers, digressing from plains; vines, roving all over; boulders and diamonds; flowers and thistles; forests and thickets; and, here and there, fens and moors. And so, the world in the Koztanza.   (p. 597)

But Melville does not allow Babbalanja to get away with this altogether, since Abrazza responds with a retort that must evoke an echo in more than one reader of *Mardi*: 'Ay, plenty of dead-desert chapters there; horrible sands to wade through' (p. 598).

Like *Typee*, *Mardi* begins with an act of desertion. Faced with the prospect of an endlessly protracted whalehunt in the seas off the coast of Siberia, the narrator decides to jump ship in mid-ocean in company with a taciturn old seaman from the isle of Skye called Jarl. They secretly lower a boat at night and are able to make their escape under cover of the cry 'Man overboard'. After sixteen days of continuous sailing without a landfall they encounter a brigantine, the *Parki*, apparently a ghost ship but which proves to have two occupants, Somoa and Annatoo, who have managed to escape with the boat from a treacherous massacre in which the captain and the rest of the crew have been killed. Subsequently they encounter the fascinating and mysterious Yillah, a maiden 'who was lovely enough to be really divine' (p. 139), who is being escorted by Aleema the priest and his guards on a journey that will end in her being offered up as a human sacrifice. The narrator falls desperately in love with her, and when she equally mysteriously disappears he embarks on an unending and fruitless quest to find her. This search, however, is largely a pretext for a protracted political and religious satire *cum* philosophical inquiry in which they visit a number of imaginary kingdoms and others that are actual ones loosely disguised – i.e. Dominora (England) and Vivenza (the United States). The narrator to impress the islanders, has assumed the name of a god, Taji, and his companions on this journey are King Media, Mohi the antiquarian–historian, Yoomy the poet, and Babbalanja the philosopher and sage. *Mardi* eclectically combines travel narrative with political satire, in the manner of *Gulliver's Travels* or Cooper's *The Monikins*, with a Romantic quest for a beautiful maiden in the footsteps of Shelley's *Alastor*. The book is Melville's mammoth attempt to get to the bottom of things – increasingly tinged by the realisation that it is *impossible* to get to the bottom of things.

In this sense, even at such an early date, Melville's work represents a transvaluation of the Romantic quest. For Melville never ceases to believe in the value of the quest, yet such is the depth of his scepticism that he is convinced it is doomed from the very start. Melville's inability firmly to believe in any religious creed, no matter how much he would like to, is, of course, characteristically Victorian, but Melville's example is of particular interest because it clearly shows that such doubtfulness did not necessarily have to have its sources in Darwinian theory but could take as its point of departure the breakdown and failure of a variety of cosmological and philosophical schemes. Melville's exposure to alien cultures, though in some sense superficial, was nevertheless highly significant in that it taught him to ask questions about the social and intellectual *function* of beliefs rather than simply classify them as true or false. For Melville belief is not a truth but a limit: it prevents and precludes any confrontation with more difficult questions. Belief is, virtually by definition, a prophylactic against doubt, and, although Melville sees the pressing social and psychological reasons for adopting it, he nevertheless remains convinced that doubt is the more natural attitude. But scepticism demands an intellectual persistence and rigorousness that will never be commonplace, whereas for most people *something* will always be better than nothing:

> And thus, my lord, is it, that the mass of Mardians do not believe because they know, but because they know *not*. And they are as ready to receive one thing as another, if it comes from a canonical source. My lord, Mardi is an ostrich, which will swallow aught you offer, even a bar of iron, if placed endwise. And though the iron be indigestible, yet it serves to fill: in feeding, the end proposed. For Mardi must have something to exercise its digestion, though that something be forever indigestible.   (pp. 455–6)

In his amusing chapter on 'those Scamps the Plujii' (pp. 262–4) Melville places all religious systems of thought in an ironic perspective, since he points out that the malicious Plujii can exercise a valuable role in plugging the gap between that which can be attributed to the action of individuals and that which can be imputed to the gods. It might seem impious to attribute a whole range of relatively minor misfortunes to the direct action of a supreme deity, and to do so might bring religion into disrepute; but to put the blame on a lower order of malignant spirits solves the difficulty admirably. However, the Plujii are themselves only another stratagem whereby men endeavour to conceal from themselves their bafflement at the capricious, inexplicable and arbitrary nature of the world. For Melville those who confidently claim to know, like the nine blind men in Babbalanja's fable each of whom claims to have found out which of the thousand embedded branches of a vast banyan tree is the aboriginal root, are necessarily charlatans. On the island of Maramma, the old blind guide Pani confidently assumes custodianship of religious faith and exacts extortionate rewards for his services, even in the midst of poverty. However, when faced with the challenge of a young boy, his posture crumbles and he is forced to concede that he really is in the dark:

> From dark to dark! – What is this subtle something that is in me, and eludes me? Will it have no end? When, then, did it begin? All, all is chaos! What is this shining light in heaven, this sun they tell me of? Or, do they lie? Methinks, it might blaze convictions; but I brood and grope in blackness; I am dumb with doubt; yet, 'tis not doubt, but worse: I doubt my doubt. Oh, ye all-wise spirits in the air, how can ye witness all this woe, and give no sign? Would, would that mine were a settled doubt, like that wild boy's, who without faith, seems full of it. The undoubting doubter believes the most. Oh! that I were he. Methinks that daring boy hath Alma in him, struggling to be free. But those pilgrims: that trusting girl. – What, if they saw me as I am? Peace, peace my soul; on, mask, again.
> And he staggered from the Morai.   (p. 339)

Pani's mistake is to believe or assume that he is in some way in possession of the answer or answers when he has scarcely even pondered the questions. When Babbalanja defends the 'antique pagan' (p. 387) author of 'A Happy Life' (p. 388) who advocates a purely secular system of ethics without any transcendental dimension, he is challenged by King Media, who insists that there must be some divine sanction and authority. The following interchange takes place:

> 'My lord! my lord! out of itself, Religion has nothing to bestow. Nor will she save us from aught, but the evil in ourselves. Her one grand end is to make us wise; her only manifestations are reverence to Oro and love to man; her only, but ample reward,

herself. He who has this, has all. He who has this, whether he kneel to an image of wood, calling it Oro, or to an image of air, calling it the same; whether he fasts or feasts; laughs or weeps; – that men can be no richer. And this religion, faith, virtue, righteousness, good, whate'er you will, I find in this book I hold. No written page can teach me more.'

'Have you that, then, of which you speak, Babbalanja? Are you content, there where you stand?'

'My lord, you drive me home. I am not content. The mystery of mysteries is still a mystery.' (p. 389)

By this Melville means that, although a secular system of ethics is attractive, especially when it seems to cut through the Gordian knot of theological speculation, its value is problematic if it exists in a vacuum. But, of course, what is also raised here is the question of *contentment* – the ultimate criterion by which religions are judged. Melville mocks his own doubt here by having Babbalanja swoon at the metaphysical confrontation with the obscurity of the universe and then instantly revive, but the issue is nevertheless a serious one. For, while contentment might certainly be preferable to the anguish of uncertainty, to give up that anguish might also be to abandon one's identity and integrity.

For Melville the only real alternative to such scepticism must be belief in a god who can be held responsible for everything that happens in the universe, the existence of evil included. As Melville sees it there can be no accidents or chance in a divine universe, and he is not content with the assumption that God simply knows all, but presses this to the conclusion that God must be the omnipresent and effective cause. In one of the crucial chapters of metaphysical speculation in *Mardi*, 'Babbalanja Discourses in the Dark', Babbalanja puts this view to Media:

'Is not Oro omnipresent – absolutely everywhere?'
'So you mortals teach, Babbalanja.'
'But so do they *mean*, my lord? Often do we Mardians stick to terms for ages, yet truly apply not their meanings.'
'Well, Oro is everywhere. What now?'
'Then, if that be absolutely so, Oro is not merely a universal on-looker, but occupies and fills all space; and no vacancy is left for any being, or any thing but Oro. Hence Oro is *in* all things, and himself *is* all things – the time-old creed. But since evil

abounds, and Oro is all things, then he can not be perfectly good; wherefore, Oro's omnipresence and moral perfection seem incompatible. Furthermore, my lord those orthodox systems which ascribe to Oro almighty and universal attributes every way, those systems, I say, destroy all intellectual individualities but Oro, and resolve the universe into him.' (pp. 427–8)

As Babbalanja points out, the emphasis on the omnipotence of God is familiar. More particularly, in the Western religious tradition from William of Ockham to Calvin and Spinoza, there has been such a concern to stress the complete freedom of God – since any qualification of it would diminish his perfection – that God's freedom has been purchased at the price of diminishing the significance of human action and marginalising human freedom as a moral issue. Such beliefs came ready to hand for Melville in the form of the New England Calvinist tradition, and Melville in the spirit of Transcendentalism sought first to question it by stressing human powers and capabilities. But the above passage shows that Melville was fascinated by the particular materialist twist that Spinoza gives this argument by directly identifying God with universal substance and thus simultaneously making God the necessary cause, since for Spinoza a strong argument for his identification of God with substance was the fact that nature abhors a vacuum. Melville rejected Spinoza's views and indeed heartily loathed them as much for their rigid systematicity as for their apparent elimination of evil and free will. But Spinoza's monism looms large in *Moby-Dick* especially.

Melville's quarrel with Spinoza, as well as with other such metaphysicians as Plato and Kant, surfaces in *Pierre*, where he is the subject of a number of disparaging references. Pierre's friend Charlie Milthorpe is invited to contribute to the *Spinozist*, which is noted for its obscurity and where nothing is admitted but 'Ultimate Transcendentals' (*Pierre*, p. 280). Pierre puts into the mouth of his author hero Vivia a rejection of Spinoza and Plato for purporting to gloss over the blackness of existence:

Hopelessness and despair are over me, as pall on pall. Away ye chattering apes of a sophomorean Spinoza and Plato, who didst all but delude me that night was day, and pain was but a tickle. Explain this darkness, exorcise this devil, ye can not.

(p. 302)

Melville's objection to the systematisers is not merely that they systematise but that they refuse the fundamental problem of existence precisely where purporting to resolve it. For Melville the most irreducible fact about the world is its 'downright positive falsity, that it seems to lie saturated and soaking with lies' (p. 208). For Melville the only true integrity comes from continually facing this fact:

> Hereupon then in the soul of the enthusiast youth two armies come to the shock; and unless he prove recreant, or unless he prove gullible, or unless he can find the talismanic secret, to reconcile the world with his own soul, then there is no peace for him, no slightest truce for him in this life. Now without doubt this Talismanic Secret has never yet been found; and in the nature of human things it seems as though it never can be. Certain philosophers have time and again pretended to have found it; but if they do not in the end discover their own delusion, other people soon discover it for themselves, and so these philosophers and their vain philosophy are let glide away into practical oblivion. Plato, and Spinoza, and Goethe, and many more belong to this guild of self-imposters, with a preposterous rabble of Muggletonian Scots and Yankees, whose vile brogue still the more bestreaks the stripedness of their Greek or German Neoplatonic originals.   (Ibid.)

But, despite the vehemence of this rejection, Spinoza was a thinker curiously congenial to Melville's purposes because he provided a schema whereby God could truly be blamed for the depressing nature of the world. In other systems of explanation there are loopholes and escape clauses, but with Spinoza God is everywhere responsible and perception of evil is simply a failure of comprehension. Melville, of course, insists that perceptions of evil are valid and it therefore follows that God himself must be malignant – and not simply the Plujii.

To cite *Pierre* in the context of *Mardi*, however, is to anticipate, for, though Melville was at work on *Pierre* only two years later, a vast spiritual odyssey lies between. In *Mardi* Melville was still attracted by the ideal of reconciliation, and the novel is genuinely dialogic in that we have not simply Babbalanja's converse with others and his trying out of different intellectual positions but also a final parting of the ways between Babbalanja and Taji.

Babbalanja decides to remain on the isle of Serenia, where it appears, the teachings of Christ (Alma) are genuinely adhered to. Babbalanja admits that Serenia does not provide the answer to all his questions, but he believes that this Christian teaching offers all that man can really hope to possess. He tries to dissuade Taji from continuing the mystical quest for Yillah:

> Babbalanja thus: – 'My voyage is ended. Not because what we sought is found; but that I now possess all which may be had of what I sought in Mardi. Here, I tarry to grow wiser still: – then I am Alma's and the world's. Taji! for Yillah thou wilt hunt in vain; she is a phantom that but mocks thee; and while for her thou madly huntest, the sin thou didst cries out, and its avengers still will follow. But here they may not come: nor those, who tempting, track thy path. Wise counsel take. Within our hearts is all we seek: though in that search many need a prompter. Him I have found in blessed Alma. Then rove no more. Gain now, in flush of youth, that last wise thought, too often purchased, by a lift of woe. Be wise: be wise.'
> (*Mardi*, p. 637)

But Taji refuses to heed Babbalanja's advice. He recklessly recommits himself to the quest for the mysterious Yillah, though he has no way of knowing whether his quest will be fruitless, whether Yillah is indeed possessed of the transcendental value he attaches to her or whether he could ever know anything about her for sure. In continuing the pursuit Taji simply dedicates himself to an unceasing struggle against the obscurity of the world, where the quest itself becomes its own validation. In its very excessiveness is its truth.

Between *Mardi* (1849) and *Moby-Dick* (1851) Melville hurriedly wrote two semi-autobiographical accounts of nautical voyages, *Redburn* (1849) and *White-Jacket* (1850), taking little more than two months over each. Even disregarding these circumstances, they are remarkably accomplished pieces of writing. Melville displays almost casually the extraordinary flexibility of his mature style that manages to weave together vivid description, curious learning, whimsical humour and intense moral indignation without any sense of awkwardness or incongruity. The lasting impression they leave with the reader is of a world filled with pain and suffering to which no conceivable meaning can be assigned.

But all the speculation that is suppressed in these books, which are, as it were, forced out between clenched teeth, spills over into *Moby-Dick*. Melville himself was almost contemptuous of them, writing to Lemuel Shaw,

> But no reputation that is gratifying to me, can possibly be achieved by either of these books. They are two *jobs*, which I have done for money – being forced to it, as other men are to sawing wood. And while I have felt obliged to refrain from writing the kind of book I would wish to; yet, in writing these two books, I have not repressed myself much – so far as *they* are concerned; but have spoken pretty much as I feel – Being books, then, written in this way, my only desire for their 'success' (as it is called) springs from my pocket, & not from my heart. So far as I am individually concerned, & independent of my pocket, it is my earnest desire to write those sort of books which are said to 'fail'. – Pardon this egotism.[17]

Melville had had enough of writing books tailored for the market, and the expostulation that greeted his infractions of the rules only served to convince him that the contrary path was best. He would be excessive or nothing.

Moby-Dick is an extraordinary book and by virtue of its extraordinariness it has established itself as one of the great classics of world literature, but the price of that classic status has been to eliminate from it everything that made it provocative and outrageous. Its puzzles and contradictions are smoothed over as it is shaped into contours more in keeping with its high status; the actual unwieldiness of the book is reconstructed as effortless formal mastery and Ahab is just one more in a long line of tragically flawed heroes. In the hands of Newton Arvin especially it acquires a Newtonian regularity. According to Arvin, 'not many imaginative works have so strong and strict a unity'[18] – indeed, 'its formal wholeness . . . is unprecedented and unique'.[19] *Moby-Dick* has a propulsion that carries it, admittedly not from climax to climax, but from 'one wave-crest to another', yet more amazingly it has a narrative line that is 'straight ahead and undeviating'.[20] We may freely concede that Ahab's fixed purpose rolls on iron rails and still rub our eyes with incredulity that this should be seriously offered as a characterisation of the book. *Moby-Dick* is nothing if not devious, oblique, peripatetic, and its digressive nature is absolutely integral to Melville's whole conception. But Arvin's formalism is no mere empty praise. It is ideologically motivated, for such a perception of the book encourages the reader to jettison his own experience of obscurity, irritation and bafflement for a posture of complacent admiration and to turn his back on all its dark sayings, just as Stubb turns his back on Pip. With Melville absolved from the guilt of having written an extravagant and tumultuous work it becomes easy to assume that only Ahab is guilty and overweening. Yet in truth the book is as excessive as its hero!

Moby-Dick is a vertiginous experience for the reader, full of abrupt and unexpected transitions. It takes Ishmael directly from a comical and unforeseen night in bed with the pagan Queequeg into the audience of the earnest and eloquent Father Mapple. After delaying the appearance of the protagonist for many pages, it follows his first appearance with a lengthy digression on the subject of 'Cetology'. It labours over many pages to establish the essential plausibility of the events that are eventually narrated, yet deliberately incorporates episodes that undermine the book's credibility. It keeps the reader dangling interminably only to conclude in a sudden and vivid flurry that leaves many questions unanswered. It offers interpretative clues that are intentionally misleading. It brandishes symbolic and allegorical meanings on every side yet seems to ask that it be read on the most pedantic and literal level. So it is salutary to return to the experiences of Melville's early reviewers, who were genuinely disconcerted at being shipped aboard the *Pequod* and were neither ashamed nor afraid to acknowledge it in their comments. Melville himself humorously acknowledged that his choice of the Leviathan as a subject represented the opportunity of writing a vast and unconfinable work that would roam over all human knowledge and raise every conceivable question:

> Unconsciously my chirography expands into placard capitals. Give me a condor's quill! Give me Vesuvius' crater for an inkstand! Friends, hold my arms! For in the mere act of penning my thoughts of this Leviathan, they weary me, and make me faint with their outreaching comprehensiveness of sweep, as if to include the whole circle of the sciences, and all the generation of whales, and men, and mastodons, past, present, and to come with all the revolving panoramas of empire on earth, and

throughout the whole universe, not excluding its suburbs. Such, and so magnifying is the virtue of a large and liberal theme. (p. 379)

Moreover, in a culture dominated by the Bible, a large and diffuse work believed to contain all the instruction necessary to human salvation, to write such an ambitious tome, especially with God as its half-hidden theme, must have had, for its author, the implication of setting it in rivalry with the Good Book. So it is by no means fanciful to think of *Moby-Dick* as an anti-Bible or to imagine that it parodies the Bible both in its diffuseness and in its rereading of Jonah, Job and Ahab. In this light it is also possible to reread the quotation from Job that stands at the head of the epilogue: 'And I only am escaped alone to tell thee' (p. 470). For *Moby-Dick* can then be read as the testimony of the single man to escape from the clutches of an all-powerful God – Melville's impious document masquerading as penitence.

Melville's early reviewers were not in much doubt about the excessiveness of *Moby-Dick* and they found it as extravagant in its ambitions as in its defiance of the reader. For the critic in *John Bull* it was the most extraordinary of all Melville's extraordinary books, characterised by a 'wild and grotesque fancy' and marred both by 'heathenish talk' and defaced by 'occasional thrusts against revealed religion' which 'cannot but shock readers accustomed to a reverent treatment of whatever is associated with sacred subjects'.[21] The reviewers were in little doubt that the sinner of *Moby-Dick* was not so much Ahab as Melville himself. At an early date Melville was marked down as a reckless and unreliable author, full of improprieties, exaggerations bordering on mendacity, as reckless of truth as of the niceties of public discourse. Far from being the redeeming glimpse of order in an output otherwise confused and inchoate, *Moby-Dick* positively capped the lot. For the London *Atlas*, *Moby-Dick* merely confirmed a general rule established by its predecessors:

> In all Mr Melville's previous works, full of original genius as they are, there was to be found lurking a certain besetting sin of extravagance. Sometimes we merely saw the tendency – at others, we traced a startling development of the tendency unchecked.[22]

But *Moby-Dick* showed that Melville was still uncured – was, as time would prove, incurable. Though praising its 'highly soaring imaginative powers' and its 'thoroughly original veins of philosophical speculation', the *Atlas* critic nevertheless objected,

> Extravagance is the bane of the book, and the stumbling block of the author. He allows his fancy not only to run riot, but absolutely to run amuck, in which poor defenceless Common Sense is hustled and belaboured in a manner melancholy to contemplate.[23]

No contemporary reader ever read the story of the whale *tout court* or even a narrative closed around Ahab, Starbuck, Ishmael and Stubb; what was impossible to evade was the presence of the author himself, constantly provoking, teasing, satirising, philosophising and blaspheming in a tale whose only principle seemed to be a resolute defiance of all order and limits. The critic in the *Morning Chronicle* was similarly bemused and his review is suggestive because it follows so closely the lineaments of the critique set forth in the London *Atlas*. He spoke of the appearance of 'a bright new star in the firmament of letters'[24] with the publication of *Typee* and *Omoo*, and praised Melville's writing for its qualities of originality, freshness, imaginativeness and intellectual energy, so he was hardly unappreciative. But he remained disquietened by the evidences of excessiveness which Melville's work displayed:

> But still, even in the best parts of the best books of the American sailor, there lurked an ominous presence which we hoped would disappear, but which, as we feared, has increased and multiplied. We could not shut our eyes to the fact that constantly before us we saw, like a plague spot, the tendency to rhapsody – the constant leaning towards wild and aimless extravagance, which has since, in so melancholy a degree, overflown and, so to speak, drowned the human interest – the very possibility of human interest – in so great a portion of Herman Melville's work. First, indeed, there was but a little cloud the size of a man's hand. Unhappily it has overspread the horizon, and the reader stumbles and wanders disconsolately in the gloom.[25]

What is significantly at stake here is the nature of Melville's relationship with his readers. The jolly jack tar who slapped you on the shoulder, spoke with a friendly and lively intimacy and regaled you with humorous and picturesque yarns of far-off climes has a sinister *Doppelgänger* who occasionally and progressively intrudes and who disturbs the illusion of straightforwardness and transparency with passages that are extravagant, speculative, obscure and disturbing. And *Moby-Dick* involves no abatement of this, but is its very quintessence. The problem is that the *Morning Chronicle* critic partly relishes this excessiveness, but in his perplexity feels duty-bound to draw the line:

> Here, however – in 'the Whale' – comes Herman Melville, in all his pristine powers – in all his abounding vigour – in the full swing of his mental energy, with his imagination invoking as strange and wild and original themes as ever, with his fancy arraying them in the old bright and vivid hues, with that store of quaint and out-of-the-way information – we would rather call it reading than learning – which he ever and anon scatters around, in, frequently unreasonable, profusion, with the old mingled opulence and happiness of phrase, and alas! too, with the old extravagance, running a perfect muck throughout the three volumes, raving and rhapsodising in chapter after chapter – unchecked, as it would appear, by the very slightest remembrance of judgement or common sense, and occasionally soaring into such absolute clouds of phantasmal unreason, that we seriously and sorrowfully ask ourselves whether this can be anything other than sheer moonstruck lunacy.[26]

Not the least reason for the combined irritation and confusion of Melville's reviewers was the way in which the book casually traversed the boundaries of a variety of genres, combining presumptive fact with indubitable fiction. The London *Britannia* was 'at a loss to determine in what category of works of amusement to place it',[27] the *Athenaeum* described it as an 'ill-compounded mixture of romance and matter-of-fact',[28] while even Evert Duyckinck, writing in the New York *Literary World*, expressed the view that Melville's books could be classified neither as fact, as fiction nor as essay and ingeniously tagged *Moby-Dick* 'a most remarkable sea-dish – an intellectual chowder of romance, philosophy, natural history, fine writing, good feeling, bad sayings'.[29]

At first glance the determined factuality of *Moby-Dick* seems like masochism on Melville's part. That he should have embarked on his literary career with autobiographical works of travel was under the circumstances only natural, and the generally favourable reception they were accorded more than made up for the occasional raised eyebrow. Melville's revolt into transparent romance with *Mardi* had, of course, won him few friends, and he had felt compelled with *Redburn* and *White-Jacket* to show that he still had his feet firmly planted on the ground. Nevertheless, given his own personal dissatisfaction with those books it seems odd that he should have attempted to propitiate his readers with a substantial bone of whaling-knowledge, especially when the result provoked some hostility all the same. But the truth of the matter was that Melville had begun to realise that there was no way he could entirely satisfy his critics, since their real objection was to his determination to write in the Carlylean mode of *Sartor Resartus*, to open up, fragment and interlard his narrative with philosophical inquiry and metaphysical speculation instead of closing it down to provide a seamless and continually unfolding recital of events within an airtight fictional world. But Melville *did* want to be taken seriously and he did want the symbolic and allegorical dimension of *Moby-Dick* to be given full weight by readers who brought to the novel an unthinking and anti-intellectual cast of mind. By presenting man's encounter with God and the opacity of the universe in the guise of a whaling-voyage he could show that this confrontation was one of the utmost strenuousness, tension, frustration and danger and could in no wise be dismissed as airy wool-gathering or frothy romance. What *Moby-Dick* proclaims in every line is not only the reality of the real but the reality of *thought* as it is brought up against and endeavours to structure that real.

Yet even here there are paradoxes. It was important for Melville that his readers should believe that it was possible for a whale to sink a ship as the *Pequod* is sunk by Moby-Dick, and quite early in his narrative, in the chapter entitled 'The Affidavit', Melville adduces a number of more or less well authenticated cases. There is Owen Chace's 'plain and faithful' narrative (pp. 178–9) describing the sinking of the *Essex*, the damage to an American sloop of war commanded by Commodore J——, and the hearsay report of the loss of the ship *Union* under similar circumstances. In such calculations the putative size of the sperm whale enters importantly into the calculations. Melville draws attention to the difficulties of arriving at a true estimate of the whale's size, and in chapter 55, 'Monstrous Pictures of Whales', he insists that no adequate idea of it can be formed from the whale's skeleton:

> and the only mode in which you can derive even a tolerable idea of his living contour, is by going whaling yourself; but by so doing, you run no small risk of being eternally stove and sunk by him. Wherefore, it seems to me you had best not be too fastidious in your curiosity touching this Leviathan. (p. 228)

Yet, much later in the book, in that curious and curiously little discussed chapter 'A Bower in the Arsacides', Melville addresses himself precisely to the problem of the dimensions of the whale's skeleton. It comes after a whole series of documentary chapters in which various aspects of whaling and the whale's anatomy have been gone into in great detail. And he then brings up the question of Ishmael's credentials:

> But how now, Ishmael? How is it, that you, a mere oarsman in the fishery, pretend to know aught about the subterranean parts of the whale? Did erudite Stubb, mounted upon your capstan, deliver lectures on the anatomy of the Cetacea; and, by help of the windlass, hold up a specimen for exhibition? Explain thyself, Ishmael. Can you land a full-grown whale on your deck for examination, as a cook dishes a roast-pig? Surely not. A veritable witness have you hitherto been, Ishmael; but have a care how you seize the privilege of Jonah alone; the privilege of discoursing upon the joists and beams; the rafters, ridge-pole, sleepers, and under-pinnings, making up the framework of the leviathan; and belike of the tallow-vats, dairy-rooms, butteries, and cheeseries in his bowels. (p. 373)

What is the basis for the authoritative exposition of whales that Ishmael–Melville has provided? Well, it seems that for his 'exact knowledge of the bones of the leviathan in their gigantic, full grown development, for that rare knowledge I am indebted to my late royal friend Tranquo, king of Tranque, one of the Arsacides' (ibid.). It was within an Arsacidean wood that 'the great, white, worshipped skeleton lay lounging' (p. 375) and there that Ishmael with the aid of a green-measuring-rod ascertained that the length of the skeleton to be seventy-two feet and had this information tattooed on his right arm.

And so Melville pulls the reader's leg unmercifully. The whole massive structure of evidence about the whale that Melville has so carefully and exhaustively analysed and sifted is found to be supported by nothing more substantial than a Polynesian tall tale, as preposterous as any that Melville ever ventured in *Typee* or *Omoo*. At a stroke the indispensable distinction between sober fact and fanciful fiction is placed in the direst jeopardy. So Melville plays with his audience by drawing out how much of what we believe we know is based on report, legend and hearsay, and that nothing is really ever established beyond doubt no matter how much we might wish to be so. At the same time Melville throws in question the careful distinction that modernism has been so anxious to draw between Melville as author and Ishmael the narrative voice, even if it were not imperilled already by the carelessness with which Melville takes Ishmael up and puts him down. For the Ishmael that speaks here is more than a brother to Tommo and Taji. And behind that serious and sober mask lurks the irreverent, fantastic and irresponsible author that Melville's reviewers always knew him to be. Melville cannot help but be excessive, and his whimsical humour here is, or should be, the last straw that breaks the camel's back – or the whale's!

Yet for all his jests Melville is in deadly earnest about whaling, for whaling epitomises man's desire to give meaning to the world, whether through thought or by action. Although to seek the whale may be to court destruction, it is nevertheless the sole remedy for an incipient melancholia or paralysis of the will. At the opening of *Moby-Dick* Ishmael stresses not merely that to go to sea is a sovereign remedy for an inward bruise in his own particular case but that his own expedition is but a special case of a more universal curiosity:

> But look! here come more crowds, pacing straight for the water, and seemingly bound for a dive. Strange! Nothing will content them but the extreme limit of the land; loitering under the shady lee of yonder warehouse will not suffice. No. They must get just as nigh the water as they possibly can without falling in. . . . Yes, as everyone knows, meditation and water are wedded forever.   (p. 13)

The sea is a perennial image of 'the ungraspable phantom of life' (p. 14) and as such it exercises a powerful fascination even if those, such as Ahab, who insist on coming to some kind of ultimate reckoning with it are remarkably few. What needs to be stressed is that Melville wishes to insist on the representativeness of both Ishmael and Ahab. True, Ahab is possessed by 'monomania' (p. 160) and doubtless 'monomania' is fraught with meaning, but it is quite false to Melville's purpose to lay excessive emphasis on Ahab's abnormality. Ishmael is the shifter between the thoughts and feelings of ordinary men and the excessive ambitions of Ahab. He leaves the shore behind as other men do in their imagination and in doing so becomes caught up in Ahab's desperate struggle against the forces in life that continually seem to thwart him. Ahab is the Romantic Superman certainly, but at the same time, like Shelley's Prometheus, he symbolises the indomitable character of the human spirit as it refuses to yield or succumb before an unjust universe. But Melville is clear that, though there may be a massive difference in degree between Ahab and the mass of men, there is no difference in kind. There comes a time when every man must face up to the implications of existence and be ready to abandon peace and tranquillity, as Ahab casts aside his pipe. For it is only at such a moment that man can achieve his full intellectual potential. For Kant and Schiller true sublimity resided in the awakening of the human spirit when faced with the vastness of nature. To Melville the infinite is more malignant and threatening and the consonance between man and nature not to be assumed, but the encounter must take place all the same:

> All deep, earnest thinking is but the intrepid effort of the soul to keep the open independence of her sea; while the wildest winds of heaven and earth conspire to cast her on the treacherous, slavish shore.
>
> But as in landlessness alone resides the highest truth, shoreless, indefinite as God – so, better is it to perish in that howling infinite, than be ingloriously dashed upon the lee, even if that were safety! (p. 97)

Man achieves dignity by the resoluteness with which he maintains his purpose, by the very clarity with which he pits himself against a universe blurred and obscure.

There is, of course, an alternative way of viewing man's place in the world and that is provided by Father Mapple's sermon. But this chapter has been shamefully misused in persistent and intellectually unscrupulous attempts to read Melville against the grain and drown the very perplexities and ironies in which he revelled. Father Mapple's sermon is important certainly, and its positioning before the epic voyage even begins highly significant, but it has been transformed into an authoritative master discourse that can suppress every doubt and question and iron out every convoluted curve in Melville's narrative. The sermon spells out what is to be the focus of intellectual inquiry in *Moby-Dick*, the issue of man's independence. As far as Father Mapple is concerned, independence is a sin and the story of Jonah can be seen as a symbolic repetition of the rebellion of Adam and Eve which is more positively resolved in that Jonah is forcibly recalled by divine intervention to the mission from which he has strayed, and because the vomiting-up of Jonah out of the belly of the whale signifies spiritual rebirth. But by the same token, however, Jonah is a man who is compelled by God and by the power of God to give up his autonomy, and who, in Melville's later terms, is cast on 'the treacherous, slavish shore'. In Father Mapple's terms, man must be nothing more than a cypher.

In Melville's and Mapple's retelling of it the story of Jonah becomes an allegory of God's all-encompassing and all-engrossing nature. Moreover, Melville makes it quite explicit that this commitment to God necessarily involves a denial of man, by laying a curious emphasis on the fact that Mapple draws the ladder up after him into the pulpit, thereby symbolising his severance from the world of human fellowship and his withdrawal from 'all outward worldly ties and connections (p. 43). Jonah's guilty flight from God is quintessentially an act of disobedience, so much so that in introducing the story Father Mapple deliberately refuses to mention that Jonah was required to preach against the wickedness of Nineveh, but only refers to his 'wilful disobedience of the command of God – never mind now what that command was, or how conveyed' (p.45). For the lesson of countless biblical narratives from Abraham to Jonah is that God's commands are to be obeyed without question. Man's only role is to be an instrument of the divine will. God is omnipresent, vengeful and punitive – to Father Mapple, as to Jonah, chiefly known by his rod – and there is nowhere in the world that Jonah can escape him. Jonah's being swallowed up by the whale of course makes explicit the God–leviathan trope that pervades *Moby-Dick*, and here it is unmistakably an image of the engulfment and extinction of human personality in which Father Mapple positively rejoices:

> Yet what depths of the soul does Jonah's deep sea-line sound! What a pregnant lesson to us is this prophet! What a noble thing is that canticle in the fish's belly! How billow-like and boisterously grand! We feel the floods surging over us, we sound with him to the kelpy bottom of the waters; seaweed and all the slime of the sea is about us!   (Ibid.)

Yet we may well reflect that Jonah is vomited out onto dry land with the last vestige of his independence eradicated and that Mapple himself is no longer a seafaring sailor and takes his pulpit for a prow. Melville underlines the parallel between Ahab and the Jonah of Father Mapple by having both men wear a slouched hat, but there the resemblance ends. Where Jonah is guilty, cowardly and skulking, Ahab is bold, daring and defiant. For Melville Jonah is a rebel in bad faith, without either the conviction or the courage to follow it through. In the final analysis, Jonah's real crime is to give up, admittedly under extreme pressure: 'Jonah, bruised and beaten – his ears, like two seashells, still multitudinously murmuring of the ocean – Jonah did the Almighty's bidding' (p. 50). And we are thereby reminded of the pertinence of that strategically placed quotation that concludes Melville's anthology of whaling-lore and legend: of the rare old whale who is

> A giant in might, where might is right,
> And King of the boundless sea.
>   (p. 11)

As Melville sees it, God's omnipotence makes a mockery of all claims that the universe is just, since we are bound to find it just and crushed if we question that it is so. Melville heavily ironises Mapple's whole presentation of the issues raised by Jonah's humiliation by incorporating within it expressions that are glaringly out of place. According to Father Mapple, 'Delight is to him – a far, far upward, and inward delight – who against the proud gods and commodores of this earth, ever stands forth his own inexorable self' (p. 51). What Father Mapple has in mind, of course, is a man in the mould of the Old Testament prophets, who will maintain his commitment to Yahweh against false gods and worldly rulers, but his reference to 'inexorable self' fatally undermines the panegyric of self-abnegation, obedience and humility to which his parable of Jonah is devoted. The man with an inexorable sense of self, who truly stands up against proud gods insteads of cringing before them, is Ahab.

Transcendentalism has already promulgated a variety of such imperious conceptions of the self, insisting that man, far from being lowly creature totally dependent on God's grace as depicted by New England Calvinism, was always potentially Godlike. For Emerson, though man is currently diminished, this is not so much the result of Original Sin as a falling away from nature. If he is at present the dwarf of himself, the prospect of achieving his full stature lies close at hand. For Emerson everything in the universe is linked, everything is meaningful, everything teems with spirituality. When he exclaims, 'I am God in nature; I am a weed by the wall',[30] the Emersonian ego becomes the shuttle that weaves the world, linking the highest with the lowest. Transcendentalism in its Emersonian vestments abhors boundaries. The pantheistic mysticism of Emerson's notorious proclamation,

> Standing on the bare ground, – my head bathed by the blithe air and uplifted into infinite space, – all mean egotism vanishes. I become a transparent eyeball; I am nothing; I see all; the currents of the Universal Being circulate through me; I am part and parcel of God[31]

merges the individual into the world and sees no need to set him in opposition to it. But Melville sees man as necessarily creating his identity through struggle; it is a reactive formation or it is nothing. In 'The Masthead' Melville forcibly articulates his disquiet at this pantheistic, harmonising mood of Transcendentalism:

> but lulled into such an opium-like listlessness of vacant, unconscious reverie is this absent-minded youth by the blending cadence of waves with thoughts, that at last he loses his identity; takes the mystic ocean at his feet for the visible image of that deep, blue, bottomless soul pervading mankind

and nature; and every strange, half-seen, gliding beautiful thing that eludes him; every dimly-discovered, uprising fin of some undiscernible form, seems to him the embodiment of those elusive thoughts that only people the soul by continually flitting through it. In this enchanted mood, thy spirit ebbs away to whence it came; becomes diffused through time and space; like Wickliff's sprinkled Pantheistic ashes, forming at last a part of every shore the round globe over.

There is no life in thee, now, except that rocking life imparted by a gently rolling ship; by her, borrowed from the sea; by the sea, from the inscrutable tides of God. But while this sleep, this dream is on ye, move your foot or hand an inch; slip your hold at all; and your identity comes back in horror. Over Descartian vortices you hover. And perhaps, at mid-day, in the fairest weather, with one half-throttled shriek you drop through that transparent air into the summer sea, no more to rise for ever. Heed it well, ye Pantheists!   (p. 140)

Melville's rhetoric is both powerful and suggestive. The figure of the masthead faces two ways. On the one hand, as the highest point of the ship, at 'a thought-engendering altitude' (p. 139), it is a fitting place to succumb to Transcendental ambitions; on the other hand as the place where the look-out stands it is the site of care and continual vigilance. The Transcendentalist takes his imaginings for reality and succumbs to the delusive fascination of the mirage that floats before him. But the pantheist thereby loses not merely any tangible sense of the world but imperils his own identity. In the imaginary fusion of the two both are sacrificed. So that, although Transcendentalism purports to restore the sense of human identity and significance that Calvinism had sacrificed, it achieves this in so ambiguous a manner that the balance struck seems highly problematic. God, man and nature whirl round in an endless circle, and what starts out as miraculous self-assertion all too often ends up looking remarkably like a complacent and uncritical resignation.

Unfortunately that same resignation is attributed all too often to Melville himself, in what must constitute some of the most pertinacious misreadings ever perpetrated on a major writer. In *Moby-Dick*, as 'The Whiteness of the Whale' and many other chapters attest, Spinozist monism is the nightmare from which Melville is desperately trying to awake, yet for Newton Arvin and others it was a prospect that Melville allegedly could face with a truly Spinozan indifference. Arvin writes as follows:

> Some years after he had written *Moby-Dick*, Melville was sufficiently struck by a sentence of Spinoza's, quoted by Matthew Arnold, to mark the passage in his copy of Arnold's essays. The sentence is this: 'Our desire is not that nature may obey us, but, on the contrary, that we may obey nature.' Already in *Moby-Dick* there had been an intimation of this cosmic submissiveness. The desire to understand, to fathom, the whole truth about the White Whale – the desire that is manifest at every turn in the explanatory and meditative passages – this is at least the true beginning of wisdom. The willingness to submit, to accept, to 'obey', in that sense, would naturally follow. Father Mapple, indeed, in his sermon – employing, of course, the familiar language of faith – makes provision for this when he says that 'all the things that God would have us do are hard for us to do. . . . And if we obey God, we must disobey ourselves; and it is in this disobeying ourselves, wherein the hardness of obeying God consists.' The 'will' of nature, even if there is something godlike in it, is hardly synonymous with God's will in the Christian sense. Yet *Moby-Dick* seems to say that one might arrive at a kind of peace by obeying it.[32]

Arvin's interpretative strategy here is certainly curious. To elucidate *Moby-Dick* he resorts to a marking made many years later, when any reading of Melville would suggest how difficult to decipher such a marking might be, and he does so despite the fact that Melville made his hostility to the general tenor of Spinoza's philosophy abundantly apparent in *Pierre*, written immediately after *Moby-Dick*. But significantly the passage is required to buttress the authority of Father Mapple's sermon as a privileged moment in the text so that it can serve as an authoritative meta-discourse that cannot be shaken, no matter what efforts Melville may make, over hundreds of pages, to undermine it. With a similar highhandedness and apodeictic certainty Marius Bewley announced that the greatest chapter of *Moby-Dick* is 'The Grand Armada', and then, since both this chapter and canto XXVIII of Dante's *Paradiso* employ imagery of concentric circles, he proclaims that the book articulates an affirmative conception of religion and a vision of a good God.[33] Such propositions and such logic leave one gasping like the whale itself. But the approaches employed are structurally similar. A proposition from outside Melville is keyed in with a selected utterance within the text, and the powerful insinuation with which we are presented is that Melville, by allegedly agreeing with Spinoza, Dante, Shakespeare, Sophocles or whoever it may be, is to be incorporated into vague and undifferentiated Western cultural tradition, which at the same time serves as Melville's ticket of admission to the literary pantheon.

The menace that hovers so threateningly over *Moby-Dick* is of a world without difference. The question it provokes is whether in the face of it man can remain *in*different. For a universe that lacks specificity, individuation and particularity or response would seem to be one that possesses no meaning. Melville associated such a prospect with two philosophers in particular, Plato and Spinoza, and the way he linked their names in *Pierre* is evidence of the connections he posited between them. Plato devalued the material world by suggesting that it offered only degraded copies of a pure world of forms. For Spinoza God is the indwelling presence in all things and sole cause of everything that happens in the universe. If man loves God this is only to say that God, in man, loves himself. According to Spinoza all attempts to posit an autonomous centre in man are illusory, based on the fact that human reason seeks an explanation of things in proximate causes, whereas the search for causes must involve a regress to the first cause in God himself and the recognition that the necessity that governs the universe is beyond human understanding. For Spinoza our discourse about human identity is a mythology:

> *Prop. XLVIII* There is in no mind absolute or free will, but the mind is determined for willing this or that by a cause which is determined in its turn by another cause, and this one again by another, and so on to infinity. . . .
> *Note.* In the same manner it may be shown that there cannot be found in the mind an absolute faculty of understanding, desiring, loving, etc. Whence it follows that these and such like faculties are either entirely fictitious, or nothing else than metaphysical or general entities, which we are wont to form from individual things: therefore intellect or will have reference in the same manner to this or that idea, or to this or that

volition, as 'stoneness' to this or that stone, or man to Peter or Paul.[34]

Plato and Spinoza warn us against immersion in the particular, for in this way we form a distorted and imperfect picture of things which will disappear if we stand back and grasp the principle of unity that in reality pervades all things. For Spinoza wisdom and truth reside in a recognition of human limitations and an acceptance of the inscrutable principles of necessity that govern the universe. He concludes the fourth book of the *Ethics* by saying,

> But human power is considerably limited and infinitely surpassed by the power of external causes, and therefore we have not absolute power of adapting things which are outside us for our usage. But we shall bear with equanimity those things which happen to us contrary to that which a regard for our advantage postulates, if we are conscious that we have performed our duty and cannot extend the power we have to such an extent to avoid those things, and moreover, that we are a part of nature as a whole, whose order we follow. If we understand this clearly and distinctly, that part of us which is called our understanding, or rather intelligence, that is, the best part in us, will acquiesce in this entirely, and will endeavour to persist in that acquiescence. For in so far as we understand, we can desire nothing save that which is necessary, nor can we absolutely acquiesce in anything save what is true: and therefore in so far as we understand this rightly, the endeavour of the best part of us agrees with the whole order of nature.[35]

Man places himself in harmony with the natural order of things by accepting it, though there is a deadly twist even in this, since we must assume that the disposition by which man accepts this divine order must in some sense be understood as God loving and acquiescing in a world which he has himself made and which he totally permeates. The way in which Melville connects Spinoza with the sperm whale in *Moby-Dick* is thus full of irony. Melville meditating on the contrasted whale heads that lie on either side of the *Pequod* writes,

> Can you catch the expression of the Sperm Whale's there? It is the same he died with, only some of the longer wrinkles in the

forehead seem now faded away. I think his broad brow to be full of a prairie-like placidity, born of a speculative indifference as to death. But mark the other head's expression. See that amazing lower lip, pressed by accident against the vessel's side, so as firmly to embrace the jaw. Does not the whole head seem to speak of an enormous practical resolution in facing death? This Right Whale I take to have been a Stoic; the Sperm Whale a Platonian, who might have taken up Spinoza in his later years.   (pp. 283–4)

For Melville implies that all aspects of the Spinozan universe, God, man and nature, are equally to be characterised by indifference. Indifference and lack of difference are one and the same thing.

Moby-Dick is the symbolic crystallisation of this indifference. But neither Ishmael nor Ahab can regard him with the same equanimity. For Spinoza emotions are to be distrusted. In the *Ethics* he writes,

> He who rightly knows that all things follow from the necessity of divine nature, and come to pass according to the eternal natural and regular laws, will find nothing at all that is worthy of hatred, laughter, or contempt, nor will he feel compassion.[36]

For Melville, on the other hand, our very identity is bound up with our ability to feel, and feel powerfully. When Starbuck asks Ahab what price his vengeance will yield in barrels of oil on the Nantucket market, he answers, striking his breast, 'Let me tell thee, that my vengeance will fetch a great premium here' (*Moby-Dick*, pp. 143–4). Likewise the whiteness of the whale arouses in Ishmael not aesthetic admiration so much as *fear*. The chapter entitled 'The Whiteness of the Whale' is one long incantation of the feelings that whiteness invokes – we find 'dread' used twice, 'appall' three times, 'fear' and its derivatives five times, 'terror' and 'terrible' eight times. To question whiteness and to find it hideous as Ishmael does verges on the sacrilegious, since white has traditionally been the colour which the Christian and other religions have used to express purity, sanctity and divinity. Melville certainly becomes excessive and crosses the boundaries of decorum when, in the self-same sentence, he describes 'the Holy One that sitteth there white like wool' and yet depicts that whiteness as striking 'more of a panic to the soul than that redness which affrights in blood' (p. 164). Arguably a significant difference is to be drawn between Ahab's proud defiance and Ishmael's horror, since Christianity has always stressed that the Lord is to be feared and the grounds for doing so are fully dramatised in Father Mapple's citation of Jonah. But the fact remains that in *Moby-Dick* God is presented wholly as negativity, and it is to that negativity that Ahab and Ishmael both respond. Ishmael is incensed by the inscrutable nature of the world and integral to that impenetrability is the problem of assigning motivation and causality. Ahab's vow, 'be the white whale agent, or be the white whale principal, I will wreak that hate upon him' (p. 144), is crucially formulated because it focuses on the problem thrown up by Spinoza's doctrine of God as an indwelling presence in all creation. If this is the case then Starbuck's description of Moby-Dick as 'a dumb brute' who 'simply smote thee from blindest instinct' (ibid.) is naïve. For a notion of blind instinct provides no explanation and prompts a regressive search for further causes. To Ahab, the ruin of a man, standing on a dead stump, it is all the same whether the loss of his leg was apparently motiveless or not, since he experiences that wound as malignant and, not altogether unjustifiably, feels that something in the universe is responsible for it. Spinoza would claim that we must simply acquiesce in the working of cosmic forces according to certain inexorable laws, but Ahab is just not prepared to be so sanguine. And neither is Ishmael, as his blasphemous musings attest. Ishmael swears Ahab's oath like the other members of the crew and all become involved in a common crusade:

> How it was that they so aboundingly responded to the old man's ire – by what evil magic their souls were possessed, that at times his hate seemed almost theirs; the White Whale as much their insufferable foe as his; how all this came to be – what the White Whale was to them, or how to their unconscious understandings, also, in some dim, unsuspected way, he might have seemed the gliding great demon of the seas of life, – all this to explain would be to dive deeper than Ishmael can go. The subterranean miner that works in us all, how can one tell whither leads his shaft by the ever shifting, muffled sound of his pick? Who does not feel the irresistible arm drag? What skiff in

tow of seventy-four can stand still? For one, I gave myself up to the abandonment of the time and the place; but while yet all a-rush to encounter the whale, could see naught in the brute but the deadliest ill. (pp. 162–3)

It is in this way that Melville introduces Ishmael's reflections on the whiteness of the whale. Of course it cannot be doubted that Ahab's vendetta against the whale is supremely his own or that Melville attributes the welding of the crew into a common cause to the magnetic force of his personality. But at the same time it is perfectly clear that Ishmael is himself deeply disturbed by all the whale represents. If Ishmael is deliberately endowed with a certain tentativeness – i.e. 'to dive deeper than Ishmael can go' (p. 162) – this is because he, like the other characters, is a foil for the grandeur of Ahab, who alone is Superman and Prometheus. Only Ahab dares to be the excessive hero, or is crazy enough to venture it. But, as Melville well knew, with the example of *King Lear* in mind, those who seem craziest are those who have faced the truth. Ahab's higher representative stems from the fact that he takes it upon himself to assume the burden of Adam and question, like Milton's Adam in *Paradise Lost*, how the endless catalogue of disaster and misfortune can possibly be justified. It is for this that he has forsaken the peaceful land for forty years, so that he is 'deadly faint, bowed, and humped, as though I were Adam, staggering beneath the piled centuries since Paradise' (p. 444).

Ahab is an anachronistic hero – a man who seeks a direct confrontation with God in a return to the manner of the Old Testament, when Moses, Abraham and the prophets parleyed with Yahweh on strangely intimate terms. For New England Calvinism God's presence was felt more obliquely in signs, portents and omens – coded messages that had to be deciphered – but Ahab insists that the gods communicate with him directly: 'If the gods think to speak outright to man, they will honourably speak outright to man; not shake their heads, and give an old wives' darkling hint' (p. 452).

The world has lost its pristine immediacy. Of old, men knew who they were and what they were dealing with. But, after two thousand years of philosophy, thought and action have become fatally entangled and even the simple gesture of going to sea is fraught with metaphysical implications. So Ahab's confrontation with Moby-Dick has a double significance: it is both an attempt to cut through the Gordian knot of speculation and challenge God directly, and at the same time a desperate affirmation of man's ontological significance in a universe that seems to deny it. To say this is of course to recognise that the play of meaning in *Moby-Dick* is not reducible to mere distinctions between Ishmael's and Ahab's 'point of view' in the allegedly sophisticated manner of the new criticism. The intellectual argument of *Moby-Dick* is complex and continuous and is articulated through all the characters in the book. Melville asks us to face up to the implications of a world of indifference as much through Ishmael as through Ahab; to respond to a complex movement of thought that encircles and envelops the whale. To translate this ambitious and indeed excessive project into a mere whaling-man's cautionary tale in which Ishmael, like Jane Austen's Fanny Price, alone conducts himself with perfect rectitude is indeed to serve the whale without the head.

Within that overall argument the ivory leg that Ahab wears to replace the limb that he lost to Moby-Dick has a considerable importance. Certainly it represents Original Sin and thus for Melville a deliberate attempt by God or gods to diminish man's powers. The many flaws in Ahab's nature – his overbearingness, obsessiveness, apparent hard-heartedness – can be directly attributed to his mutilation by the whale. So that, philosophically considered, the responsibility for the disastrous cruise of the *Pequod* in an endless regress of causes can finally be laid at the door of God himself. But Melville addresses himself also to the implication that God is not only the indwelling presence and cause of all things but is himself universal material substance. Symbolically speaking Ahab's leg of whalebone represents the invasion of his human integrity and autonomy by a vindictive and jealous God who seeks to engulf him completely. For Melville man is not to be assimilated to the world of nature as Spinoza and the American Transcendentalists, in their quite different ways, would wish him to be. This would be to deny that which most crucially distinguishes man – his independence. Man is by definition a rebel, articulating himself through protest, defiance and rage against a cosmic order that continually and demoralisingly crushes him.

The carpenter who is assigned the task of replacing Ahab's leg after he splinters it in his hasty departure from the *Samuel Enderby* quite clearly stands for a Spinozan orientation to experience, since he merges the most diverse phenomena together in a comprehensive indifference. The carpenter draws no distinction between one task and another or between man and matter. He remains as completely unruffled and unperturbed as Spinoza believed one should be. In composing this portrait of him as a technician who exists as a pure instrumentality and extension of his tools Melville must have had Spinoza's occupation as a grinder of lenses in mind:

> Thus, this carpenter was prepared at all points, and alike indifferent and without respect in all. Teeth he accounted bits of ivory; heads he deemed but top-blocks; men themselves he lightly held for capstans. But while now upon so wide a field thus variously accomplished, and with such liveliness of expertness in him, too; all this would seem to argue some uncommon vivacity of intelligence. But not precisely so. For nothing was this man more remarkable, than for a certain impersonal stolidity as it were; impersonal, I say; for it so shaded off into the surrounding infinite of things, that it seemed one with the general stolidity discernible in the whole visible world; which while pauselessly active in uncounted modes, still eternally holds its peace, and ignores you, though you dig foundations for cathedrals. Yet was this half-horrible stolidity in him, involving, too, as it appeared, an all-ramifying heartlessness; – yet was it oddly dashed at times, with an old, crutch-like antediluvian, wheezing humorousness, not unstreaked now and then with a certain grizzled wittiness; such as might have served to pass the time on the bearded forecastle of Noah's ark. Was it that this old carpenter had been a life-long wanderer, whose much rolling, to and fro, not only had gathered no moss; but what is more, had rubbed off whatever small outward clingings might have originally pertained to him? He was a stript abstract; an unfractioned integral; uncompromised as a new-born babe; living without premeditated reference to this world or the next. You might almost say, that this strange, uncompromisedness in him involved a sort of unintelligence; for in his numerous trades, he did not seem to work by reason or by instinct or simply because he had been tutored to it, or by any intermixture of all these, even or uneven; but merely by a kind of deaf and dumb, spontaneous literal process. He was a pure manipulator; his

> brain, if he had ever had one, must have early oozed along into the muscles of his fingers. He was like one of those unreasoning but still highly useful, *multum in parvo*, Sheffield contrivances, assuming the exterior – though a little swelled – of a common pocket knife; but containing, not only blades of various sizes, but also screw-drivers, cork-screws, tweezers, awls, pens, rulers, nail-filers, countersinkers. So, if his superiors wanted to use the carpenter for a screw-driver, all they had to do was to open that part of him, and the screw was fast: or if for tweezers, take him up by the legs, and there they were. (pp. 388–9)

Apart from their philosophical pertinence other details in Melville's description of the carpenter also allude to Spinoza. Spinoza was born into a community of Spanish Jews in exile in Holland and his excommunication from the synagogue left him without cultural identity or 'outward clingings'. The 'cunning life-principle' in him that nevertheless keeps him soliloquising like the unreasoning humming wheel is Spinoza's philosophical system endlessly circulating from one proposition to another. The carpenter epitomises the inert insentient existence that to Ahab is anathema, and in their comic encounter Melville relishes the irony whereby Ahab is to be reconstructed by a 'manmaker' (p. 390), by a man who is himself a living death. As Ahab says, 'Take the hint, then; and when thou art dead, never bury thyself under living people's noses' (p. 396).

The invasion of Ahab's body by the carpenter typifies the threat which a materialistic universe poses to the human spirit. The fact that Ahab can still feel his lost leg – 'Canst thou not drive that old Adam away?' (ibid.) – suggests that man can never forget the paradisal period 'When Adam walked majestic as a God' (p. 165). In true Transcendental spirit, Melville affirms the priority of mind over matter. On the second day of the chase, when Ahab's leg snaps, Melville cashes the accumulated significance that he has so carefully built up. For Ahab insists that no external force or pressure can ever reach the deepest sources of his identity:

> Aye! and all splintered to pieces, Stubb! d'ye see it. – But even with a broken bone, old Ahab is untouched; and I account no living bone of mine one jot more of me than this dead one that's lost. Nor white whale, nor man, nor fiend, can so much as graze old Ahab in his own proper inaccessible being. (p. 458)

Ahab is therefore also a martyr who maintains an unquenchable spirit of resistance in the face of divine persecution. Ahab is the principle of fire, the Promethean spark of human independence, that remains in perennial opposition to the duller elements of earth and water. Ahab is the self-created Superman who has created his own internal spiritual kingdom that is truly not of this world.

It is characteristic of the rich, subtle and subversive irony of *Moby-Dick* that Melville should take the whale itself as the model for everything that man should be. For the inescapable implication is that man must model himself on God. For Melville the inscrutable nature of the hieroglyphical markings on the skin of the whale represents the opacity and illegibility of God's purposes. But equally the whale's massive blanket of blubber that keeps him comfortable and well insulated from his external environment signifies God's imperviousness to human suffering – as Ahab later says, 'see the omniscient gods oblivious to suffering man' (p. 428). The conclusion that Melville points to in 'The Blanket' is that man's only resort and refuge is to model himself on God and to remain as indifferent and impervious to the lamentable world that God has created as the divinity himself:

> It does seem to me, that herein we see the rare virtue of a strong individual vitality, and the rare virtue of thick walls, and the rare virtue of interior spaciousness. Oh, man! admire and model thyself after the whale! Do thou, too, remain warm among ice. Do thou, too, live in this world without being of it. Be cool at the equator; keep thy blood fluid at the Pole. Like the great dome of St Peter's and like the great whale, retain, O man! in all seasons a temperature of thine own. (p. 261)

But even in positing it Melville could not but acknowledge the hopelessness of such a satanic parody of Transcendentalist ambitions. To remain so totally insulated and so impervious to feeling he would have to be tougher than Ahab himself and made according to Ahab's specification: 'No heart at all, brass forehead, and about a quarter of an acre of fine brains' (p. 390). He would have to be super-superhuman.

Ahab's own declaration of independence comes when he smashes the quadrant and decides to steer by dead-reckoning, with rod and line. The quadrant that points toward the heavens and calculates a position with reference to the sun and stars becomes the symbol of the dependence of the sublunary world on the heavens, of man's inability to separate himself from the possibility of divine or transcendental guidance and of his abject position in relation to higher powers. Moreover, since astrology has always taught that men's lives are determined by the movements of the stars, Ahab's gesture can be seen as representing a determination to act freely and repudiate necessitarianism. Similarly the transposed compasses that Ahab uses can be seen as his use of a counter-magic to turn against the divine power. Needless to say, Melville is acutely conscious of the irony whereby Ahab, relying solely on his own resources, steers skilfully and directly to the final encounter with Moby-Dick and thus precipitates the last desperate struggle and the sinking of the *Pequod*.

The frightful spectre that stalks the death-ship of the *Pequod* is that all man's pretensions to independent action may be nothing more than a mirage. The image that runs through the novel – in 'The Mat-maker', 'A Bower in the Arsacides', 'The Castaway' – is of the universe as a gigantic loom constantly interlocking warp and weft in a remorseless and uncheckable rhythm. In 'A Bower in the Arsacides' in particular Melville presents us with sinister intimations of the world as sheer process, in which the God who shapes events is as unreflective and bemused as those who are on the receiving end: 'the weaver-god he weaves; and by that weaving is he deafened, that he hears no mortal voice; and, by that humming, we, too, who look on the loom are deafened' (p. 374).

We may surmise that the reason for the particular interest and sympathy that Ahab shows in Pip is that he too has grasped the terrifying indifference of the world and been overwhelmed by a sense of its relentless, implacable power as he sees 'God's foot upon the treadle of the loom' (p. 347). Ahab himself is tortured by the suspicion that even he may lack any true autonomy, that his every action however wilful may nevertheless be part of some predetermined pattern laid down from above. In the face of what is perhaps the most ominous portent of all, when the *Pequod* is struck by lightning, Ahab nevertheless proclaims his independence. Addressing his tutelary spirit of fire he proclaims,

> I now know thee, thou clear spirit, and I now know that thy right worship is defiance. To neither love nor reverence wilt

thou be kind; and e'en for hate thou canst but kill; and all are killed. No fearless fool now fronts thee. I own thy speechless placeless power; but to the last gasp of my earthquake life will dispute its unconditional, unintegral mastery in me. In the midst of the personified impersonal a personality stands here. (pp. 416–17)

Yet despite his determined revolt he cannot escape the suspicion that he is the tool of fate, that to strike through Ahab's own mask might be to encounter the visage of an omnipresent, omnipotent deity:

Is Ahab, Ahab? It is I, God, or who, that lifts this arm? But if the great sun move not of himself; but is an errand-boy in heaven; nor one single star can revolve, but by some invisible power; how then this one small heart beat; this one small brain think thoughts; unless God does that beating, does that thinking, does that living, and not I? (p. 445)

Yet he is able to accept the same premiss and transpose its significance when during the battle with Moby-Dick he proudly exclaims, 'Ahab is forever Ahab, man. This whole act's immutably decreed. 'Twas rehearsed by thee and me a billion years before this ocean rolled. Fool! I am the Fates' lieutenant; I act under orders' (p. 459).

This is a riddling utterance indeed, since almost immediately afterwards he insists, 'know that Ahab's hawser tows his purpose yet' (ibid.). In strangely Spinozan fashion that fate that is Ahab and the fate that is Moby-Dick become one and it becomes impossible to tell them apart. This is an ineluctable aporia which Ahab himself recognises. His cry, '*I'll, I'll* solve it, though!' (ibid.), is addressed to just this dilemma. Within the same speech Ahab follows his own acknowledgement that he acts under order with the command to Starbuck, 'Look thou, underling! that thou obeyest mine' (ibid.).

On the face of it Ahab's hypocrisy is abundantly clear. He denies Starbuck the right of rebellion that he arrogates to himself; he constantly rails against God yet insists on unquestioning obedience to himself. He is ready to use the musket on Starbuck, yet Starbuck cannot respond in kind. However, it needs to be stressed that rebellion is not indisputably the free act that it appears to be. As Starbuck hesitates by Ahab's bed with the musket in his hand, pondering the fact that by killing Ahab he might save the whole crew, it is significant that he could contemplate it if he felt that such an action were in accordance with the divine purpose! But of course he cannot know. In failing to kill Ahab he lacks the determination of his captain, but, as he stands by the door, is the angel he is wrestling with a good or a bad one? Starbuck does nothing because the morality of his action has become inscrutable – but so also has Ahab's.

Of many impious suggestions in *Moby-Dick* perhaps the most heretical is that the gods are as flawed as man; that the imperfection in man mirrors that of his creator. The livid scar that runs down Ahab's body and which he taunts the blacksmith to remove is matched by a like deformity in Moby-Dick – 'the wrenched hideousness of his jaw' (p. 448). As Melville suggests, 'the ineffaceable, sad birth-mark in the brow of man, is but the stamp of sorrow in the signers' (p. 386). And, as Ahab says addressing the spirit of fire, 'thou too hast thy incommunicable riddle, thy unparticipated grief' (p. 417). The gods themselves face the problem of imperfection, the mystery of imperfection, the prospect of infinite regress, the enigma of origins.

But in the face of fatality and the inscrutability of the world Ahab knows that his power to feel that had engendered his monomaniac purpose is nevertheless the core of his identity and human value:

> but Ahab never thinks; he only feels, feels, feels; *that's* tingling enough for mortal man! To think's audacity. God only has that right and privilege. Thinking is, or ought to be, a coolness and a calmness; and our poor hearts throb, and our poor brains beat too much for that. (p. 460)

Feeling is the uniquely human capacity, which distinguishes man both from God and from the material, insensate world. In a humorous mock dialogue with the masthead, Ahab both plays with the carpenter's perspective on the world and denies it:

> But good-bye, good-bye, old masthead! What's this? – green? aye, tiny mosses in these warped cracks. No such green weather stains on Ahab's head! There's the difference now between

man's old age and matter's. But aye, old mast, we both grow old together; sound in our hulls, though, are we not my ship.

(p. 462)

As the *Pequod* is pulled into the terrifying vortex of the ocean, Melville underlines the fact that absolutely no distinctions are to be made: 'the lone boat itself, and all its crew, and each floating oar, and every lance-pole, and spinning, animate and inanimate, all round and round in one vortex' (p. 469). It all makes no difference to an indifferent God, yet Melville insists on the difference just the same.

Moby-Dick was so powerful and so comprehensive an artistic statement that with it Melville virtually exhausted his creative resources. Yet he published *Pierre* only a year later. *Pierre* is a parallel work to *Moby-Dick*, articulating many of the same intellectual concerns, but in a manner that is more idiosyncratic and which, superficially, is more difficult to untangle. Much of the distinctiveness of Melville's fiction comes from the fact that its reference points are in travel literature and philosophy rather than in the tradition of the novel. But in *Pierre* Melville determined to address the theoretical problematics of the novel through a critique of contemporary romantic fictions as exemplified by the best-selling novelist Lord Lytton. As Leon Howard and Hershel Parker have pointed out, Pierre is conceived of as an antitype to Glyndon in Bulwer-Lytton's *Zanoni*, who is overly anxious about what people will think of him and who mistrusts his own powers (*Pierre*, pp. 370–2). But the novel also has as its target Bulwer-Lytton's two-volume romance *Ernest Maltravers* and *Alice, or the Mysteries*, from which the incestuous theme is directly drawn. Ernest Maltravers is a romantically handsome youth in the Byronic mould, but Bulwer-Lytton ostentatiously claims his novelistic allegiance to the example of Goethe's *Wilhelm Meister*, and thus to the tradition of the *Bildungsroman*, both by a prefatory acknowledgement and by a dedication to 'the Great German People'.[37] Ernest is a romantic hero in the Byronic mould, but he is also a 'wild, enthusiastic, odd being,'[38] 'full of strange German romance and metaphysical speculations'.[39]

Ernest Maltravers opens on a blasted heath in the vicinity of a northern manufacturing town, where the hero almost instantaneously falls in love with the beautiful fifteen-year-old daughter of a desperate ruffian called Luke Darvil. Alice warns

Ernest to make a hasty departure, since her father plans to murder him. They leave together and at his country cottage Alice is instructed by Ernest in reading, writing and music. Their passion is consummated, but Ernest is almost immediately called away to Germany to see his dying father. Alice sees Ernest again for a brief moment as he is proclaiming his attachment to another woman, but apart from this they do not meet again for many years and many protracted pages. Many years later Ernest meets the beautiful Evelyn, who is ward of Lumley Ferrers, now Lord Vargrave, an unscrupulous acquaintance of his. Maltravers is strangely drawn towards Evelyn and haunted by her image, which strangely reminds him of Alice, the girl he has lost. Hitherto he has imagined that he could never love again, but through his love for Evelyn he begins to live again: 'This enchanting child – this delightful Evelyn – this ray of undreamt of sunshine – smiled away all my palaces of ice',[40] so that 'in Evelyn he half loved Alice again'.[41] But his hopes are brutally dashed by Lord Vargrave, who covets Evelyn for himself and who tells him that Alice Darvil is Evelyn's mother and that there is a strong probability that he himself may be Evelyn's father. However, the dreadful spectre of incest so disconcertingly raised is soon laid to rest. Ernest finally meets Alice herself again and discovers that Evelyn is in fact the child of a sensual clergyman, Richard Templeton, who seduced a simple-minded girl called Mary Westbrook. The obstacle to any union with Evelyn is removed, but Maltravers, recalled to a sense of duty and his early love, marries Alice instead.

By giving *Pierre* the alternative title of 'The Ambiguities', Melville alluded quite unmistakably to Bulwer-Lytton's work, and it was to be an important part of his own project to retain the sense of ambiguity which Bulwer-Lytton has so rapidly dissipated. For Melville, in the spirit of Carlyle, life is inescapably mysterious, and therefore the novelistic stratagem of creating an initial mysteriousness only to resolve it all in a fatuous happy ending was nothing less than a calculated evasion of the very problem of existence. *Pierre*, like life, will leave the individual no alternative but to confront recalcitrant and inscrutable events. Of the mysterious heroine, Isabel, Melville writes,

> In her life there was an unraveled plot; and he felt that unraveled it would eternally remain to him. No slightest hope or dream had he, that what was dark and mournful in her would ever be

cleared up into some coming atmosphere of light and mirth. Like all youths, Pierre had conned his novel-lessons; had read more novels than most persons of his years; but their false, inverted attempts at systematizing eternally unsystematizable elements; their audacious, intermeddling impotency, in trying to unravel, and spread out, and classify, the more thin than gossamer threads which make up the complex web of life; these things over Pierre had no power now. Straight through their helpless miserableness he pierced; the one sensational truth in him, transfixed like beetles all the speculative lies in them. He saw that human life doth truly come from that, which all men are agreed to call by the name of *God*; and that it partakes of the unravellable inscrutableness of God. By infallible presentiment he saw, that not always doth life's beginning gloom conclude in gladness; that wedding-bells peal not ever in the last scene of life's fifth act; that while the countless tribes of common novels laboriously spin veils of mystery, only to complacently clear them up at last; and while the countless tribes of common drama do but repeat the same; yet the profounder emanations of the human mind, intended to illustrate all that can be humanly known of human life; these never unravel their own intricacies, and have no proper endings; but in imperfect, unanticipated, and disappointing sequels (as mutilated stumps), hurry to abrupt intermergings with the eternal tides of time and fate. (p. 141)

For Melville life is necessarily powerful, complex and overwhelming, and fate is the name that we give to an unforeseen and unforeseeable pattern of events that resists all our human attempts at explanation and analysis. By purporting to play God himself and by weaving only to unweave, the novelist does not merely fly in the face of our assured sense of the intransigence of the world through the banality of his optimism: he creates an illusion of transparency that is as mystifying as it is false. The difficulty of existence derives from the fact that there are no clear landmarks by which we can plot our course, and in reality that novelistic moment when obscurity suddenly and dramatically lifts never comes. The writer's moral duty to enforce this unpalatable conclusion is fatally at odds with the expectation that he should engross and entertain, and Melville's own aborted career as a novelist after *Pierre* has as much to do with his own recognition of this as with his own continuing lack of success. But in *Pierre* at least he had convinced himself that he could write a successful romantic novel that would nevertheless dismantle the genre completely, like a collapsing futurist sculpture.

Pierre seeks to expose the instability that is at the heart of things. At the opening of the novel Pierre as a youth is encompassed by the enchanting rural world of Saddle Meadows. His existence, his happiness, seems complete. He lacks nothing, materially or spiritually. He is loved completely, rapturously, devotedly by two women, his mother and his future bride, Lucy Tartan, and in each case there is no rival for his affections. Saddle Meadows seems to epitomise the strength and solidity of rural life and traditional virtues, yet even in announcing this rustic bliss Melville gestures towards the shadows that hover over it: 'In the country that Nature planted our Pierre; because Nature intended a rare and original development in Pierre. Never mind if hereby she proved ambiguous to him in the end; nevertheless, in the beginning she did bravely' (p. 13).

Pierre's identity seems secure because it seems that everything in his life is clear and unproblematic. There is no place for doubt. But from the very moment that Pierre begins to doubt, after his first encounter with Isabel, the foundations of his existence are irretrievably and fatally shattered. Pierre, as Melville so obviously intends, is as traumatised by this event as Hamlet is by the revelations of his father's ghost. Melville's literary borrowings and appropriations in *Pierre*, from *Hamlet* and Dante to Bulwer-Lytton, the Gothic tradition, and Romantics such as De Quincey, are so extensive that *Pierre* seems inescapably a novel of bricolage – and thus as perplexing to encounter as a building in which domes, turrets, spires and minarets are piled on pell-mell behind a classical portico. But what is certain is that Isabel's meaning and significance are undecidable. Isabel is the blackness in the world that fractures all theories, fancies and stabilising structures. Isabel is simply the name for the void that opens up in Pierre's existence. But Isabel is also importantly linked with the power of the imagination. Even before Pierre sees Isabel he is haunted by the power of a mysterious female face:

> Oh tree! so mighty thou, so lofty, yet so mournful! This is most strange! Hark! as I look up into thy high secrecies, oh, tree, the face, the face, peeps down on me! – 'art thou Pierre? Come to

me' – oh, thou mysterious girl, – what an ill-matched pendant thou, to that other countenance of sweet Lucy, which also hangs, and first did hang within my heart! Is grief a pendant then to pleasantness? Is grief a self-willed guest that *will* come in? (p. 41)

By introducing the face in this way, as Pierre sits beneath a pine tree emblematic of sadness, which has outlived 'a century of that gay flower's generations' (p. 40), Melville indicates that the mysterious face is representative of a continuous presence of grief in human existence – a grief of which Isabel is merely a contingent, though pregnant, instance, and that inexplicably invades the individual's existence and thus deprives it of the transparency that is joy.

Nevertheless this mysterious face is only the premonition of its actualisation in the person of Isabel. With the appearance of Isabel, Pierre is not merely haunted and provoked but totally possessed:

The face haunted him as some imploring, and beauteous, impassioned, ideal Madonna's haunts the morbidly longing and enthusiastic, but ever-baffled artist. And even as the mystic face thus rose before his fancy's sight, another sense was touched in him; the long-drawn unearthly, girlish shriek pealed through and through his soul; for now he knew the shriek came from the face – such a Delphic shriek could only come from such a source. And wherefore that shriek? thought Pierre. Bodes it ill to the face, or me, or both? How am I changed, that my appearance on any scene should have power to work such woe? But it was mostly the face – the face, that wrought upon him. The shriek seemed as incidentally embodied there.

The emotions he experienced seemed to have taken hold of the deepest roots and subtlest fibres of his being. And so much the more that it was so subterranean in him, so much the more did he feel its weird inscrutableness. What was one unknown, sad-eyed, shrieking girl to him? There must be sad-eyed girls somewhere in the world, and this was only one of them. And what was the most beautiful sad-eyed girl to him? Sadness might be beautiful, as well as mirth – he lost himself trying to follow out this tangle. 'I will no more of this infatuation', he would cry; but forth from regions of irradiated air, the divine beauty and imploring sufferings of the face, stole into his view.

Hitherto have I ever held but lightly, thought Pierre, all stories of ghostly mysticalness in man; my creed of the world leads me to believe in visible, beautiful flesh, and audible breath, however sweet and scented; but only in visible flesh, and audible breath, have I hitherto believed. But now – now! – and again he would lose himself in the most surprising and preternatural ponderings, which baffled all the introspective cunning of his mind. Himself was too much for himself. He felt that what he had always before considered the solid land of veritable reality, was now being audaciously encroached upon by bannered armies of hooded phantoms, disembarking in his soul, as from flotillas of specter-boats.

The terrors of the face were not those of Gorgon; not by repelling hideousness did it smite him so; but bewilderingly allured him, by its nameless beauty, and its long-suffering hopeless anguish.

But he was sensible that this general effect upon him, was also special; the face somehow mystically appealing to his own private and individual affections; and by a silent and tyrannic call, challenging him in his deepest moral being, and summoning Truth, Love, Pity, Conscience, to the stand. Apex of all wonders! thought Pierre; this indeed almost unmans me with its wonderfulness. Escape the face he could not muffling his own in his bedclothes – that did not hide it. Flying from it by sunlight down the meadows was as vain.   (pp. 48–9)

The face represents not only the mysteriousness of the world but the imperious claims of the Romantic imagination. The reference to 'specter-boats' links the image to Coleridge's 'spectre bark' in 'The Rime of the Ancient Mariner', while the face itself deliberately recalls the celebrated passage in De Quincey's *Confessions of an English Opium Eater* in which De Quincey describes the most powerful and disturbing dreams that he experienced under the influence of opium:

The waters now changed their character, – from translucent lakes, shining like mirrors, they now became seas and oceans. And now came a tremendous change, which, unfolding itself slowly like a scroll, through many months, promised an abiding torment; and, in fact, it never left me until the winding up of my case. Hitherto the human face had mixed often in my dreams, but not despotically, nor with any special power of tormenting. But now that which I have called the tyranny of the human face began to unfold itself. Perhaps some part of my London life may be answerable for this. Be that as it may, now it was that upon the rocking waters of the ocean the human face began to appear: the sea appeared paved with innumerable faces, upturned to the heavens: faces, imploring, wrathful, despairing, surged upwards by thousands, by myriads, by generations, by centuries: – my agitation was infinite, – my mind tossed – and surged with the ocean.[42]

It is under the influence of the imagination that the individual is disjoined from the complacency of the everyday world and finds abysses not broad meadows before his feet. It is the imagination that challenges our sense of the facts and acts as a solvent on the notion of reality. The face opens up a duality in Pierre's perception of the world where formerly there had been unity and harmony. In the gallery of his mind alongside the image of Lucy is now a contrary dark image; alongside the large, ponderous and respectable picture of Pierre's father as paterfamilias appears the small, provocative chair portrait. Significantly it is through his encounter with Isabel that Pierre is transformed into a writer, but in recognising this we must remain conscious that for Melville the imaginative is not some autonomous higher world but rather itself a sceptical principle that places everything in doubt. The chair portrait finally is no truer or more final than the large portrait at Saddle Meadows or the later resemblance that Pierre comes across; what is significant about it is its power to put its antitype in question and thus open up a process of interrogation and contradiction in which all finalities are abandoned.

Pierre's action in leaving Saddle Meadows is a self-conscious and deliberate attempt to sail into uncharted waters regardless of the risks or of the consequences. Hitherto everything in his life has been mapped out for him in advance, but now he positively embraces chance and uncertainty with all the recklessness of a fifth-act Hamlet. To face the possibility of incest is, philosophically considered, merely to recognise the multifariousness of the world and the complexity of human destinies. For Pierre to refuse his affinity with Isabel would be an impoverishment of his existence, and therefore he refuses to accept that limit just as Thoreau refuses to accept the meanness of life as it is lived in his rendezvous with destiny at Walden. Only their trajectories are reversed, as Thoreau forsakes Concord for the woods, Pierre the country for the town. Pierre cannot tear up Isabel's letter just because to do so would have been the easy way. Melville theologically thus defines goodness as the path of difficulty:

> The good angel seemed mildly to say – Read, Pierre, though by reading thou may'st entangle thyself, yet may'st thou thereby disentangle others. Read, and feel that best blessedness which, with the sense of all duties discharged, holds happiness indifferent. The bad angel insinuatingly breathed – Read it not, dearest Pierre; but destroy it and be happy. (*Pierre*, p. 63)

Pierre's actions prove as catastrophic for himself and for everyone else as do those of Ahab, but Melville is in no doubt that he has acted under the sway of an ineluctable moral necessity. To act selfishly and to avoid risk may well be prudent and profitable but it can never be either honourable or intelligent. Pierre adopts the horological standard of virtue and rejects the opportunism of a Plotinus Plinlimmon that denies either the possibility or relevance of acting according to an absolute moral standard. By trying to act out a superhuman love in the world's despite, Pierre, Isabel and Lucy aspire to the ranks of angels and seraphim. They are excessive, hero and heroines together. But, even if they tragically fail, Melville suggests that they have demonstrated a human potentiality for greatness, and their downfall is brought about as much by the world as by themselves.

Finally, however, the philosophical and moral preoccupations of *Pierre* are swamped by Melville's own disillusionment with America and the possibilities that it offered for the writer and artist. Until *Pierre*, with the possible exception of *White-Jacket*, Melville had never really addressed himself to the actual conditions of American life, so that it is in *Pierre* that his deep bitterness of spirit finally comes out. Melville never ceased to feel that America had never truly lived up to its revolutionary promise or that the American agenda remained still to be carried out, and in his most optimistic moments he fondly imagined that the banner raised by the generation of 1776 would be carried forward by the writers and artists of mid century. The pen would supplant the sword. It is for this reason that Pierre is given an impeccable revolutionary pedigree. But the failure of America to sustain the artist feeds back into a critique of America itself, for in this way the nation has failed its own best sons and daughters – already in *Pierre* we find outlines of the stance taken up by Ezra Pound, that it is by their treatment of the arts and artists that civilisations are to be judged. The pathos of Pierre's predicament is that he is always struggling against invisible enemies. As he gazes at his father's old campaign bedstead Melville observes,

> But has that hard bed of War, descended for an inheritance to the body of Peace? In the peaceful time of full barns, and when the noise of the peaceful flail is abroad, and the hum of peaceful commonsense resounds, is the grandson of two Generals a warrior too? Oh, not for naught in the time of this seeming peace, are warrior grandsires given to Pierre! For Pierre is a warrior too; Life his campaign, and three fierce allies, Woe and Scorn and Want, his foes. The wide world is banded against him; for lo you! he holds up the standard of Right, and swears by the Eternal and True! But ah, Pierre, Pierre, when thou goest to that bed, how humbling the thought, that thy most extended length measures not the proud six feet four of thy grand John of Gaunt sire! The stature of the warrior is cut down to the dwindled glory of the fight. For the more glorious in real tented field to strike down your valiant foe, than in the conflicts of a noble soul with a dastardly world to chase a vile enemy who ne'er will show his front.   (pp. 270–1)

Either the writer achieves a fortuitous and arbitrary success, as Melville himself had done with *Typee*, or else he finds himself continually thwarted, baffled and obstructed by an unresponsive, uncomprehending and unseen audience that becomes the more resistant as he struggles toward intensity of statement. As Melville writes,

> Who shall tell all the thought and feelings of Pierre in that desolate and shivering room, when at last the idea obtruded, that the wiser and profounder he should grow, the more and more he lessened his chances for bread?   (*Pierre*, p. 305)

The paradox is that a country that prides itself on the freedom and independence of the individual should be so hostile to actual manifestations of such a spirit in its writing. But Melville is also haunted by the fear of the second and third generation after the Revolution that they may themselves fall short of the stature of their illustrious sires. So part of the difficulty in being an excessive hero is that, although the world may perceive one as excessive, in reality one may not be nearly excessive enough; that in a shrunken, Lilliputian world the whole scale of action and achievement may have been profoundly altered. The determination to fly in the face of the world no matter what the cost may give way to the fear that true greatness may yet be impossible, no matter how terrible the price.

Melville's disillusioned mood persisted, though in a more sardonic mood, in *Israel Potter* (1855) and *The Confidence-Man* (1857). The denial of recognition, experienced by Pierre as tragic, is transposed into a humorous key. Melville's suggestion that Israel Potter's birthplace in Berkshire, Massachusetts, is the home of Titans and thus a fitting birthplace for such a devoted patriot renders farcical a mythic analogy which in *Pierre* he had explored in deadly earnest. Israel is an excessive hero who is forced into a whole series of desperate measures, adventures and escapes simply in order to return home, and the ironic focus is on the disproportion between the effort and the result. But for his pains the veteran of Bunker Hill is not greeted like a long-lost hero but narrowly escapes being knocked down by a triumphal car flying the legend,

BUNKER HILL
1775
GLORY TO THE HEROES THAT FOUGHT[43]

In *The Confidence-Man* Melville sharpened his knives to expose the gap between an American spirit of optimism based on a universal need for confidence, on the one hand, and the canny shrewdness with which each individual calculated his own advantage, on the other. In effect, to show confidence was to be a dupe. Melville felt that American culture was sadly lacking in idealism. When closely scrutinised, even such representative cultural figures as Benjamin Franklin and Emerson emerged as deeply flawed, concealing a definite opportunism and eye for the main chance behind a pose of lofty and disinterested idealism. What Melville called Franklin's 'working wisdom' involved a decided italicisation of the modifier. Similarly, Mark Winsome, *The Confidence-Man*'s Emerson figure is described as 'a kind of cross between a Yankee peddler and a Tartar priest, though, it seemed as if, at a pinch, the first would not in all probability play second fiddle to the last'.[44] The efficaciousness of the Emersonian philosophy lies in the fact that, since it places so much stress on the judgement and autonomy of the individual, it leaves abundant scope for the evasion of any serious commitment. It is for this reason that, 'moonshine as it in theory may be, yet a very practical philosophy it turns out in effect'.[45] Although at the end of 'Self-Reliance' Emerson eloquently insisted that nothing but the triumph of principle could ever bring the individual peace, that triumph could in practice always be postponed until the Greek Kalends. Melville could not believe in such a painless virtue.

Nevertheless, the most trenchant expression of Melville's war with American society is a short story, first published in *Harper's New Monthly Magazine* in November and December 1853, in the year after the publication of *Pierre*. Though Melville was never a Transcendentalist pure and simple, it is this seemingly humble and unpretentious story about a seemingly humble and unpretentious man that most powerfully expresses the rejection of American society and its emergent capitalist order by its idealists and intellectuals, a development that Emerson referred to in his lecture 'The Transcendentalist':

> It is a sign of our times, conspicuous to the coarsest observer, that many intelligent and religious persons withdraw themselves from the common labors and competitions of the market and the caucus, and betake themselves to a certain solitary and critical way of living, from which no solid fruit has yet appeared to justify their separation. They hold themselves aloof; they feel the disproportion between their faculties and the work offered them, and they prefer to ramble in the country and perish of ennui, to the degradation of such charities and such ambitions as the city can propose to them.[46]

On a symbolic level it is not hard to perceive Bartleby as a representation of the superfluous American writer. The argument presented in this book that there was no social space available to the American writer is perfectly exemplified by Melville's hero, who does not belong, has nowhere to go, and whose apparently strange refusal to leave suggests both the writer's sense of himself as an importunate and unwelcome hanger-on amid the bustle and solemn earnestness of the marketplace and at the same time his persistent and seemingly perverse belief that he really does have some sort of a claim on the American world and some sort of right to a place within it. Early in the tale Melville, in describing the monotony of the scrivener's task of verifying his copy, writes,

> It is a very dull, wearisome, and lethargic affair. I can readily imagine that, to some sanguine temperaments, it would be altogether intolerable. For example, I cannot credit that the mettlesome poet, Byron, would have contentedly sat down with Bartleby to examine a law document of, say five hundred pages, closely written in a crimpy hand. (*Piazza Tales*, p. 24)

To invoke Byron in such a context must have seemed odd to Melville's contemporary readers. Why invoke the shade of the lofty Romantic poet in such a humdrum context? But Melville is entirely serious. For how can the contemporary American successors to Byron make a living if not in circumstances such as these? Melville also knows that you do not have to be a Byron to object to boring, dehumanising, alienated labour.

The unprepossessing Bartleby is the most unlikely type of excessive hero, but if he is one this is because Melville's complacent bourgeois narrator, a lawyer who prides himself on having enjoyed John Jacob Astor's good opinion, regards any manifestation of individuality whatsoever as excessive. His parade of tolerance is a tolerance that is conducted entirely on his own terms and which masks a real spirit of intolerance. He only employs the seemingly colourless Bartleby as a way of whipping the other clerks into line. For he finds their every attempt to express their personality, their every suggestion of dissatisfaction with their grinding, relentless, ill-paid work, intolerable. He is incensed by the elderly Turkey's 'too energetic behaviour', by his 'strange, inflamed, flurried, flighty recklessness of activity' (p. 18) which at times leads to blots on the manuscript and indecorous outbursts of passion over damaged pens. He regrets his 'kindly' (p. 19) gesture in giving Turkey a coat (the wages he pays are too low to permit Turkey to buy one for himself), because he feels that this gives him an inflated idea of himself: 'In fact, precisely as a rash, restive horse is said to feel his oats, so Turkey felt his coat. It made him insolent. He was a man whom prosperity harmed' (p. 21).

Indeed, it is only men of the class of John Jacob Astor and the narrator who are not so impaired. The narrator finds the ways of the younger Nippers equally irksome. He is annoyed that Nippers, not satisfied with the boring copying-work, has the effrontery to claim to be able to draw up legal documents, and that his 'diseased ambition' (p. 20) leads him to receive a succession of seedy clients within the hallowed portals of the office. Nippers's 'irritable, brandy-like disposition' (p. 21) is bad enough, but his pretensions to independence are unforgivable. The narrator believes that through the agency of Bartleby he will be able to put down altogether such fractious and importunate displays of individuality and resistance, however marginal. He will place Bartleby between the clerks and himself and separate himself off from Bartleby with a screen. Bartleby will be always available yet always unseen, the perfect *factotum*:

> I should have stated before that ground glass folding-doors divided my premises into two parts, one of which was occupied by my scriveners, the other by myself. According to my humor, I threw open these doors or closed them. I resolved to assign Bartleby a corner by the folding-doors, but on my side of them, so as to have this quiet man within easy call, in case any trifling thing was to be done. I placed his desk close up to a small side-window in that part of the room, a window which originally had afforded a lateral view of certain grimy backyards and bricks, but which, owing to subsequent erections, commanded at present no view at all, though it gave some light. Within three feet of the panes was a wall, and the light came down from far above, between two lofty buildings, as from a small opening in a dome. Still further to a satisfactory arrangement, I procured a high green folding screen, which might entirely isolate Bartleby from my sight, though not remove him from my voice. And thus, in a manner, privacy and society were conjoined.   (p. 23)

Bartleby has no autonomous space of his own, unlike the other clerks, who at least have their own office. He is made to lurk on the fringes of his employer in a lonely, isolated and wholly subservient existence. His enclave is nothing more than a prison. Indeed, it is one of the many subtle ironies of the tale that, when Bartleby's erstwhile employer visits him in the Tombs prison, he can point out to him advantages of his lot there such as he never enjoyed at the office: 'And see, it is not so sad a place as one might think. Look, there is the sky, and here is the grass' (p. 51). For the Transcendentalist certainly, prison would be preferable.

The narrator's plan fails to work. Bartleby is prepared to work endlessly and silently copying documents, but he is not prepared to correct and collate the documents and, above all, he is not prepared to be at his employer's beck and call. Bartleby's insidiously and persistently uttered 'I would prefer not to' (p. 26) strikes at office discipline and the hoped-for structure of power in a way that the grumbles, exhibitions and irritations of the other clerks never can. By simply refusing, albeit politely, Bartleby challenges in the most subversive way his employer's rationale of his own behaviour and his hypocritical parade of reasonableness and benevolence. In his words, his actions and his suggestions the narrator seeks to impose his view of things upon those who work for him. Whatever he asks and whatever he demands is always reasonable, no matter how excessive the demands and no matter how little the pay, simply because he is the employer. Bartleby is perverse and excessive, the employer moderate by definition. But Bartleby resists this implication. When the narrator implores him to be reasonable, '"At present I would prefer not to be a little reasonable", was his mildly cadaverous reply' (p. 36). Bartleby will not be reasonable because the price of such reason is servitude and the loss of independence.

When the narrator comes round to the office on a Sunday and discovers Bartleby there in a state of shabby undress, he is thoroughly disconcerted and feels a mixture of guilt and unease. For he is suddenly reminded that the automaton secreted behind the screen is actually a fellow human being and that he has had the temerity to transform this working-niche into a 'bachelor's hall' (p. 33). Like a mouse he lives on nothing but the crumbs of ginger-nuts and morsels of cheese. The narrator is well aware of the many victims of a capitalist system, but most of the time he prefers to forget about them. On a Sunday he may be momentarily reminded of his Christian duty to others, but Melville thereby indicates how such attitudes are also thrust into remote corners, along with Bartleby, most of the time. Bartleby's personal life and that of millions of others is something to be blotted out 'from a certain hopelessness of remedying excessive and organic ill' (p. 35). In truth it is capitalism itself that is excessive. With the best will in the world the narrator dismisses Bartleby and pays for his meals in prison when he has been removed there as a vagrant. The system and the narrator are always well intentioned and benign, always reasonable. It is *Bartleby*, they insist, who is excessive.

Billy Budd, Melville's last, posthumously published work, also concerns a conflict between the individual and the system, but one whose implications are pursued at a far more metaphysical level: the question that this deceptively simple narrative raises is whether it is possible for goodness, beauty and innocence to survive in the world – a question which, in that form, would never have crossed Melville's mind when, some forty-five years earlier, he embarked on the writing of *Typee*. Billy, the handsome and good-natured sailor, represents an ideal of moral purity too powerful, too exemplary, too dazzling for the world to bear. Billy is the divine man in sober fact, but at the same time he undermines the Transcendentalist faith that all this lies within the compass of aspiration and emulation. Billy Budd is *sui generis*. His example is intolerable just because it is so evidently out of reach. In the world, perfect goodness can be neither normal nor acceptable, only excessive. Billy provokes resentment because there is no common measure between himself and others, no element of striving or strain that could convince them that such virtue is always possible, if difficult. Billy's resolve, after witnessing a flogging, that 'never through remissness would he make himself liable to such a visitation or do or omit aught that might merit even verbal reproof' (p. 68) very naturally provokes incredulity because it is impossible. This recalls the words of the Apostles' Creed, with its reference to things that should and should not have been done, but the very language of the Creed takes it for granted that this will occur. That someone might be unable to say those words truthfully is unthinkable. But Billy's resolve is still more preposterous because it somehow assumes that his ability to stay out of trouble depends purely on his own perfection and not on how he is perceived or dealt with by others – whereas it is the very impossibility of faulting him that brings retribution upon his head. As a hypothetical reminder of what man was or could have been, Billy can be the subject of wonder or nostalgia, even bringing tears to the eyes of a Claggart, but as a living and possible/impossible instance of it he becomes unbearable. It is Billy's 'significant personal beauty' (p. 77) that first moves Claggart against him.

Billy's congenital stutter, his inability to communicate which involuntarily produces the deadly blow to Claggart's head, is indeed a fatal flaw, but it represents not so much flawed goodness as a flaw in goodness itself. Goodness, no matter how extraordinary, is simply incapable of resisting the power of interpretation. Billy's own behaviour is completely transparent and straightforward, and in his innocence he assumes that what is true of himself is true of others. As Melville says, 'To deal in double meanings and insinuations of any sort was quite foreign to his nature' (p. 49). It is only the old Dansker who can explain to him, while omitting the complex chains of reasoning that lead to this conclusion, that 'Jimmy Legs is down on you' (p. 71).

But, once interpretation begins – and, of course, interpretation can never be halted even for a second – Billy Budd is doomed. For interpretation is necessarily based on the assumption that behaviour, words and actions are not completely clear and transparent, otherwise interpretation would not be necessary. So to interpret is to search for whatever is hidden, occulted or otherwise displaced. Moreover, he who interprets also masters, since it is his interpretation that controls meaning and not the actions and events that give rise to it. The meaning of Billy Budd is never a matter for Billy himself but always a concern for Claggart, Captain Vere and anyone else who, then or now, submits the evidence to his scrutiny. But further interpretation can only proceed on the basis of assumptions about normal human behaviour, and these assumptions must necessarily exclude from their calculations impossible ideas of perfect goodness and, correspondingly, always look for the worst. So, for Billy, things will always look bad. His simple farewell to his old shipmates, his spilling the soup in Claggart's path, will always be open to misconstruction. When Claggart says, 'You have but noted his fair cheek. A man trap may be under his ruddy-tipped daisies' (p. 94), there must always be a strong presumption, to put it no higher, that Claggart is right. Billy's blow is an attempt to resist this power of interpretation, but it is a gesture in vain. Vere may intuitively recognise both Billy's goodness and his innocence but they will always lie beyond inference and demonstration, precisely because they are excessive.

Yet even such an account is idealistic, since it assumes that the object of inquiry must be the truth and justice of an overriding moral requirement, which is, of course, very far from being the case. The context of Melville's narrative is the British navy in the immediate aftermath of the Mutiny at the Nore, where the ruling class faces not only a formidable military opponent in France, but internal and justified disaffection amongst lower orders who are no longer content to know their place. As ever, considerations of democracy, liberty, justice, the righting of abuses will have to be subordinated to the overriding need to maintain, perpetuate and legitimise the system. Even if the abuses are real, the resistance justified, this can never be openly admitted, since to do so would be to undermine the system's credibility. So naval discipline cannot actually judge anything but only assert its power. So a failure to act against Bill Budd 'would tend to awaken any slumbering embers of the Nore among the crew' (p. 104) and a clement sentence would be thought 'pusillanimous' (p. 113). Like Natty Bumppo, like Hester Prynne, Billy Budd, the excessive hero, can survive only in legend.

3 Mark Twain: the Torture of Excess

From the writing of his very first story, 'The Celebrated Jumping Frog of Calaveras County', Mark Twain could never escape the imputation of being excessive. His credibility was always at stake. In this his predicament resembled that of Melville, since they were both strongly suspected of extravagantly embroidering the facts and even of shameless invention, yet on the face of it this should not have been much of a problem. Melville, after all, was presenting himself as a serious man and a truthful reporter, while Twain, as a self-confessed Western humorist, might be expected to relay tall tales as a matter of professional necessity. Yet this almost inevitably meant that Twain's narrative would be received with a raised eyebrow and a knowing wink and that any pretension he might have as a serious writer would continually run up against the massive social fact of his current reputation and the all-pervading odour of mendaciousness. So Twain's and Melville's literary careers follow entirely different trajectories. Melville has to struggle against the demand for plain and unvarnished truth in order to create space for the claims of the imagination, while Twain has to struggle to write something that will seem convincing. In this connection, of course, the manner of the Western yarn-spinner becomes a serious liability. Since his endeavour is to take in some naïve and credulous auditor by palming off some grotesquely exaggerated tale as no more than a plain account of well-attested and authenticated facts, it is incumbent on him to unburden himself of his narrative with the utmost sobriety.

In 'The Celebrated Jumping Frog' Twain introduces his Western storyteller as follows:

> Simon Wheeler backed me into a corner and blockaded me there with his chair, and then sat me down and reeled off the

monotonous narrative which follows this paragraph. He never smiled, he never frowned, he never changed his voice from the gentle-flowing key to which he tuned the initial sentence, he never betrayed the slightest suspicion of enthusiasm; but all through the interminable narrative there ran a vein of impressive earnestness and sincerity, which showed me plainly that, so far from imagining that there was anything ridiculous or funny about his story, he regarded it as a really important matter, and admired its two heroes as men of transcendent genius in *finesse*. To me, of course the spectacle of a man drifting serenely along through such a queer yarn without ever smiling, was exquisitely absurd. (*Sketches New and Old*, pp. 27–8)

Twain is at pains to distance himself from Wheeler and merely presents him as a characteristic phenomenon of the frontier culture that can only be viewed with a kind of wonder. Wheeler's tale is quite inseparable from his manner of telling it, which involves overpowering the listener by trapping him in a corner and forcing him to listen to a continuous monologue that is saturated with circumstantial detail. Although the events he describes seem far-fetched, they acquire a certain weightiness through the evident involvement of their narrator, through his apparent concern to get the facts right ('in the winter of '49 – or maybe it was the spring of '50' – p. 28) and through the deftness with which the occasional litotes ('You never seen a frog so modest and straightfor-ard as he was, for all he was so gifted' – p. 30) is scattered amongst the hyperbole. The tale seeks to make its point with the tactics of the heroes it celebrates, by masking a high degree of sophistication and cunning behind an apparently artless and unprepossessing appearance. The illusion that Simon Wheeler conjures up is so powerful that Smiley looms up vividly in his mingled astonishment, bafflement and subsequent rage. But it seems that such a powerful rhetoric is almost going to waste by being lavished on so insubstantial a cause.

In reading Twain we become distinctly conscious of the United States as a new nation that lacks the stable and well-established social levels from which authoritative or apparently authoritative pronouncements can be issued. Excessiveness signifies that many battles are simultaneously in progress and, equally, that there is no particular confidence on anybody's part either that they should believe or be believed. The pretence of objectivity is simultaneously out of reach and scarcely worth trying for as a variety of groups and individuals struggle to impose their views upon the rest. Settlers are lured to remote and desolate places in the West by boastful and boosting promotion. The incipient art of advertising acquires potency and force. In the general hurly-burly a certain tolerance is called for, and many a Western tall-tale may pass unchallenged if its veracity can always be supported by an appeal to violence. Faced with many conflicting and assertive claims, the individual develops the art of assessing everything he hears carefully. Like a pawnbroker he fixes his estimate at a figure that is invariably on the conservative side. He takes his shrewdness for granted since it is almost habitual, and he prides himself on his ability to avoid being taken in. Yet at the same time his emotional loyalties are heavily tied up in such inflationary currency and he is quick to resent any potential slight or oblique suggestion that the causes and enterprises in which he takes pride are in any way less than he claims them to be. The world of hyperbole is at once at expansive, easy-going, prideful web of sociability and a treacherous, enveloping web of deceit. And Twain is a man completely at home here, attuned to realities that words inflate or belie.

Twain's America is a combative sort of place and it is in such a combative spirit that Twain and his fellow passengers set forth aboard the *Quaker City* for 'the great Pleasure Excursion to Europe and the Holy Land' (*The Innocents Abroad*, I, 45), the journey that produces *The Innocents Abroad*. Their motives are decidedly mixed. The puritan culture epitomised in the name of their vessel favours modestly, control, sobriety and restraint, yet their journey seems frankly dedicated to enjoyment; it is to be 'a picnic on a gigantic scale' (ibid.). Abroad itself is a kind of excess, since it involves exposing oneself to a positive superflux of cultural difference. Tangiers, Twain comments, 'is a foreign land if ever there was one' (I, 114), since the exaggerated pictures they have seen of it 'have not told half the story' (I, 113–14). Tangiers is replete with alienness. It is the real thing. But the journey of the *Quaker City* piles excess upon excess, since it offers virtually all the known wonders of the world from France and Italy to Egypt and the Holy Land. On the other hand, 'the pilgrims' (II, 436) embarked on their excursion in a serious frame of mind, expecting to be uplifted and edified. As Twain commented in his letter to the New York *Herald*,

The venerable excursionists were not gay and frisky. They played no blindman's buff; they dealt not in whist; they shirked not the irksome journal, for alas! most of them were even writing books. They never romped, they talked but little, they never sang, save in the nightly prayer-meeting. The pleasure ship was a synagogue, and the pleasure trip was a funeral excursion without a corpse. (Ibid.)

In such a frame of mind the real goal of the journey appeared to be the Holy Land, and the preceding progress through the sights of Europe something of a Bunyanesque confrontation with wickedness, moral corruption and spiritual pride. Certainly Twain and his fellow passengers felt obliged to struggle against Europe, while the desolate wastes of the Holy Land presented no resistance. In Europe God's people have to fight the good fight – 'we bore down on them with America's greatness until we crushed them' (II, 438) – but in the Holy Land they enter into their birthright: 'we were at home in Palestine' (II, 439). The cultural world of the eastern Mediterranean – Greece, Turkey, Egypt, Palestine – can be safely kept at a distance, since its past is remote, its monuments are largely ruins. And no sagacious Westerner is going to be taken in by oriental tall tales. But in Europe Twain is faced with great cathedrals, splendid palaces, celebrated works of art, with an excessiveness of culture that seems positively overbearing.

The problem of *The Innocents Abroad* is that of finding an appropriate response. The patriotic American tourist finds himself in an inescapable dilemma. He comes to Europe to admire and wonder, and to refuse to do so might seem uncultivated and churlish. Yet to allow himself to be overwhelmed and glutted by a surfeit of spectacle would be to betray his own sense of cultural identity and to abdicate his independence of judgement by simply adding one more voice to an interminable chorus of praise. It is a matter of nice judgement to strike precisely the right balance, to be above all 'innocent' – enthusing spontaneously and apparently unprompted where appropriate yet not being inhibited from offering forceful and outspoken criticism. So the excessiveness of Europe meets its match in an American style that can rise to magniloquent rhetorical heights but which can excoriate its evils with a comparable eloquence. Twain's language struggles to gain the mastery by the very virtuosity with which it can render the

European scene. For the claim to find Europe wanting is validated by the unstinting flow of hyperbole, which, as it were, would flow *even more* profusely if only the occasion warranted it. But in any event Twain cannot help feeling that to go to Europe is to participate in a servile and mechanical routine. Approaching Rome – a sensitive topic for Americans, because of its claims to a cultural and religious imperialism – Twain is careful to let the reader down. In the spirit of Emerson he proclaims that genius and originality are the supreme delight, as against which the mere pleasures of tourism pale into insignificance. So Twain fights fire with fire, excess with excess. The supreme joy in life is discovery:

> To give birth to an idea – to discover a great thought – an intellectual nugget, right under the dust of a field that many a brain-plow had gone over before. To find a new planet, to invent a new hinge, to find the way to make the lightnings carry your message. To be the *first* – that is the idea. (I, 338)

Moreover, Twain both here and subsequently gives the process a strongly American flavour by presenting it in terms of Californian prospecting and by citing patriotic examples – Morse code, the steamboat, Columbus. As compared with this pioneering spirit of adventure, tourism, for all its pretensions, offers only repetition:

> What is there in Rome for me to see that others have not seen before me? What is there for me to touch that others have not touched? What is there for me to feel, to learn, to hear, to know, that shall thrill before me before it pass to others? What can I discover? – Nothing whatsoever. One charm of travel dies here. (I, 339)

Twain inverts the terms of the debate and suggests that the Romans, in their ignorance, could learn far more from visiting America than the Americans can ever learn from visiting Rome, for America exceeds Italy in its profusion of everyday wonders – political, technological and topographical. So that after this we are scarcely surprised when Twain finds that 'St Peter's did not look nearly so large as the capitol and certainly a twentieth part as beautiful, from the outside' (I, 345).

Alas, the voyage of the *Quaker City*, ostensibly a pleasure cruise, had become more and more of an ordeal. We cannot but marvel at the fortitude of these stalwart Yankee folk as they maintain their composure in the face of immense provocations and interminable cultural excesses. Increasingly they figure as storm-tossed cockleshell heroes, bedraggled and weary perhaps, but with a cheery grin stoically pasted on their faces. No matter what the challenge was, they could outface it. As Twain noted,

> We never showed any but impassive faces and stupid indifference in the presence of the sublimest wonders a guide had to display. . . . We have made some of those people savage at times, but we have never lost our serenity. (I, 368)

What is *The Innocents Abroad* in all its abundant length if not a virtuoso display of an American self-confidence *in extremis*, of humour as sustained aggression? Twain will not be shaken from his belief that America is the yardstick by which the world must be judged, and, in truth, the world would be disappointed to find an American who did not think so. It is scarcely surprising that Twain should fail to get a decent shave in all the length and breadth of Europe or that he should find the majority of women ugly by comparison with the American girl. But America looms larger than this. America is the true Sublime, Europe the shadow. As the travellers hurtle by train through France past cathedrals and feudal castles they see 'glimpses of Paradise', 'visions of fabled fairy land' (I, 149), but they are less than impressed with the trains. 'Stage-coaching is infinitely more delightful', observes Twain (ibid.), and he invokes

> thirteen hundred miles of desert solitudes; of limitless panoramas of bewildering perspective; of mimic cities, of pinnacled cathedrals, of massive fortresses, counterfeited in the eternal rocks and splendid with the crimson and gold of the setting sun; of dizzy altitudes among fog-wreathed peaks and never-melting snows, where thunders and lightnings and tempests warred magnificently at our feet and the storm-clouds above swung their shredded banners in our very faces.
> (I, 150–1)

Twain has to nudge and jostle himself out of his delightful reveries to remind himself that he is actually 'in elegant France now' (I, 151) and by comparison bored out of his mind. When they arrive in Italy they see one of Europe's most celebrated sights, Lake Como, and Twain does not hesitate to find it picturesque: 'Beyond all question, this is the most voluptuous scene we have yet looked upon' (I, 261). And yet Twain seems quite genuinely disappointed. It is not completely enclosed by mountains, it is not as big as he had expected and its waters are dull by comparison with the 'wonderful transparence of Lake Tahoe' (I, 262). By comparison with the splendours of Lake Tahoe, 'Como would only seem a bedizened little courtier in that august presence' (I, 263). The image suggests that America is the world of nature, Europe that of effete culture, that the pretensions of Lake Como are on a par with the inflated pretensions and puffery of lords and dukes. Twain subsequently compares the Sea of Galilee with Lake Tahoe, but the battle is over before it is begun. Galilee is not even in the same league.

It may well be that the *Quaker City* was never Fun City, but Twain nevertheless takes the reader of *The Innocents Abroad* on an excruciating, hair-raising rollercoaster ride that is likely to leave him feeling battered and slightly queasy, as every breathtaking verbal ascent is followed by an abrupt, stomach-churning descent into the social abysses of the European scene. The pattern is both persistent and predictable. Confronted with Versailles, Twain spares no effort in his attempt to overpower the reader with the stupendous nature of the spectacle that it presents:

> Versailles! It is wonderfully beautiful! You gaze, and stare, and try to understand that it is real, that it is on the earth, and that it is not the garden of Eden – but your brain grows giddy, stupefied by the world of beauty around you, and you half believe you are the dupe of an exquisite dream. The scene thrills out like military music! A noble palace stretching its ornamented front block upon block away, till it seemed that it would never end; a grand promenade before it, whereon the armies of an empire might parade; all about it rainbows of flowers, and colossal statues that were almost numberless and yet seemed only scattered over the ample space, broad flights of stone steps leading down from the promenade to the lower grounds of the park – stairways that whole regiments might stand to arms upon and have room to spare; vast fountains whose bronze effigies discharged rivers of sparkling water into the air and mingled a hundred curving jets together in forms of

matchless beauty; wide grass-carpeted avenues that branched hither and thither in every direction and wandered to seemingly interminable distances, walled all the way on either side with compact ranks of leafy trees whose branches met above and formed arches as faultless and as symmetrical as ever were carved in stone; and here and there were glimpses of sylvan lakes with miniature ships glassed in their surfaces. And everywhere – on the palace steps, and the great promenade, around the fountains, among the trees, and far under the arches of the endless avenues, hundreds and hundreds of people in gay costumes walked or ran or danced, and gave to the fairy picture the life and animation which was all of perfection it could have lacked. (I, 204–5)

Here is enough and more than enough to sate the armchair traveller, but this is just the trouble. The very excessiveness of Versailles and the verbal celebration that it provokes seems to preclude further apostrophes in this vein, especially when it occurs so early in the narrative. A further uneasiness is created by the fact that it seems improper for a democratic American to applaud a monument that represents the most overbearing demonstration of kingly arrogance, wastefulness and power. But Twain deliberately excludes criticism under this head and for the moment is content to note the deaths involved in its construction and the fact that splendid royal sleighs in the shape of lions and swans are now dusty and decaying. But he does feel the need to correct excessiveness of one kind with excessiveness of another, and concludes the chapter with a search for 'its antipodes', the Faubourg St Antoine:

Little narrow streets; dirty children blockading them; greasy, slovenly women capturing and spanking them; filthy dens on first floors, with rag stores in them (the heaviest business in the Faubourg is the chiffonier's); other filthy dens where whole suits of second and third-hand clothing are sold at prices that would ruin any proprietor who did not steal his stock; still other filthy dens where they sold groceries – sold them by the half-pennyworth – five dollars would buy the man out, goodwill and all. Upon these little crooked streets they will murder a man for seven dollars and dump the body in the Seine. And up some other of these streets – most of them, I should say – live lorettes. (I, 209)

What makes this turn so rhetorically effective is not simply the sharp contrast between space and enclosure – for the Faubourg with its dens beyond dens has a sublime of its own – or between squalor and magnificence, but rather the characteristics that link them, fine clothes, sexual licence and immorality. The truth of Versailles that is not yet glimpsed in Twain's excessive apostrophe is to be found in the Faubourg St Antoine; each is only the distorted reflection of the other and each can only acquire significance as part of a binary set. Twain's descriptive method permits him to be innocent and experienced. He can seem to yield before the European spectacle and then place his earlier response in perspective by a reassertion of American realism and clarity of perception.

Similarly Twain paints a lyrical picture of the 'Venice of poetry and romance' 'under the mellow moonlight' (I, 280) but by day he discovered what had mercifully been hidden under the 'charitable moon' (I, 283), the fact that the palaces are stained and dingy, the sculptures battered, the streets filthy and polluted. The prospect of Naples in the early dawn is 'a picture of wonderful beauty' (II, 30), but close to it cannot be denied that 'the people are filthy in their habits' (II, 31). Yet, though the truth emerges from all these multiple depictions and although the reader is led to believe that he has been given a fully rounded view of things, it is not one that involves either cautious or restrained assessment or the building-up of a composite picture. Though Twain as narrator creates the powerful impressions of the book, it is as if they come to assume control and that he, as much as his readers, is left floundering in a welter of confused impressions. Though the desire may be to cut Europe down to size, it nevertheless figures as an interminable and preposterous Western yarn.

Of Twain's early reviewers it seems significant that virtually the only journal to be impressed by Twain's sobriety was the Buffalo *Express*, of which he was part owner. The *Express* emphasised Twain's ability to form 'his own impressions of things, as they actually presented themselves, not as he had been taught to expect them'.[1] Twain allegedly brings to his task a scrupulous faithfulness that enables him to see the object as it really is:

> What he saw he tells, and we believe there is more true
> description in his book than in any other of the kind that we

have read. What is to be told soberly he tells soberly, and with all the admiration or reverence that is due to the subject. But he does like to wash off false colors, to scrape away putty and varnish, to stick a pin into venerable moss grown shams – and it is a perpetual delight to his reader to see him do it in his droll, dry way.[2]

But other commentators found it rather more difficult to treat Twain's fizzing, heavily spiked and extravagantly mixed concoction as a glass of cool, clear water. The *Nation* found in it 'All the prominent characteristics of our peculiar school of humorists – their audacity, their extravagance and exaggeration.'[3] *Packard's Monthly* admitted that some parts of the book contained 'correct, unexaggerated descriptions'[4] but added, 'there is no pretence, other than of a humorous and extravagant account of a memorable voyage'.[5] More severely, the London *Athenaeum* found that Twain destroyed his own credibility both by 'the reckless manner in which he makes his assertions'[6] and by his habitual exaggeration: 'By putting a number of exaggerations together he deprives any little grain of truth of its value.'[7]

Perhaps the most severe assessment of Twain's early style was provided by his fellow Western humorist Bret Harte, who wrote,

> Before the *Quaker City* reached Fayal, the first stopping-place, he had worked himself into a grotesque rage at everything and everybody. In this mock assumption of a righteous indignation, lies we think, the real power of the book, and the decided originality of Mr Clemens' humour. It enables him to say his most deliberately funny things with all the haste and exaggeration of rage; it gives him an opportunity to invent such epithets as 'animated outrage' and 'spider-legged gorilla', and apply them, with no sense of personal responsibility on the part of the reader or writer. And the rage is always ludicrously disproportionate to the cause.[8]

Evidently what is involved in Twain's style is the way in which he abuses both the anonymity and authoritativeness of print by writing in a style which is quite deliberately exaggerated, but the excessiveness is more convoluted than Harte suggests because, although Twain's rage and indignation is always transformed into a manner that appears genial and urbane, it is never altogether feigned. Twain's extravagance becomes so all-embracing that it completely smothers and envelops its ostensible objects, and the question of the relation of his writing to real objects, experiences and events becomes quite impossible to determine. Twain's 'professional exaggeration'[9] has become an end in itself.

On the Grand Tour the fact that Twain was describing sights that were either familiar or well known meant that there was always some notional point of reference from which Twain's divagations might be deemed to depart. In *Roughing It*, however, subtitled 'The Innocents at Home' and published three years later in 1872, Twain writes of his experiences in Virginia City as a journalist and prospector, of diverse episodes in the West and of a trip to Hawaii. Here all bearings are lost as Twain plunges into a series of anecdotes ranging from hearsay, rumour and near fact to legend and autobiographical yarn. But the question of veracity scarcely matters. For one thing Twain writes as a Western humorist and a man vastly more successful than the majority of his predecessors, and his task is above all to entertain. Twain is a professional, knows it and is proud of it. Not for nothing did he preface the co-written *Gilded Age*, published the following year, with a disclaimer of the usual disclaimer that it was written for amusement only or for circulation among friends. But in any event Twain seeks to give the reader some sense of the life and spirit of the West and therefore it seems scarcely apposite to sift and scrutinise tales which in their overblown and inflated forms epitomise that spirit better than anything else. After retailing various accounts of the Nevada 'nabobs' Twain remarks,

> But why go on? The traditions of silverland are filled with instances like these, and I would never get through enumerating them were I to attempt to do it. I only desired to give the reader an idea of a peculiarity of the 'flush times' which I could not present so strikingly in any other way, and which some mention of was necessary to a realizing comprehension of the time and the country. (*Roughing It*, p. 293)

What Twain implies is that you cannot understand the West and the flush times unless you recognise that such anecdotes were commonplace and formed the opinions, dreams and expectations of those who lived through it. Twain writes, 'The first twenty-six graves in the Virginia cemetery were occupied by *murdered* men. So everybody said, so everybody believed, and so they will always say and believe'(p 366).

Belief determines truth. It is the only thing that matters. Twain's Westerner is like Henry Brierley in *The Gilded Age*, who is an indefatigable optimist and who always talks in six figures:

> Harry had the most buoyant confidence in his own projects always; he saw everything connected with himself in a large way and in rosy hues. The predominance of the imagination over the judgement gave that appearance of exaggeration to his conversation and to his communications with regard to himself, which sometimes conveyed the impression that he was not speaking the truth. His acquaintance had been known to say that they invariably allowed a half for shrinkage in his statements and held the other half under advisement for confirmation.[10]

The difference, however, is that not everyone in Washington is necessarily like Henry, so it is still possible to invoke such notions as falsehood and not speaking the truth. In the West, on the other hand, everyone deals in the same inflationary currency. In Virginia City absolutely everyone has confidence:

> Virginia had grown to be the 'livest' town, for its age and population, that America had ever produced. The sidewalks swarmed with people – to such an extent, indeed, that it was generally no matter to stem the human tide. The streets themselves were just as crowded with quartz wagons, freight teams, and other vehicles. The procession was endless. So great was the pack that buggies frequently had to wait half an hour for an opportunity to cross the principal street. Joy sat on every countenance, and there was a bald, almost fierce intensity in every eye, that told of the money-getting schemes that were seething in every brain and the high hope that held sway in every heart. Money was as plentiful as dust; every individual considered himself wealthy, and a melancholy countenance was nowhere to be seen. There were military companies, fire companies, brass bands, banks, hotels, theaters, 'hurdy-gurdy houses', wide-open gambling palaces, political powwows, civic processions, street fights, murders, inquest, riots, a whiskey mill every fifteen steps, a board of aldermen, a mayor, a city

> surveyor, a city engineer, a chief of the fire department, with first, second and third assistants, a chief of police, city marshal, and a large police force, two boards of mining brokers, a dozen breweries and half a dozen jails and station houses in full operation, and some talk of building a church. The 'flush times' were in magnificent flower! Large fireproof brick buildings were going up in the principal streets, and the wooden suburbs were spreading out in all directions. Town lots soared up to prices that were amazing.   (*Roughing It*, p. 274)

Virginia City is truly excessive, but the wonder of it is that it is not merely a gleam in the prospector's eye or the subject of some extravagant traveller's tale. For a moment at least it has a curious substantiality, and each person's possibly illusory sense of his personal substance and worth seems confirmed by the massive solidity and multifariousness of the enterprises to which the gold rush has given rise. Virginia City is not merely a place: it is a state of mind. Yet this state of mind has constructed monuments that seem to demonstrate the truth of its own excessiveness. So, if prospectors dream, they are scarcely aware of doing so, since they participate in a mood that is omnipresent and universal.

Twain is infected by this all-pervading spirit and sees no need to apologise for the fact. Journalism both reflects and intensifies the world in which it functions, since reports of value are of more significance than the actual existence of the minerals themselves. Reality is itself constructed through language. As Twain reports it, he was instructed by his chief editor and proprietor as follows:

> Never say 'We learn' so-and-so, or 'It is reported', or 'It is rumored' or 'We understand' so-and-so, but go to headquarters and get the absolute facts, and then speak out and say 'It *is* so-and-so'. Otherwise, people will not put confidence in your news. Unassailable certainty is the thing that gives a newspaper the firmest and most valuable reputation.   (p. 268)

Excellent advice, no doubt; but Twain discovers that it is infinitely more important to be interesting, and he decides to incorporate a covered wagon that is passing through into the list of those killed and wounded:

> I put this wagon through an Indian fight that to this day has no parallel in history.

> My two columns were filled. When I read them over in the morning I felt that I had found my legitimate occupation at last. I reasoned with myself that news, and stirring news, too, was what the paper needed, and I felt that I was peculiarly endowed with the ability to furnish it. Mr Goodman said that I was as good a reporter as Dan. I desired no higher commendation. With encouragement like that, I felt that I could take my pen and murder all the emigrants on the plains if need be and the interest of the paper demanded it. (pp. 269–70)

In an excessive world excessiveness ceases to exist and even the most outrageous fabrication can simply blend in with the background as if part of the natural order of things. Twain sees no need to distance himself from the Western mode as he had in 'The Celebrated Jumping Frog'. He can report on what he has seen and heard by merging with the motley carnival and by adding his own voice to the exultant and vaguely preposterous chorus.

Yet, in this Western world, if it is essential to inflate and exaggerate it is equally indispensable to be believed. Twain is infected by this too. Every now and again the reader is proffered his assurance that this is the undisputed truth, unquestionable fact and testimony of the highest value, and this with an earnestness that seems hard to fathom. Perhaps Twain did once briefly own a valuable claim, and perhaps his assurance that he did so casts an amiable and familiar glow over reports of more doubtful veracity, but in the final analysis does it really matter? Part of Twain's reminiscences of San Francisco incorporates the story of a huge bearded miner who offers $150-worth of gold dust for the privilege of kissing a little girl. 'That anecdote', says Twain, 'is true' (p. 372), though it is hard to see what grounds he has for the affirmation, since he hears the story from a young lady who herself heard it from her father. Twain is thereby reminded, however, of his own 'experience' of queueing up in Star City in order to squint through a crack in a cabin 'and get a sight of the splendid new sensation – a genuine live woman' (ibid.), who, it turns out, was 165 years old and without a tooth in her head. Twain does not actually affirm that this first-hand report is true, though he does add a vestige of verisimilitude by reducing her age by a hundred years in a footnote. It is all very entertaining, but why drag in the truth?! The answer, presumably, is that to be a Westerner you have to be a believer, and Westerners like to feel that, if they are not to be taken entirely seriously, at least they live in a world where their solemn asseverations are felt to have a certain substance.

The American West creates a universe that is strangely formidable, and faced with this imposing edifice the newcomer, as long as he remains one, finds that it takes a certain temerity to question it. Long before Twain ever meets Slade, the notorious desperado, he has heard all about him:

> And a deal the most of the talk was about Slade. We had gradually come to have a realizing sense of the fact that Slade was a man whose heart and hands and soul were steeped in the blood of offenders against his dignity; a man who awfully avenged all injuries, affronts, insults or slights, of whatever kind – on the spot if he could, years afterward if lack of earlier opportunity compelled it; a man whose hate tortured him day and night till vengeance appeased it – and not an ordinary vengeance either, but his enemy's absolute death – nothing less; a man whose face would light up with a terrible joy when he surprised a foe and had him at a disadvantage. A high and efficient servant of the Overland, an outlaw among outlaws and yet their relentless scourge, Slade was at once the most bloody, the most dangerous, and the most valuable citizen that inhabited the savage fastnesses of the mountains. (p. 90)

By any standards Slade is excessive, but when Twain actually meets the man of whom he has heard such blood-curdling reports he finds him friendly, polite and gently spoken. But of course this in no way disproves what he has heard. Slade's cruelty is notorious. Twain relates how he tortured his longstanding enemy, Jules, before killing him and cutting off his ears as a souvenir. He adds, 'That is the story as I have frequently heard it told and seen it in print in California newspapers. It is doubtless correct in all essential particulars' (p. 96). The fact is that Slade, a man who has killed twenty-six men (a number with certain magical connotations in the West), is so singularly excessive that no account of him can possibly do him justice. No matter what evils are attributed to him, they will nevertheless fail to convey the extraordinary vengefulness and malevolence of the man. The reports, tales and legends that circulate about the man still fall short of the truth. Slade epitomises a Western reality that the

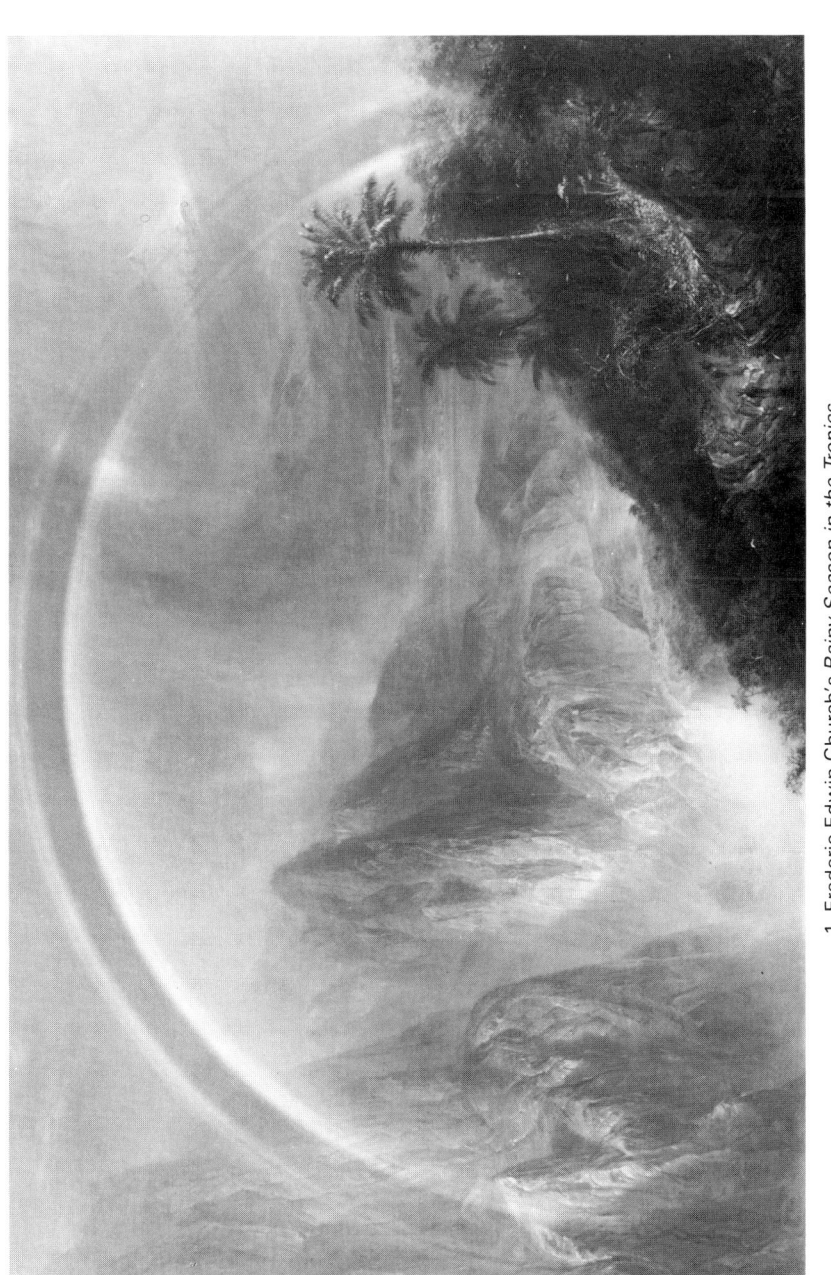

1 Frederic Edwin Church's *Rainy Season in the Tropics*.

2 *The Republican Party Going to the Right House*: from a contemporary campaign cartoon published by Currier & Ives.

3a Matthew Brady's *Lincoln in Washington, 1862.*

3b The seated Lincoln in Grant Park, Chicago.

4 The frontispiece to Mark Twain's *A Tramp Abroad* (1880).

outsider will have to come to terms with, the *terra incognita* for which a new vocabulary must be found. Not to believe in Slade, out West, is akin to not believing in God.

After Slade, Twain's ludicrous tale of the unridable Mexican plug, his preposterous account of facing death in a snowy wilderness that turns out to be only fifteen feet from the offices of the Overland stage, seem like mere foothills in the Himalayas. Truth implies a sense of perspective that can no longer be applied. The West is the West is the West.

With *Roughing It* Twain became the supreme Western humorist by the sheer dizziness of his invention. The reviewer for the *Overland Monthly* commented,

> Artemus Ward, Doesticks and Orpheus C. Kerr, who have been the favorite purveyors of mirth for the Eastern people, were timid navigators, who hugged the shore of plausibility, and would have trembled at the thought of launching out into the mid-ocean of wild, preposterous invention and sublime exaggeration, as Mark Twain does.[11]

Even Howells could not fail to acknowledge the excessiveness of the book, but he argued, 'The grotesque exaggeration and broad irony with which the life is described are conjecturably the truest colors that could have been used.'[12] Twain's style is the only style that can do the West justice, and with this flamboyant, patched and baggy overcoat of a book he becomes its authentic interpreter.

By contrast, *The Adventures of Tom Sawyer*, we may surmise, was conceived of as an enterprise in a lower key. In it Twain would depict the world of his boyhood and attempt to show how in the mind of a child even the most mundane events and escapades could be invested with excitement and glamour. Not the least surprising thing about *Tom Sawyer* is Twain's curious prefatory claim – one that has understandably been disregarded – that the narrative is substantially factual: 'Most of the adventures in this book really occurred' (*Mississippi Writings*, p. 3). It is difficult to see why such a preamble is necessary. If the book answers its purpose of entertaining boys and girls and perhaps some adults as well, if it offers them a gripping and amusing read, then surely that is enough. Why is it necessary to conceive of it as a more or less true story? Of course, we may respond by saying that Twain's authorial nudging must be interpreted within the specific context of children's fiction, and, just as Twain's own characters are anxious to believe in the authenticity of Robin Hood, so by the same token Twain's readers will be gratified and reassured to hear that Tom Sawyer's adventures really did happen and that therefore the kind of superhuman role he is conceived of as playing is not entirely beyond their own capabilities. Twain can offer this assurance more or less in good faith, and the question as to how it is to be understood is very much a matter for Twain's readers themselves. But we also add that Twain has a distinct emotional investment in the book and it is his earnest wish that it shall be taken as having a certain level of verisimilitude and not merely be dismissed as yet another hair-raising yarn. The world of Tom Sawyer *matters* to Twain and he wants it to matter to his audiences as well.

In the early part of the story a sense of proportion is maintained. Our first glimpse of Tom is as a shabby boy in 'the poor little shabby village' (p. 13) of St Petersburg, both easily impressed and eager to impress, with an active fantasy life. Here it is an achievement to be able to perform a birdlike warble and to balance a straw on the end of one's nose. Brass and iron knobs and pinch-bugs in a box figure as tangible wealth. But, as *Tom Sawyer* develops, the claims of the hero on our attention become more and more imposing. He is no longer just a little boy who impresses his friends with the ability to spit through a gap in his teeth, but a commanding presence in the town, a figure to be looked up to for his celebrated exploits, a 'glittering hero' (p. 120). Though Tom Sawyer is not yet a man when the work is concluded, he is a man in all but name.

Twain conjures up a primitive warrior world of boyhood, where male authority figures are largely absent, and where the youthful desperadoes who have taken their place sally forth to do battle on mysterious errands and quests while a wailing woman is left at home to grieve, hope and pray. Tom's adventures become more and more tremendous: he is the terrified witness of a nocturnal killing and subsequently bravely comes forward at the trial of the innocent Potter to give evidence against Injun Joe. With the other boys he travels down river on a raft and makes a camp, but to satisfy himself that his Aunt Polly is truly grieving during his lengthy absence he makes an undetected visit home. Here, as on many occasions in the book, child/adult roles are reversed and it is Tom who leans over his sleeping aunt to give her a kiss, as if a symbolic token of his other life, of which she, poor thing, remains in ignorance. Huck saves the Widow Douglas, whose occasional acts of kindliness towards Tom Sawyer have caused her to be marked down for vengeance by Injun Joe. Tom and Becky are finally rescued after a terrifying three-day ordeal in the dark labyrinthine caves. Tom and Huck discover Injun Joe's treasure box after his death. It contains $12,000 and they are famous:

> The Reader may rest satisfied that Tom and Huck's windfall made a mighty stir in the poor little village of St Petersburg. So vast a sum, all in actual cash, seemed next to incredible. It was talked about, gloated over, glorified, until the reason of many of the citizens tottering under the strain of the unhealthy excitement. Every 'haunted' house in St Petersburg and the neighbouring villages was dissected, plank by plank, and its foundations dug up and ransacked for hidden treasure – and not by boys, but men – pretty grave, unromantic men, too, some of them. Wherever Tom and Huck appeared they were courted, admired, stared at. The boys were not able to remember that their remarks had possessed weight before; but now their sayings were treasured and repeated; everything they did seemed somehow to be regarded as remarkable; they had evidently lost the power of doing and saying commonplace things; moreover, their past history was raked up and discovered to bear marks of conspicuous originality. The village paper published biographical sketches of the boys. (p. 210)

Doubtless much of this rocketing inflation can be justified on the grounds both that it makes for a more exciting story and that it faithfully reflects the importance with which children like to invest their actions. It is obviously gratifying that Tom Sawyer and Huck shall not merely loom large in the imagination of their schoolfellows and companions but that they should make their mark in the adult community as well. But, even so, Twain's conclusion still seems monstrously excessive. To boys such as Tom and Huck $100 would have represented a princely sum and $1000 wealth beyond their own – if not Twain's – wildest dreams. By giving his heroes the sum of $12,000, a sum as much beyond their comprehension as their ability to spend it, and by making them the cynosure of all eyes as a model for earnest adults, Twain takes his tale well beyond the reach of credibility and destroys altogether the sense of an enclosed, scaled-down world of childhood, where imagination alone could invest the world with wonder, value and excitement.

Twain's excesses in *Tom Sawyer* were nevertheless productive, for his determination to avoid them in its successor, *The Adventures of Huckleberry Finn*, enabled him to produce a work of extraordinary vividness and conviction. With the passage of time his attitude to the Old South had become simultaneously nostalgic and more critical. Despite its determined unpretentiousness, *Huckleberry Finn* was to be a vastly more ambitious work; a presentation not so much of a childhood world as of the South as seen through the eyes of an acute, clear sighted boy, through which Twain could puncture all its illusions without incurring any direct responsibility. What makes Twain's use of the vernacular positively startling is not so much the fact that he uses it, though that would have been breakthrough enough, but that he is able to make it modulate through so many different registers, so that Twain can slide effortlessly back and forth between the most astringent social criticism and a mellow, enchanted evocation of the sights and sounds of a bygone world. But from the very outset the spectre of *Tom Sawyer* must be exorcised. What is so distinctly ingenious about the opening of *Huckleberry Finn* is that Huck appears positively to plead for *Tom Sawyer* and its author, to seem determined to find a good word to say in its defence despite his obvious recognition of its shameless excesses:

> You don't know about me, without you have read a book by the name of *The Adventures of Tom Sawyer*, but that ain't no matter. That book was made by Mr Mark Twain, and he told the truth, mainly. There were things which he stretched, but mainly he told the truth. That is nothing. I never seen anybody but lied, one time or another, without it was Aunt Polly, or the widow, or maybe Mary. Aunt Polly – Tom's Aunt Polly, she is – and Mary, and the Widow Douglas, is all told about in that book – which is mostly a true book; but with some stretchers, as I said before. (*Mississippi Writings*, p. 625)

Huck's loyal stress on the ostensible veracity of the previous narrative only serves to foreground more emphatically the fact of its excessiveness. He is reluctant to concede that it is so, but his

Mark Twain

honesty nevertheless forces him into some kind of qualification. Huck's honesty – here as elsewhere – does not so much manifest itself as a vainglorious and self-righteous transparency as it evidences a stubborn determination to avoid going too far beyond the facts. Since Huck has no particular interest in impressing people, and since, as a boy, he has no particular axe to grind, we can rely on him to maintain a sense of proportion and shortcircuit the excessiveness that literariness ordinarily induces. The vernacular is a plain speech that cuts through pretentiousness and hypocrisy. It can capture the texture of life in all its freshness and immediacy because it speaks from within the experience and not from without. The effect of Huck's speech is to situate him within a particular cultural horizon. Twain will not present the South from an external viewpoint that might become censorious and complacent, or through the self-validating, self-justifying, unseeing eyes of Dixie itself. Rather he will present an unrelenting immanent critique that will be the more forceful because it seems to issue from no particular direction to serve no partisan ends and to be prompted by nothing more than a desire to give a straightforward report on some fairly humdrum events that took place somewhere in the Mississippi valley forty to fifty years ago.

Just to cite the title page is to foreground a striking aspect of *Huckleberry Finn*, that, improbably and unlooked for as it might seem in view of Twain's obsessive polemics and animadversion against the author of *Waverley* and his alleged fatal influence on the American South, the book is nevertheless very much in the tradition of Scott and the historical novel. The strategy that Scott adopted in *Waverley* was to write of a period 'sixty years since', a period recent enough to remain just within the confines of living memory and personal recollection, yet one that is the same time receding into the historical past. It is sufficiently recent for the passions and loyalties of that time still to find an echo, yet sufficiently distant for it to be possible to view the participants with a degree of impartiality and detachment, to enter into their state of mind without being wholly carried away by their own fervour or fanaticism. The world that is gone, instead of seeming broken, fragmentary and confused, begins to cohere again and it becomes evident that all have been caught up in a common cultural web. If the bigotry and intolerance of a bygone age stand out in greater relief, so too do the folkways, pastimes and customs of a vanishing way of life. The historical novel is born of multiple

...ere the past, deeply divided within itself,
...s integral when set against the present. Just as
...llion marked the end of an era of Highland
...he destruction of a whole way of life that would
... for Twain, the provincial culture of the
... with all its striking contrasts and
contradictions had, with the Civil War, become lost irretrievably.

Moreover, it should not be forgotten what a compelling model Scott offered to a writer who wished to free himself from the inhibiting and demoralising influence of metropolitan culture. Scott was concerned to bring out the contrast in Scottish culture between the tribal Highlands and the commercial Lowlands and to articulate many nuances and shades by means of a careful rendition of the varieties of dialect, idiom and patterns of speech. Scott demonstrated that to do so was not mere pedantry or wilful obscurantism but a way of bringing to life distinctive ways of thinking and feeling that polite speech and literary prose simply obliterated. Twain by his painstaking attention to dialects of the Missouri and the South-West gives us not merely a narrator but the South itself. It is through speech that we come to recognise that, although the townships on the banks of the Mississippi are in many ways raw, primitive and unsophisticated, they constitute a world that, when seen by its own lights, is nevertheless diverse and complex.

Lastly, Huck Finn himself is a lineal descendant of that recurrent figure in the Waverley novels, the wavering hero. As I pointed out in *Romanticism: A Structural Analysis*, this wavering hero is also a 'lost hero',[13] a young man who, having been either cut off from or rejected by his family, lacks any secure place in the world and who as a result is led to identify or align himself with those who stand outside the mainstream of society. As a result he finds himself implicated in actions that are from the point of view of respectable society disreputable if not actually seditious and disloyal. In Scott this psychological movement is often the result of a journey into remote and unfamiliar territory where new companions and unforeseen experiences have the effect of widening the hero's perspectives. Many of these characteristics are recapitulated in *Huckleberry Finn*. Huck is at odds with his brutal drunken father yet ill at ease with his respectable guardians, Judge Thatcher, the Widow Douglas and Miss Watson. The sheer plenitude of these authority figures only serves to bring out the more strongly how thoroughly isolated Huck really is. Huck escapes and his journey down the majestic Mississippi river takes him far from the customary reference points of his habitual existence and forces him to think about moral issues of which he had either been unaware or given very little thought to. His friendship with Jim, a black man and a runaway slave, places him in the most acute moral dilemma, since by staying with Jim and not betraying him he thereby contradicts the most fundamental axiom of the South: that a black man is nothing more than a white man's property. Huck is a wavering hero because his experiences compel him to accept the validity of the oppositional and subversive cause, which goes against the grain of everything he has been taught. Of course, the Southern context of the novel significantly alters the nature of the message which this structure can transmit, since it is scarcely possible for Twain to maintain the evenhandedness which Scott displayed in relation to the struggles between Protestant and Catholic; the issue of black equality and freedom is too actual, urgent and absolute to admit of any compromise. And this is really Twain's problem. The balance and poise that Twain sought to maintain in relation to the Old South is both aesthetically right in that a fuller and more detailed picture can result, but ethically false in that the peculiar institution penetrates so deeply into all aspects of Southern life that its significance can be neither counterweighted nor evaded. Twain tries to rectify the imbalance created by the experiences of Huck on the raft by a return to the status quo that is purely imaginary and patently threadbare, but the only real solution is to have Huck light out for the new territory – not so much, one suspects, for the opportunities that it offers, as because it is neutral ground, neither North nor South.

What is significant about *Huckleberry Finn* is that Twain becomes aware of the South as an excessive culture at the same moment as he recognises an excessiveness in his own writing and thus grasps the need for an alternative style. 'Tom Sawyer' is simply the name for this wrongly taken path, and Scott the scapegoat on whom Twain unloads all the blame. But really Scott was in no way responsible for Twain's self-created problems. It was the twin roles of frontier humorist and American patriot that created his problem, a mode of writing so forceful and exaggerated that it pulverised its ostensible object. Instead of adopting, in *Huckleberry Finn*, a high viewpoint that appears to offer the possibility of mastery, Twain chooses a low viewpoint that will allow the excessive to establish its own register by contrast. Instead of forcing his writing to maintain the same insistent level, it can now encompass pianissimo and adagio as well as presto and fortissimo. Twain's writing becomes at its best an immensely subtle and flexible instrument that can evoke a whole panorama of feelings and moods without ever bringing the reader up with a jolt. The overbearing narrative presence has gone. Huck's willingness to admit his inability to express everything satisfactorily is not significant just as a moral gesture: it opens up a world of shared experience which the reader can recognise and in which he can participate, instead of simply remaining on the receiving end of a rhetorical barrage. The vastness of the Mississippi, for example, is conveyed through suggestion rather than through grandiloquent description, grasped through a visual and auditory blurring:

> The first thing to see, looking away over the water, was a kind of dull line – that was the woods on t'other side – you couldn't make nothing else out; then a pale place in the sky; then more paleness, spreading around; then the river softened up, away off, and warn't black any more, but gray; you could see little dark spots drifting along, ever so far away – trading scows, and such things; and long black streaks – rafts; sometimes you could hear a sweep screaking; or jumbled up voices, it was so still, and sounds come so far. (*Mississippi Writings*, p. 740)

The punctuation seeks to capture the hesitations of speech, and the almost invisible repetitions 'away off . . . ever so far away . . . so far' communicate the immensity of the river in a manner that is almost subliminal. It would be a mistake to assume that the style Twain uses for Huck is one of clear direct statement alone, for it is also masterfully oblique and suggestive. One reason for this is that Twain sees more clearly that it is as necessary to avoid excessive precision as it is to avoid excessive abstraction.

Storms were a favourite literary challenge for Twain and he takes every opportunity he can to describe them. In *The Innocents Abroad* the style is predictably inflated and marked by both the vagueness and conventionality of the literary sublime:

> But the vessel climbed aloft as if she would climb to heaven – then paused an instant that seemed a century, and plunged headlong

down again, as from a precipice. The sheeted sprays drenched the decks like rain. The blackness of darkness was everywhere. At long intervals a flash of lightning clove it with a quivering line of fire that revealed a heaving world of water where was nothing before, kindled the dusky cordage to glittering silver, and lit up the faces of the men with a ghastly lustre! (I, 95–6)

This could be any ship in any storm at any time. By contrast Twain's description in *Life on the Mississippi* aims for a high level of precision. The writing endeavours to pick out the many different forms of turbulence created by the wind and demonstrate how it becomes progressively heightened stage by stage:

> The wind bent the young trees down, exposing the pale underside of the leaves; and gust after gust followed, in quick succession, thrashing the branches violently up and down, and to this side and that, and creating swift waves of alternation green and white, according to the side of the leaf that was exposed, and these waves raced after each other as do their kind over a wind-tossed field of oats. No color that was visible anywhere was quite natural – all tints were charged with a leaden tinge from the solid cloud-bank overhead. The river was leaden, all distances the same; and even the far-reaching ranks of combining whitecaps were dully shaded by the dark, rich atmosphere through which their swarming legions marched. The thunder-peals were constant and deafening; explosion followed explosion with but inconsequential intervals between, and the reports grew steadily sharper and higher-keyed, and more trying to the ear; the lightning was as diligent as the thunder, and produced effects which enchanted the eyes and set electric ecstasies of mixed delight and apprehension shivering along every nerve in the body in unintermittent procession. The rain poured down in amazing volume; the ear-splitting thunder-peals broke nearer and nearer; the wind increased in fury and began to wrench off boughs and tree-tops and send them sailing away through space; the pilot house fell to rocking and straining and cracking and surging, and I went down in the hold to see what time it was.
>
> (*Mississippi Writings*, p. 522)

Twain's determination to make this a *real* storm and not just an imaginative one begins to seem pedantic not because his endeavour has no value but because it becomes a conscious effort in word-painting, manifested in its diction of colours, tints, tinges and shades. By its very carefulness the language neutralises the violence of the storm; it becomes so objectified that Twain then has to humanise it with anthropomorphic touches. The 'I' that is invoked at the end of the paragraph seems almost unexpected as if Twain can only permit it to emerge when the describing is done. By comparison, Huck's description of a storm in *Huckleberry Finn* is blatantly subjective and incomparably more vivid, despite the fact that it deploys much of the observation from the earlier passage:

> Pretty soon it darkened up and begun to thunder and lighten; so the birds were right about it. Directly it begun to rain, and it rained like all fury, too, and I never see the wind blow so. It was one of these regular summer storms. It would get so dark that it looked all blue-black outside, and lovely; and the rain would thrash along by so thick that the trees off a little ways looked dim and spider-webby; and here would come a blast of wind that would bend the trees down and turn up the pale underside of the leaves; and then a perfect ripper of a gust would follow along and set the branches to tossing their arms as if they were just wild; and next, when it was just about the bluest and blackest – fst! it was as bright as glory and you'd have a little glimpse of tree-tops a-plunging about, away off yonder in the storm, hundreds of yards further than you could see before; dark as sin again in a second, and now you'd hear the thunder let go with an awful crash and then go rumbling, grumbling, tumbling down the sky towards the underside of the world, like rolling empty barrels down stairs, where it's long stairs and they bounce a good deal you know.
> (*Mississippi Writings*, pp. 671–2)

In *Life on the Mississippi* Twain writes self-consciously as a connoisseur and consumer of storms who has sampled them the world over and found the best to be – naturally – in the Mississippi Valley. As a result he misses the basic element *storminess*, which in the guise of Huck, he is able to capture. Huck's ostensibly unpretentious account is faithful to the storm as a developing and unfolding experience in time, a succession of events that make their distinctive impact, punctuated by a series of markers: 'and here... and then... and next... fst... dark as sin again... and now ... and then'. The barrels image works so forcefully here because, besides being imaginatively so apt, it stretches the time scale still further in rhythms that mimic the protracted and desultory activity of the thunder.

With the appearance of the King and the Duke the casual and unforced register of Huck Finn undergoes its severest test. For it is at this moment that Twain, having indiscriminately mingled with the excessiveness of frontier culture in *Roughing It* and *The Adventures of Tom Sawyer*, will endeavour to stand aside and simply disclose that excessiveness as the ludicrous and sometimes frightening phenomenon that it is. Twain recognised that these small and often isolated communities were afflicted by a desperate scarcity of striking events with which to diversify the banality of their customary existence. When, in *Huckleberry Finn*, Twain describes his little one-horse town in Arkansas, immediately after the King and the Duke have stuck up their handbills proclaiming a 'thrilling, masterly and blood-curdling Broadsword conflict' (*Mississippi Writings*, p. 760), he presents it as a place where almost any entertainment would be grasped at as a lurid moment of colour:

> Then we went loafing around the town. The stores and houses were most old shackly dried-up frame concerns that hadn't even been painted; they were set up three or four foot above ground on stilts so as to be out of reach of the water when the river was overflowed. The houses had little gardens around them, but they didn't seem to raise hardly anything in them but jimpson weeds, and sunflowers, and ashpiles, and old curled-up boots and shoes, and pieces of bottles, and rags, and played-out tin-ware. The fences was made of different kinds of boards, nailed on at different times; and they leaned every which-way, and had gates that didn't generly have but one hinge – a leather one. Some of the fences had been white-washed, some time or another, but the duke said it was in Clumbus's time like enough. There were generly hogs in the garden and people driving them out.
>
> All the store was along one street. They had white-domestic awnings in front, and the country people hitched their horses to the awning-posts. There were empty dry-goods boxes under the

awnings, and the loafers roosting on them all day long, whittling them with their Barlow knives; and chawing tobacco, and gaping and yawning and stretching – a might ornery lot. (pp. 760–1)

The description for all its humour is strangely menacing. Time seems to have been suspended; neither hours, months nor years are registered. Though whiteness is invoked as the only colour, since it lacks its customary associations of freshness and cleanliness it figures rather as an absence of colour, the mark of an overpowering drabness. The description is punctuated by repetitive invocations of stores, houses, fences, awnings, as if searching compulsively for features that might somehow characterise them; yet every narrative path leads to a vacancy – to 'played-out tinware' and 'empty dry-goods boxes'. In such an unmarked existence, camp-meetings lynchings, murders, circuses, fights and vendettas are gratefully received as events that can structure these great tracts of time, like pylons striding across the desolate wastes. Yet even dogs and pigs can be the very stuff of entertainment. Twain has a kind of pity for the terrifying hollowness of it all, but this is blended in with a mixture of amusement and withering contempt. Even in Huck Finn, Twain's humour has an element of harshness that consorts awkwardly with the determination of Huck to live and let live. There is no way in which Twain is going to suffer fools gladly, and as a result we are plunged into a narrative vortex that is simultaneously tolerant and merciless.

For Twain theatricality has a deep and abiding fascination. Undoubtedly he relishes the preposterous excesses of the 'histrionic muse' (p. 750) of which the King and the Duke are the devoted acolytes, yet at the same time he cannot but distrust the imposition that they represent. The puritan hostility to the performing arts goes deep in American culture, and Twain is not unaffected by it, because, although he has no serious objection to frivolity, he is deeply opposed to any blurring of the division between fantasy and fact and hostile to the vanities and falsities implicit in human finery. When we are first presented with the King, his ragged jeans, greasy blue woollen shirt and battered slouch hat give a truthful impression of what he is, but decked out in fancy clothes he creates a far more powerful illusion:

The king's duds was all black, and he did look real swell and starchy. I never knowed how clothes could change a body before. Why, before, he looked like the orneriest old rip that ever was; but now, when he'd take off his new white beaver and make a bow and do a smile, he looked that grand and good and pious that you'd say he had walked right out of the ark, and maybe was old Leviticus himself. (p. 780)

Since the miraculous transformations in *Huckleberry Finn* are often presented humorously, it is easy to misrecognise the seriousness of Twain's intentions. At bottom Twain sees the whole of social life as a masquerade in which people, by playing a part, seek to manipulate others and impose their will on them. So in reading *Huckleberry Finn* it is essential to keep in mind that it is just as much an allegory of the deceitfulness of the world as is that other depiction of a journey on the Mississippi, Melville's *The Confidence-Man*. In *Pudd'nhead Wilson* Twain used the device of exchanging black and white babies not only to criticise racial prejudice but to expose the cruelty and injustice that is always implicit in the assumption or imposition of social roles. 'Tom', 'Chambers' and all the other characters in the novel are caught in a network of convention against which they struggle blindly and in vain. The arbitrariness of the world is foregrounded by the transposition, but, of course, it would have been equally constricting had Tom been Tom and Chambers Chambers. Pudd'nhead is symbolically important for the story both because he has a concern for truth that Twain sees as so exceptional as to border on utter eccentricity, and because his own life has been blighted also by the prejudice and ignorance that constructs a false identity for him. The part of truth-seer in the social masquerade is thus a crucial one for Twain, and in *Huckleberry Finn*, of course, it is played by Huck himself.

For Twain the small-town craving for drama, excitement and excess is deeply corrupting, because the distinction between the real and the unreal becomes unimportant. All that matters is that people shall be entertained, and theatricality permeates every aspect of life. The King and the Duke make no distinction between the part they play on the boards and the part they play in life, and even in their plans to turn Jim into hard cash they are mindful of preserving the illusion:

> Handcuffs and chains would look still better on Jim, but it wouldn't go well with the story of us being so poor. Too much like jewellery. Ropes are the correct thing – we must preserve the unities, as we say on the boards.
>
> (*Mississippi Writings*, p. 755)

The shooting of Boggs by Colonel Sherburn is instantaneously transformed into a dramatic spectacle, and all the disturbing aspects of the situation are quite forgotten. The lanky individual who represents Sherburn becomes Sherburn:

> Then he stood up straight and stiff where Sherburn had stood, frowning and having his hat-brim down over his eyes, and sung out, 'Boggs!' and then he fetched his cane down slowly to a level, and says 'Bang!' staggered backwards, says 'Bang!' again, and fell down flat on his back. The people that had seen the thing said he done it perfect; said it was just exactly the way it happened. Then as many as a dozen people got out their bottles and treated him. (p. 766)

This incident is all of a piece with the act that Huck Finn sees in the circus where the audience is entertained by the spectacle of a drunken man riding a horse in such a way as to risk a serious accident. The incident, of course, is a fake, but Twain has a moral point to make about it nevertheless. For, although the episode has been rigged, the crowd actually enjoys the prospect of a serious accident and in fact is just as deceived as Huck. Huck's concern, though misconceived, is a more genuine human response. The carelessness that the mob shows about truth ultimately manifests itself as cruelty, hysteria and violence.

The King and the Duke play out their imposture to its bitter end in a ritual tarring and feathering, and their effrontery almost commands admiration. They realise that if they play their parts to the hilt they will always, if the mob are to be their judge, have the edge over rival claimants who have nothing but truth and justice on their side. Far from being abashed and demoralised when the genuine heirs turn up, they face the crisis with considerable sangfroid:

> I reckoned they'd turn pale. But no, nary a pale did *they* turn. The duke he never let on he suspicioned what was up, but just

went a goo-gooing around, happy and satisfied, like a jug that's googling out buttermilk; and as for the king, he just gazed and gazed down sorrowful on them newcomers like it give him the stomach-ache in his very heart to think there could be such frauds and rascals in the world. (p. 816)

There is something almost sublime in the King's desperate resource of inventing a thin blue arrow as an identification mark on the body of the deceased, not just because of improvisatory imagination it displays but because it demonstrates how reckless and total is his disregard for truth. The King, the Duke and their audience deserve one another, but Twain is more concerned for the innocent victims of their greed and mendaciousness: Jim, whom they humiliate; the black families they casually destroy; Mary Jane; even Huck himself. As Huck returns to the raft in the face of a possible lynching to find Jim attired as King Lear, all humour is finally gone from the masquerade. In Huck's indignation the biblical overtones are inescapable:

> After all this long journey, and after all we'd done for them scoundrels, here was it all come to nothing, everything busted up and ruined, because they could have the heart to serve Jim such a trick as that, and make him a slave again all his life, and amongst strangers, too, for forty dollars. (p. 832)

The King and the Duke lack all decency and integrity, as might have been expected. Their intervention turns a lyrical idyll into a bitter charade.

And so we are inescapably brought to the greatest paradox of all. Faced with the social falsity which the King and the Duke represent, Huck cannot but acknowledge his kinship with Jim and thus repudiate the whole value system of slave society. For so long merely a spectator of the actions of others, the unlikeliest of dissenters, Huck now becomes the excessive hero who, by tearing up the letter that identifies Jim as an article of property, violates the deepest of taboos. Yet the power of this moment is almost instantaneously dissipated as Twain presents us with an even more stupid and ignominious charade: the imaginary freeing of Jim as a childish game of Tom Sawyer. Evidently, even in the aftermath of the Civil War Twain knew that he had gone too far. The gesture was indeed excessive, so it must be emptied of meaning in a farcical episode that makes the freedom of a black man appear the most trivial and insignificant matter. Twain can appear to criticise the absurdities of a chivalric code and thus realign the thrust of the book against a target to which no one could object. Jim and Huck are rendered harmless. Rebellion dissolves. Such is the predicament of a writer who seeks to be both critic and entertainer, a truth-seer who flinches from his own excesses. From a reading of *Huckleberry Finn* we must conclude that his fear of the mob is utterly sincere and that therefore he admires no one more than the man who has the courage to stand up to it.

It has become commonplace to regard *A Connecticut Yankee in King Arthur's Court* as a deeply flawed book, yet such an assessment, in truth, seems only to indicate that the critics who see it in this way have not enjoyed reading it. On Twain's own terrain at least, it appears as his most courageous and articulate book, in which, for once, he does not pull any punches. But it is significantly misread by being approached as a perverse belabouring of a vanished past instead of a despairing allegory of the present. The real target of *A Connecticut Yankee* is the persistence of inequality, exploitation and oppression in society, of which Arthurian England is simply the unideal type. This contemporary address was never concealed. The likeness of a slave-driver, in one of the illustrations, to the arch-capitalist Jay Gould was inescapable, and even Howells recognised that Twain was using the past as a mirror for the present. Describing the scene in which a starving mother is executed for stealing, Howells writes,

> It is one of many passages in the story where our civilisation of today sees itself mirrored in the cruel barbarism of the past, the same in principle, and only softened by custom. With shocks of consciousness, one recognises in such episodes that the laws are still made for the few against the many, and that the preservation of things, not men, is still the ideal of legislation[14]

– though he does significantly blur the clarity of this perception by adding, in a fashion which Twain in his usual manner had partially encouraged, 'But we do not wish to leave the reader with the notion that Mr Clemens's work is otherwise than obliquely serious.'[15]

In the case of *A Connecticut Yankee* I would rather want to say that Twain is obliquely *humorous*. When it came to taking a stand on public events, Twain cut a distinctly less prepossessing figure than Howells, but, while conceding this, we must nevertheless acknowledge the boldness of his attack on the law as an instrument of class oppression and his unwavering insistence that the democratic programme, far from having been accomplished, is still very much on the agenda of unfinished business. Arthurian Britain, significantly, is a slave society, and Twain does not fail to underline the parallels with the American South. In *A Connecticut Yankee* Twain reveals that he has finally worked his way out of the ideological delusion, still implicit in *Huckleberry Finn*, that slavery is in general relatively benign and only cruel or harmful somewhere further down the river. In the Arthurian mirror he can state unequivocally that slavery is always morally corrupting and vicious through and through. For once Twain's correlation between the South and a romanticised West carries more than rhetorical weight. Moreover, as a Southerner (as well as a Westerner and a Yankee in Twain's chameleon identity) he understood only too well the massive power of tradition and custom to condition men's minds in inflexible patterns of behaviour. When Twain writes of the King,

> There it was, again, he could see only one side of it. He was born so, educated so, his veins were full of ancestral blood that was rotten with this sort of unconscious brutality, brought down by inheritance from a long procession of hearts that had each done its share towards poisoning the stream. To imprison these men without proof, and starve their kindred, was no harm, for they were merely peasants and subject to the will and pleasure of their lord, no matter what fearful form it might take; but for these men to break out of unjust captivity was insult and outrage, and a thing not to be countenanced by any conscientious person who knew his duty to his sacred caste
> (*A Connecticut Yankee*, p. 338)

it is not just Hapsburgs, Hohenzollerns and Romanovs that he has in mind. Twain recognises that equality is not just an economic demand but one based on the autonomy and dignity of every individual. Such indifference is everywhere to be found and it is always wrong. Like William Morris, Twain believes that no man is good enough to be another man's master.

The distinguishing characteristic of Twain's relationship with his readers is that he may try to disarm them or deflect their attention but he never seeks to ingratiate himself with them Twain's 'lack of taste' is produced by his distinct unwillingness to refrain from striking a jarring note and his determination thereby to defend what he sees as his professional integrity. Twain's truculence is not simply a personal characteristic: it reflects the strengthened position of the freelance writer and the increased, though by no means total, readiness of a socially diversified reading public to respond favourably to an outspoken and lively manner. It is within such parameters that Twain's style and especially that of *A Connecticut Yankee in King Arthur's Court*, should be understood. In its berating of European institutions and the feudal past *A Connecticut Yankee* ostensibly returns to the assertive, patriotic and excessive manner of *The Innocents Abroad*. Twain's customary stridency of tone reasserts itself. Indeed, for a humorist is unflinchingly didactic. He seems convinced that his every word will do the world and the public some good. Which is both to say that Twain is not unaffected by his celebrity and that, at bottom, he is a very serious man. William Lyon Phelps's characterisation of Twain –

> The essentially American qualities of common sense, energy, enterprise, good humour and Philistinism fairly shriek from his pages. . . . Without being an offensive and blatant jingo, I think he is well satisfied to be an American.
>
> Mark Twain is our great democrat. Democracy is his political, social and moral creed. His hatred to snobbery, affectation and assumed superiority is total. His democracy has no limits; it is bottomless and far-reaching[16]

– has a perfect aptness to *A Connecticut Yankee*. For Twain's message cuts through the genial puffs of smoke with all the piercingness of a locomotive whistle, and the peculiar achievement of the book is to make the usually bland credo of nineteenth-century democracy seem positively excessive.

Having said this, however, I must immediately add that, although Twain believed in democracy, he did not believe in the capacity of people to want it for themselves; hence the paradox by which it must be brought to them by the excessive and all-powerful figure of Hank Morgan, the deliverer from the future, 'The Boss'. This is not to say that, at this point at least, Twain had no faith in human nature: it was rather that he felt that potentially generous impulses were inhibited and overlaid by social conditioning – the position of *Huckleberry Finn*. Of a flogging Twain writes,

> All our pilgrims looked on and commented – on the expert way in which the whip was handled. They were too much hardened by lifelong every-day familiarity with slavery to notice that there was anything else in the exhibition that invited comment. This was what slavery could do, in the way of ossifying what one may call the superior lobe of human feeling; for these pilgrims were kind-hearted people, and they would not have allowed that man to treat a horse like that.
> (*A Connecticut Yankee*, pp. 245–6)

The remark may seem ironic, but Twain is invariably ready to invoke the Romantic distinction between natural and acculturated man. Hank Morgan epitomises the progressive as it was understood in his era in terms of such technological innovations as the telephone, the newspaper and the use of guns and explosives. Yet there is no faith in progress understood as an automatic, continuous process of constructive evolution. It is here that the excessive comes in. For, as Henry Nash Smith has suggested, Hank is 'a man with a world-historical mission'.[17] Left to themselves, Twain suggests, men would always reject progress and continue in their customary ways, so that progress can only come about if they can be persuaded by a combination of brainwashing and brute force. Hank Morgan is always the showman. As he observes early on in *A Connecticut Yankee*, 'You can't throw too much style into a miracle' (p. 265). People must be convinced by methods that are themselves irrational. It is not truth that matters but rhetoric, not substance so much as a flashy and flamboyant way of projecting things. As Hank notes of his plans for rescuing the King: 'It would be showy and picturesque enough, all things considered, though I would have preferred noonday, on account of the more theatrical aspect the thing would have' (p. 416).

Even the final massacre is an 'effect' (p. 493). Twain's sense of appearance as truth reflects the power of advertising, publicity and image-building in the America of his day, and his demoralising conclusion, if implicit, can be explicitly stated. The people would only want freedom if they had been conditioned into wanting it! We should not therefore assume that Twain shares our horror at his Armageddon-like conclusion to the book. Just as John Brown is prepared to purge the land with blood, so Twain believes quite sincerely that the destruction of the forces of reaction and oppression would be an unmitigated blessing. Like Ahab, Hank Morgan wills the end regardless of consequences. Since it rejects all accommodation, the American mission will necessarily figure as excessive.

4 Henry James: Refusing the Limit

As Henry James, in his work on the New York Edition, once again looked over the manuscript of *Roderick Hudson* after an interval of many years, he began vividly to recall the emotions that had attended its composition. Though he was now the acknowledged master of both novel and short story, James could not but acknowledge the mixture of trepidation and daring with which he had originally embarked on this his first considerable enterprise and, retrospectively, the first that he was prepared to recognise as his own. This tale of a young American artist was a reckless and presumptuous, if necessary, venture in which the lineaments of the brash and opinionated hero offered a definite clue to the many and various moods of his creator also. Though far less daunting to the reader, *Roderick Hudson* was James's *Mardi*, an exploratory journey into unchartered waters, an essay in artistic self-definition:

> *Roderick Hudson* was my first attempt at a novel, a long fiction with a 'complicated' subject, and I recall again the quite uplifted sense with which my idea, such as it was, permitted me at last to put quite out to sea. I had but hugged the shore on sundry previous small occasions; bumping about, to acquire skill, in the shallow waters and sandy coves of the 'short story' and master as yet of no other vessel constructed to carry a sail. The subject of *Roderick* figured to me vividly this employment of canvas, and I have not forgotten, even after long years, how the blue southern sea seemed to spread immediately before me and the breath of the spice-islands to be already in the breeze.
>
> (*The Art of the Novel*, p. 4)

Though the mature artist still feels affection and even respect for the fledgling work he is nevertheless conscious of a certain hubris mingled with incapacity, reflected in his use of such words as 'reckless' and 'rash'.

If there is one fault that James particularly fastens on, it is the lack of sufficient development either in the plot or in the character of the hero – everything 'moves too fast' (p. 12). In fact James retrospectively discerned in his first novel the problem that he was to encounter in his more substantial works: the fact that, for all their length, they seemed to possess a beginning and an end, without having anything very substantial in the way of a middle. James felt that Roderick's rapid distintegration in Europe, after venturing there with such high hopes – and, indeed, after following up with such signal achievements – was such as to place him 'Beyond our understanding and our sympathy' (ibid.). Roderick seems contradictory since his collapse seems to render nugatory the high talent attributed to him in the first place. In presenting his hero as a man oscillating wildly between extremes, James seems to have created a hero so paradoxical as to be beyond even his own powers of explanation. James remarks,

> We conceive going to pieces – nothing is easier, since we see people do it, one way or another, all round us; but this young man must either have had less of the principle of development to have had so much of the principle of collapse, or less of the principle of collapse to have so much of the principle of development. (p. 13)

So Roderick's character seems not merely excessive but inexplicable as well.

In his latter-day Preface, James concedes that certain aspects of his theme may nevertheless have escaped him with the passage of time, despite all his endeavours to restore it to its pristine freshness:

> I have felt myself then, on looking over past productions, the painter making use again and again of the tentative wet sponge. The sunk surface has here and there, beyond doubt, refused to respond: the buried secrets, the intentions are buried too deep to rise again, and were indeed, it would appear, not much worth the burying. (p. 11)

But in so saying it seems to me that James is being too severe on his earlier creation and perhaps insufficiently ready to acknowledge that the novel may indeed have an interest and complexity of another order from that which he now specifies. *Roderick Hudson* is not only the myth of the artist; it is also a myth which suggests how deeply American confidence has been fissured and shattered by the experience of the Civil War.

The Civil War was not only a bloody and bitter conflict, which was to leave lasting psychological scars on the collective American memory, but it dealt a seemingly irrevocable blow to the myth of American identity. When American had fought American in desperate enmity barely half a century after the framing of the Constitution, that imaginary American so confidently gestured towards by Crèvecoeur or Whitman seemed as remote and insubstantial as a faded portrait in a family photograph album, kept as a memorial of happier and more prosperous times. There was no longer an American, only Americans; the term 'American' seemed an over-optimistic portmanteau word, rather than one brimming with existential meaning. *Roderick Hudson* (1875) is the record of an attempt imaginatively to reconstruct the idea of American identity in the darkest hours of national consciousness, but one which cannot hope to ignore the shadows and spectres that menace it. The novel is an attempt to put the American Humpty Dumpty back together again in a full awareness that the damaged object, though superficially impressive, can scarcely hope to be as durable as before.

Roderick Hudson is a complex, composite construction of Americanness, patched together from North and South. So although he possesses a higher typicality this nevertheless makes him 'a very odd creature' (*Roderick Hudson*, p. 37). Rowland Mallett, his future patron, encounters Roderick in the New England village of Northampton, Massachusetts, but learns that his family actually comes from Virginia. The family plot thickens still further when it is revealed that Roderick's mother herself came from Massachusetts but married a Southern planter and slaveholder, who dissipated his fortune and drank himself to death. Roderick's elder brother Stephen finds that New England blood runs thicker in his veins than Virginian and elects to fight the war on the Northern side, but Roderick, being too young to fight, is spared any tendentious commitment and is allowed to grow up wild, irresponsible and horribly spoiled. Since he is presented as more addicted to novel-reading and billiards than to mathematics, Greek or the law, he seems to have had a fairly typical Southern education. In appearance the young sculptor displays true Dixie flamboyance and bravado. He wears a white linen suit adorned with a big sombrero, yellow gloves and a bright red cravat and accentuates his speech with suitable flourishes of a silver-topped cane. Yet his more recent upbringing has been in Northern surroundings. James links him with earlier national ambitions by calling him Hudson, after the Hudson river, emblem of the American Sublime, and thereby presenting him as the incarnation of spontaneous natural force.

Through the figure of Roderick Hudson, James seeks to recover and reassert an earlier mood of American optimism, to insinuate that the Civil War has been no more than a detour from the preordained path, the prelude to a renewed sense of national destiny. Yet the novel is unable to sustain these hopes, and the fate of Roderick as hero expresses James's anxiety about American prospects in the post-war era. The 'ache of fear' that James speaks of in his Preface (*Art of the Novel*, p. 4) is not only there in the struggle to write the book but in his whole sense of the predicament of the American writer, whose presumed special identity may simply be part of an all-embracing national mirage.

One particular scene in *Roderick Hudson* crystallises James's lurking disquiet that America may not, after all, be destined to be the artistic leader of nations. In the final pages of the novel Roderick Hudson and Rowland Mallett are sitting outside the door of a Swiss mountain inn watching the beauty of the sunset, when Roderick suddenly sees a gigantic figure outlined against the crimson background of the sky. It seems like a superhuman presence, and as it approaches Roderick asks what it can possibly want with them, since they are small people and cannot aspire to keep company with giants. Finally, the mystery is dispelled:

> The dusk meanwhile had thickened, and they had not perceived a figure approaching them across the open space in front of the house. Suddenly it stepped into the circle of light projected from the door and windows and they beheld little Sam Singleton stopping to stare at them. He was the giant they had seen so strikingly presented.   (p. 307)

Sam Singleton is an honest, hard-working, unpretentious American painter of landscapes, who possesses only a slender and restricted talent – evoked as much by his name as by his stature;

who will never be a genius and who knows it. Yet the optical illusion whereby he is transformed into a far more imposing figure serves to express symbolically the possibly illusory and ephemeral nature of American greatness. The point is explicitly made by Roderick himself: '"He's like me", Roderick rejoined; he'll have passed for ten minutes for far bigger than he is"' (ibid.). James acknowledges that the American's need to believe in his heroic destiny is always in danger of taking the will for the deed, and the novelist or sculptor, in essaying a great work, will not necessarily accomplish one. For James, therefore, in his own career, the act of realising and working through the initial inspiration was of the utmost importance, and by those standards he criticised *Roderick Hudson* itself. But what James forgot was that the novel was itself *about* this anxiety, and to have resolved the problem in these terms would have been to cancel everything with which it is imaginatively concerned.

Sam Singleton is generous in his praise of Roderick Hudson and sufficiently unself-regarding to recognise him as his artistic superior. Yet in the light of the novel as a whole Singleton's assessment of his fellow American pioneer seems distinctly odd. For in explaining why he cannot deprecate Roderick, even when he forces upon him a sense of his own comparative inadequacy, Singleton says,

> Oh, I don't envy Hudson anything he possesses . . . because to take anything away would be to spoil his beautiful completeness. 'Complete', that's what he is; while we little clevernesses are like half-ripened plums, only good eating on the side that has had a glimpse of the sun. Nature has made him so, and fortune confesses to it!   (p. 133)

It is as if Singleton prefers to dwell on Roderick's completeness in theory while carefully avoiding the question whether or not it is substantiated in practice. In the symbolic scheme of the novel Sam Singleton represents America's tentative artistic beginnings; Gloriani, European cynicism and decadence; while only Roderick can be allowed to stand for the moment of high heroic representation, the possibility of an art that is altogether ripe and final. Yet in proposing this *Roderick Hudson* is gripped by the anxiety that the United States has nevertheless missed its artistic moment, as the young painter misses his; that the moment of triumphal optimism of the 1830s and 1840s has slipped elusively by, never to return.

This sense of the United States as spiritually exhausted yet eager to renew its faith and to carry forward once more the torch of American possibility is articulated through the character of Rowland Mallett, Roderick's indulgent patron, of whom James was to write, 'The centre of interest throughout *Roderick* is in Rowland Mallett's consciousness, and the drama is the very drama of that consciousness' (*Art of the Novel*, p. 16). Unlike his protége Rowland belongs to the pre-war generation, and, while Roderick has been virtually untouched by the conflict, Rowland finds his whole life dislocated by 'submitting to the great national discipline' (*Roderick Hudson*, p. 29) in obtaining a commission in 1861. After the war Rowland has no desire to return to the world of business. He feels restless and disatisfied. He is looking for some errand or purpose that can fill the spiritual vacuum in his life and he finds it in the opportunity of aiding Roderick to become a sculptor:

> And I want to care, don't you see? with a certain intensity; even, if you can believe it, with a certain passion, I can't just now be intense and passionate about a hospital or a dormitory. Do you know I sometimes think that I'm a man of genius half-finished? The genius has been left out, the faculty of expression is wanting; but the need for expression remains, and I spend my days groping for the latch of a closed door. (p. 25)

The diffracting of Roderick Hudson through the perception of Rowland Mallett in the novel has the effect of suspending a full commitment to Roderick's personal goals and of placing his representativeness in brackets. Mallett would, of course, like to believe in Roderick, since this would restore his confidence both in America and in himself, but there is always the lurking possibility that Rowland, in taking the young sculptor as his *beau ideal*, has committed a serious error of judgement: taking the wish for the reality as Roderick himself is disposed to. Roderick is the double who will offer a reflected image of completeness to the half-finished Rowland, yet he cannot sustain the burden of such transcendant representation and proves incomplete himself. Through his use of Rowland, James suggests that in the 1870s American idealism, however well-meaning, cannot be presented without a trace of distancing irony, since the American future was predicated on some unified notion of what it was to be an American, which the Civil War itself put in question. Mallett's indecisiveness and wishful thinking is James's own. Yet, contrariwise, in so far as he has shown confidence in Roderick, Rowland has also been a vain idealist and a dreamer. His faith has been excessive and its final, inescapable collapse leaves him feeling as hollow and empty as before:

> He recognised a sudden collapse of his moral energy; a current that had been flowing for two years with a breath of its own seemed at last to submit to shrinkage and thinness. He looked away at the sallow vapours on the mountains; their dreariness has an analogy with the stale residuum of his own generosity. At last he had arrived at the very limit of the deference a sane man might pay to other people's folly; nay, rather, he had transgressed it, he had been befooled on a gigantic scale.
> (p. 316)

At redemption time all those promissory notes isued by the Bank of Emerson in the heyday of Transcendentalism have finally proved as worthless as Confederate Bonds.

Roderick Hudson is an excessive hero in the antique Transcendental manner. He is bewitched with hyperbole. His talk brims with 'the superlative and the sweeping' (p. 35). He is convinced that America has a special destiny and that he will be the one to manifest it. He is in absolutely no doubt about the correlation between geographical size and artistic excellence: 'We are the biggest people and we ought to have the biggest conceptions. The biggest conceptions, of course, would bring forth the biggest performance' (p. 40). James knew the dangers of this doctrine then, and he was to be still more convinced of them in the future, through his relationship with the blond Norwegian American Henrik Anderson, who cherished such colossal ambitions for his gargantuan statues that James felt in duty bound to warn him against megalomania. The presumed link between national greatness and art, far from producing great art, might actually militate against it. For there is more to art than grandiose conceptions. There *is* a psychological dimension to art, and Roderick, in true Romantic fashion, absolutely insists upon it. You really can pick up colossal weights if you look at the bar with sufficient aggression:

> For me it's either that or nothing. It's against the taste of the day I know; we've really lost the faculty to understand beauty in the large ideal way. We stand like a race with shrunken muscles, staring helplessly at the weights our forefathers easily lifted. But I don't hesitate to proclaim it – I mean to lift them again! I mean to go in for big things; that's my notion of my art. I mean to do things that will be simple and sublime. (p. 88)

But the novel suggests that limits may still be encountered by those who refuse to speak of them, and that Roderick lacks the inner strength that would enable him to realise his goals. Over all his speculative endeavours there hangs the stern, prophetic rebuke of the philistine Barnaby Striker, who nevertheless brings a Yankee shrewdness to his assessment of men: 'He may be the biggest genius of the age: his potatoes won't come up without his hoeing them' (p. 58). Roderick lacks application as he lacks stoicism and fortitude. He cannot face even the slightest discouragement. Looking back at Transcendentalism across the smoking battlefields of the Civil War, it is as if the optative mood has been found out.

Roderick Hudson is the novel in which James announces the international theme, the opposition between Europe and America, that was to prove a lasting obsession. So it should be noted that here the scales are seen as heavily weighted against the new nation, even if the Europeans do play second fiddle. James suggests that Americans will do well to be in awe in Europe, as 'immemorial, complex, accumulated' (p. 219), since it is just this that America lacks. Initially it might seem surprising that Roderick should meet his nemesis through his love for a beautiful girl who is herself American, but James's purpose is to present a desperate either/or. Christina is the American acquiescence in and acculturation to Europe where the American identity becomes almost wholly extinguished. Christina finally has to give up her Bostonian higher self and reconcile herself to a prosperous match with the Prince Casamassima. But Roderick signifies the bafflement and frustration of an American idealism when it encounters alien phenomena which it cannot confront on its own terms. American idealism becomes excessive when seeks to cancel the world in the very ecstacy of its self-intoxication.

With *The American* (1877) James set out to make a completely fresh start, purging himself of all nostalgia. His hero, Christopher

Newman, is an essentially post-war hero, a man who can represent America to Europe for the very reason that he owes nothing to the past and is freed from narrow, sectional loyalties. That James's disillusionment with the Transcendental mood, as manifested in Roderick Hudson, has turned to something very like impatience is indicated by his withering characterisation of Mrs Tristram, a typically flighty American abroad:

> Restless, discontented, visionary, without personal ambitions but with a certain avidity of imagination, she was, as I have said before, eminently incomplete. She was full – both for good and for ill – of beginnings that came to nothing, but she had nevertheless, morally, a spark of the sacred fire. (p. 38)

Christopher Newman is made of sterner stuff. He is a self-sufficient, self-possessed, self-made man of the new American type, who can look on even the most exalted of Europeans with an inquisitive but wholly unblinking eye. Whereas in *Roderick Hudson* it was Northampton, Massachusetts, that epitomised narrowness and provinciality, and Europe that was the great world, in *The American* the polarities are reversed. It is Christopher Newman, with his vast experience of life, who is the man of the world, and the aristocratic Bellegardes – whose daughter, Claire, Newman vainly seeks to marry – who seem enclosed in an elaborately circumscribed world, so that they are scarcely conscious of anything that goes on beyond the confines of the Faubourg St Germain. On the road to making his fortune in copper and railroads Newman has knocked about a good deal. He has sold leather, manufactured washtubs, had dealings in a needle factory, and mingled with Western humorists in rowdy saloons. He is at home in almost any human context – except perhaps the Faubourg St Germain. Yet in general he is prepared to view all European quirks and foibles in a tolerant if quizzical spirit. James endows Newman with a singular patience and generosity of disposition in order to show how terribly exiled Americans are imposed upon, so that at times he recalls the long-suffering pilgrims of *The Innocents Abroad*. Though Newman is far more resilient than his artistic precursor, he nevertheless finds that a visit undertaken for pleasure is turned, step by step, into the most strenuous trial and test of the spirit, from which even he can scarcely emerge unscathed – and which is the more severe precisely because he is so unprepared for it. Young Valentin de Bellegarde, who idolises him, sees him as 'a man who stands at his ease, who looks at things from a height' (*The American*, p. 38), as casual and unperturbed as Whitman in 'A Song of Myself'; but by the end he is an angry and frustrated man.

Although James shows himself concerned to offer a careful and convincing depiction of both American and European types and to present a finely focused rendering of a specific Parisian milieu, the novel unexpectedly comes across as a fairytale. Christopher Newman is the bold and splendid knight-errant who comes to the dark tower holding aloft the banner of the Stars and Stripes, who will rescue Clare de Cintré, the beautiful, patient and long-suffering princess, from durance vile. Like the Connecticut Yankee he will break the shackles of moribund tradition simply by the shining example he offers of a higher ethical creed. If the American hero is thwarted, this is because the age of chivalry is past and his nobility seems anachronistic. Surrounded by depravity and cynicism, he cannot help acting more honourably than the situation requires, despite the many provocations to which he is exposed. James seems to acknowledge this at many points. At the ball given to celebrate his engagement to Clare de Cintré, when Newman is looked over by the assembled Parisian elite, he figures as the Beast in 'Beauty and the Beast' and the duchess praises him for winning over the countess, who is 'as difficult as a princess in a fairy tale' (p. 190). Yet Newman has not in fact conquered, and it is the apparently insuperable nature of the obstacles he must overcome that links his task with myth and legend, even though his efforts are unsuccessful. Nevetheless James subsequently denied that he had been fully conscious of this fabulous dimension. Speaking of Newman's power over the Bellegardes, which he attains through the discovery of a dark secret in their recent past, James wrote,

> Here above all it really was, however, that my conception unfurled, with the best conscience in the world, the emblazoned flag of romance; which venerable ensign it had, though quite unwittingly, from the first and at every point sported in perfect faith. I had plotted arch-romance without knowing it.
>
> (*Art of the Novel*, p. 25)

So *The American*, though innocent, artless and charmingly unself-conscious, was always skidding out of control. In writing it the young novelist became emotionally involved with his theme to the point that the inherent improbability of the narrative was lost sight of. For the hard-up Bellegardes would have been only too delighted at this opportunity to restore the faded family fortunes. It was flagrant, extravagant, excessive.

Despite his unassuming demeanour, Christopher Newman is even more determined to storm the citadel of Europe than was Roderick Hudson. His resolution is clear and unshakable. He wants to make a match that will confirm the high valuation he places on himself as a self-made man and on his native country, and he is not going to be fobbed off with anything less. Although his early gesture of offering to buy a picture from Mlle Noémie at her extravagant asking-price seems naïve, he is still shrewd enough not to get emotionally involved with her despite her considerable attractiveness, since the plans he has made for himself are, in reality, quite as unalterable as those that the Bellegardes have made for their daughter Claire. For Newman to marry a beautiful, aristocratic Parisienne will set the seal on his success and proclaim his master of the Old World as much as the New. From the outset he regards her as a trophy: 'She is exactly, what I have been looking for. She is my dream realised.' (p. 106). Since Europe is his oyster – that, as he sees it, 'Europe was made for him, and not he for Europe' (p. 66) – it is his mission to affirm these priorities and to collect the best that it affords. All obstacles can be simply brushed aside: 'Energy and ingenuity can arange everything' (p. 113). Newman's calm refusal to recognise that any limit can be set to his ambitions in a European context establishes him not simply as an ambitious American but as positively Faustian. He reminds Tristram of 'the heroes of the French romantic poets, Rolla and Fortunio, and all those other insatiable gentlemen, for whom nothing in this world is handsome enough' (p. 45).

But, whereas James is ever conscious of the dangers attending the path of Roderick Hudson, he is sure that Christopher Newman's desires are perfectly reasonable. Surely he is the equal of the best that Europe can offer? Patriotic emotions are involved. When Newman is foiled and rebuffed by the Bellegardes, by their scheme to place Claire in a Carmelite convent, James has the choice of several possible endings. He could have his hero keep his dignity, turn his back on the absurd pretensions of the Bellegardes and conclude that they were never worth it anyway. Although this might seem reminiscent of the fox and the grapes, it would be both more in character and more in keeping with James's sense of incommensurable cultural worlds. Alternatively he could have presented Newman and Mme de Cintré as star-crossed lovers, who genuinely care for one another but whose love has been fated from the start. James's actual ending makes it quite evident that what we actually have is an American ego-trip, in which Christopher Newman is far more the 'remorseless egoist' than Roderick Hudson ever was. Since Newman can neither forgive or forget the slight that has been offered him, which is far more demoralising than the loss of Claire, he is determined on revenge:

> I want to bring them down – down, down, down! I want to turn the tables upon them – I want to mortify them as they mortified me. They took me up into a high place and made me stand there for all the world to see, and then they stole behind me and pushed me into this bottomless pit, where I lie howling and gnashing my teeth! I made a fool of myself before all their friends; but I shall make something worse of them. (p. 257)

This extraordinary vehemence, almost preposterous in its melodrama, seems quite disproportionate and seems traceable to what Nietzsche would call *ressentiment*; to a sense of moral indignation at those European cultural pretensions that make Americans conscious of feelings of inferiority which they cannot deny but which they feel are wholly unwaranted. It is James's own overvaluation of Europe that becomes a Sisyphean boulder against which his heroes vainly push, for to undervalue the task is also to undervalue the striving itself. There is a suggestive parallel between this attitude to Europe and that expressed by Ivan in Dostoevsky's *The Brothers Karamazov* just three years later:

> I want to travel in Europe, Alyosha, I shall set off from here. And yet I know that I am only going to a graveyard, but it's the most precious graveyard, that's what it is. . . . I know that I shall fall on the ground and kiss those stones and weep over them; though I'm convinced in my heart that it's long been nothing but a graveyard.[1]

The Russian spirit, like the American, seeks to liberate itself from the spellbinding power of Europe, but at the same time there is an eagerness to acknowledge Europe and even respect it, just so long as it is perceived as a spent cultural force that can safely be consigned to the past. The empire is to be translated elsewhere. The future is America's – or Russia's.

Christopher Newman is as mystified as Hank Morgan by the alien nature of European customs and the sheer perversity with which people continue to adhere to them – whether it is Valentin de Bellegarde's determination to fight a duel with a social inferior out of regard for the chivalry of a bygone age, the spirit of resignation in Claire that can lead her acquiesce in the life of a Carmelite nun putting up any resistance, or even the Marquise's obsession with dancing at the Bal Bullier. To Newman the world seems bafflingly opaque. He is tormented by its implacable, impenetrable resistance to his purposes. It is as if Europe is the White Whale to his remorseless Ahab. In the moment of truth when Newman pays his final visit to the site of the convent, situated in the aptly named Rue d'Enfer, this inscrutability becomes psychologically overwhelming:

> At the intersection of two of these streets stood the house of the Carmelites – a dull, plain edifice, with a high-shouldered blank wall all round it. From without Newman could see its upper windows, its steep roof and its chimneys. But there things revealed no symptoms of human life; the place looked dumb, deaf, inanimate. The pale, dead, discoloured wall stretched beneath it far down the empty side street – a vista without a human face. (*The American*, p. 305)

At this moment the European world no longer figures as a spacious theatre for the celebration of unbounded American possibility, but rather as an overpowering negativity, one that easily exceeds the most titanic energies that can be sent against it. The trajectory of *The American* is that of a bullet slowing down. At the end Newman is a spent force himself.

In *The Portrait of a Lady* (1881) the American assault on Europe is renewed, but by using a female protagonist James is able to escape from the constrictive role of masculine stereotyping and to present a central character who can be more open to the world, without thereby putting the national psyche at risk. The problem with James's earlier heroes, whether artist or businessman, was that they had to assume too great a burden of representation. Both in the massive hopes that are invested in Roderick Hudson by his patron Rowland Mallett, and in the way in which Newman's aristocratic marriage becomes a matter of life and death, the stakes have become too high; their *engagé* author asks us to believe that the fate of America itself is at risk, or at least suspended on a knife edge. Since they embody native American genius and sagacity, it is as if they court moral contamination simply by coming to Europe – if they do not succumb to the infection-laden miasmas of the Colosseum, as Daisy Miller does, such implications are never far away. For them to change or develop in response to their new environment would be tantamount to an act of betrayal. For James the America–Europe opposition was fraught with divergent possibilities. At his most enraptured he could envisage some kind of Transcendental synthesis in which the most admirable features of both would be combined; but he could also view it as some kind of moral arm-wrestling contest, where sooner or later the weaker party would be relentlessly forced down on the table. This sense of struggle is never altogether superseded, since, although the relative crudity of *The American* gives way to the greater sophistication of *The Portrait of a Lady*, the later novels are permeated with a vision of life as a battle in which no quarter can be given.

The interest of a heroine for James is that, as a woman, she eludes simple definition. The whole point of *Daisy Miller*, his first commercial success, is that Winterbourne, the narrator, can never really make Daisy out. She may well be a 'little American flirt'[2] and she may well get herself into compromising situations with mustachioed Italian gentlemen in a way that no nice girl should; it may well be that her manner is too forward – but despite all this there is still some insurmountable difficulty in the way of placing her or classifying her. Winterbourne finds himself reluctantly and embarrassingly enrolled in the task of saving Daisy Miller's 'reputation', a task made the more invidious because it is a subject for ironic comment on the part of Daisy herself. Winterbourne always has the uneasy feeling that his attempts to analyse Daisy may be ludicrously wide of the mark, that the innocence attributed to Daisy may be more in the eye of the beholder than in Daisy herself:

Winterbourne wondered how she felt about all the cold shoulders that were turned towards her, and sometimes it annoyed him to suspect that she did not feel at all. He said to himself that she was too light and childish, too uncultivated and unreasoning, too provincial, to have reflection upon her ostracism or even to have perceived it. Then at other moments he believed she carried about in her elegant and irresponsible little organism a defiant, passionate, perfectly observant and consciousness of the impression she produced. He asks himself whether Daisy's defiance came from the consciousness of innocence or from her being, essentially, a young person of the reckless class. It must be admitted that holding oneself to a belief in Daisy's 'innocence' came to seem to Winterbourne more and more a matter of fine-spun gallantry.[3]

In effect, the problem of deciphering Daisy lies in deciding whether or not Daisy is able to pick up the appropriate cues from the people she encounters. She may be innocent because she never knows when she has gone too far; but equally she might be innocent in a more complex way, where, although conscious of the fact that she is disapproved of, she nevertheless persists in behaving recklessly because she does not see what is wrong with her behaviour and does not believe that the integrity of her own personality can be touched by other people's perceptions. Daisy Miller is a woman without a handle just as surely as Hudson and Newman are men *with* a handle; the freedom that she represents is a freedom from the possibility of naming. In *Portrait of a Lady* James is able to make this moral elasticity into something more complex, whereas his male protagonists are subject to foreclosure from the start.

Isabel Archer does not come straight from the cast but is subject to a process of moulding. James is concerned to show – no doubt under the influence of the then-fashionable ideas of the French historian Hippolyte Taine – how his characters are shaped by the influence of a particular milieu. Although James does present pure and unmodified American types such as Caspar Goodwood and Henrietta Stackpole, they serve primarily as foils for the Europeanised Americans, Ralph Touchett and his father, Madame Merle and Gilbert Osmond; above all, for Isabel Archer, the heroine, whose fate, as an American newly arrived in Europe, lies suspended between all possibilities. There is no one American stereotype, no single point of view. James makes an implicit critique of his earlier novels in the opening phase of the novel when Mrs Touchett repudiates in the most strenuous terms Isabel's suggestion that she may be losing touch with American values:

> 'Now what's your point of view?' she asked of her aunt. 'When you criticise everything here you should have a point of view. Yours doesn't seem to be American – you thought everything over there so disagreeable. When I criticise I have mine; it's thoroughly American!'
>
> "My dear young lady,' said Mrs Touchett, 'there are as many points of view in the world as there are people of sense to take them. You may say that doesn't make them very numerous! American? Never in the world; that's shockingly narrow. My point of view, thank God, is personal.'   (pp. 60–1)

For James it is not enough for Americans to get on their patriotic high horse and simply complain about European decadence and feudal survivals. Americans, above all, should be open-minded about other systems of values and ready to explore alternative possibilities in an inquiring spirit. Human diversity itself is denied if all true Americans are cast from the self-same patriotic mould. Not the least ingenious aspect of James's novel is the way in which he contrives to present his Americans blending quite unobtrusively into an ostensibly alien landscape. When James introduces Gilbert Osmond outside his Italian villa, he notes that his Vandyke beard and curly moustache gave him a 'foreign, traditionary look' and that his English blood had probably received some 'French or Italian commixture' (p. 197). We are scarcely prepared for the fact that this languid aesthete, who speaks to his daughter in fluent Italian, should be an American, yet American he is. In the same way in the opening of *The Portrait* James is at pains to set a characteristically English scene – afternoon tea on the lawns of an English country house at the height of summer, yet all the participants in this ritual except Lord Warburton are American, and old Mr Touchett, with embroidered slippers, shawl and collie dog at his feet, seems most English of all. His narrow clean-shaven face is the only potential signifier of Americanness that remains. This paradoxical beginning announces the themes that the novel will explore.

While Roderick Hudson and Christopher Newman are always hard at work on the European try-your-strength machine, and so bound always to verge on a Melvillean monomania, Isabel Archer's quest for self-definition will always be more oblique and elusive, since she is called upon to articulate her identity through a variety of options that are likely to be as restricting as they are enabling. In his initial portrait of Isabel as an idealistic, open-minded, spirited young girl trapped in a musty old house, James shows himself sensitive to the contradiction that Transcendentalism opened up in the lives of many American women: they were encouraged to think of freedom and self-realisation while remaining confined within the home. It is James's great merit that he is prepared to take an Isabel Archer seriously. It may seem faintly preposterous to speak of the democratic impulse in relation to a heroine who inherits a substantial fortune, but the fact remains that in making his heroine a 'mere young thing' and in suggesting that her hopes, ambitions and sense of independence were matters of moment, James did more to align himself with Whitman's America than he had ever done before. It is no small achievement on his part to make us feel that Isabel's horizons would be as restricted by marriage to Lord Warburton as they actually were by her marriage to Gilbert Osmond. We are never allowed to patronise Isabel. In *The Portrait of a Lady*, for all its awareness of the resistance life places in the way of American dreams, we are made to re-experience the boundless vistas that Walt Whitman had opened up in his 'Song of Myself', where the world is a theatre for the surging, pulsating expansions of the spirit.

In pondering Isabel's mistakes and her failures we must not lose sight of the fact that this 'failure' is to be measured against the almost excessive sense of possibility that James calls upon her to represent. Isabel, with her 'inflated deals', with her 'fixed determination to regard the world as a place of brightness of free expansion, of irresistible action' (p. 54), is a heroine who makes excessive demands on the world, yet these are demands that James approves of even though he suspects that they can never be met or even partially met. Of course it can be argued that by appropriating a figure of New England femininity for his own transcendental purpose James thoroughly mystified the contemporary situation of women and failed to sketch in anything remotely resembling a realistic analysis of the predicament of such a person. It might have been more interesting to contemplate the fate of an Isabel Archer in an American context than to follow her progress across Europe trailing clouds in her wake. Nevertheless we cannot ignore the Nietzschean turn that American idealism has taken. The possibilities that Whitman spoke of before the Civil War and once designated as real are no longer there to be taken possession of and redeemed, but are rather to be cherished as a noble fiction. For James the spiritual grandeur of American Transcendentalism lies precisely in its sublime readiness to fly in the face of the facts, in the power of a conviction that can almost give credence to the conviction itself. But that little word 'almost' is quite crucial. America is already a mythology.

The definitive moment when the American commitment to potentiality confronts a more worldly and materialistic orientation occurs in chapter 19 of *The Portrait of a Lady*, when Isabel is first thrown together with Madame Merle. Madame Merle possesses all the talents that can make a woman the ornament of polite society: she is a brilliant pianist, an accomplished water-colourist, an expert needlewoman. In addition she is a resourceful conversationalist, a prolific letter-writer and a person adept as adapting herself to the inclinations of her guests or companions. Yet these gifts are not presented to the reader in order to be admired. On the contrary, Madame Merle is 'too perfectly the social animal' (p. 167), and in her social adroitness she has ceased to be the solely singular person that all good Americans should be. As Ralph Touchett subsequently sums her up, 'She's too complete, in a word' (p. 216).

In the American sense of things a person is altogether complete, or who affects to be so, is one who denies his or her immortal soul, who turns aside from the possibility of unlimited, unceasing spiritual development. For this Transcendental idealism the old saying 'Better Socrates unhappy than a pig happy' could well be rephrased as 'Better *anyone* unhappy than even Socrates happy', since, although American life, on the face of it, is devoted to the pursuit of happiness, to acknowledge happiness can only be regarded as a willingness to give up on higher goals. In this sense the United States can be defined as an excessive culture, since its symptomatic response to any failure of achievement is to call not for more realism but for more effort. The world must be bombarded with seemingly unlimited reserves of motivation and commitment until victory is finally achieved. James is careful to discount Madame Merle's point of view from the outset, before the following pivotal discussion occurs:

'When you've lived as long as I you'll see that every human being has his shell and that you must take the shell into account. By the shell I mean the whole envelope of circumstances. There's no such thing as isolated man or woman; we're each of us made up of some cluster of appurtenances. What shall we call our "self"? Where does it begin? where does it end? It overflows into everything that belongs to us – and then it flows back again. I know a large part of myself is in the clothes I choose to wear. I've a great respect for *things*! One's self – for other people – is one's expression of one's self; and one's house, one's furniture, one's garments, the books one reads, the company one keeps – these things are all expressive.'

This was very metaphysical; not more so, however, than several observations Madame Merle had already made. Isabel was fond of metaphysics, but was unable to accompany her friend into this bold analysis of the human personality. 'I don't agree with you. I think just the other way. I don't know whether I succeed in expressing myself, but I know that nothing else expresses me. Nothing that belongs to me is any measure of me; everything's on the contrary a limit, a barrier, and a perfectly arbitrary one. (p. 175)

The phrase that gives Madame Merle away is her parenthetical insertion 'for other people', since it demonstrates that she has no conception of what authenticity is. Isabel, in the spirit of Emerson, takes the high Transcendental ground and refuses to think the limit. If Emerson finds Jesus Christ as model an irritating constriction that blocks his own potentiality, we can scarcely be surprised that Isabel Archer declines to be viewed as some purposive agglomeration of dresses, bodices, bonnets and parasols. Human identity is to be found not in such external trappings but in the capacity to transcend them. The European point of view, as expounded by Madame Merle, represents the denial of human freedom – perfectly exemplified in the way in which she and Osmond bring up their daughter, Pansy, who is 'so formed and finished for her tiny place in the world' (p. 238). Such an education is a self-fulfilling prophecy, a looping of the cultural loop, since anyone so formed and fitted is incapacitated for life from the very start. The expansive horizons and explosive possibilities of Transcendental America simply never crop up. So, by contrast, we are meant to feel that Isabel's ideal, even if they lead to frustration or actual unhappiness, nevertheless represent an authentic form of consciousness that must never be silenced or suppressed. With Isabel there is always an openness of the novel that goes beyond the actual ending of the novel, or any possible endings, as if even the novelist cannot bring her to a halt.

But having said this there is still a problem about the rapidity with which James attempts to dispose of Madame Merle's point of view. Madame Merle, quite sensibly, suggests that the whole idea of the self as conceived of by either Romanticism or Transcendentalism is far more problematic than those who habitually speak of it would be prepared to admit. She rightly draws attention to the fact that personality is significantly structured by an envelope of conditioning circumstances and is therefore not to be conceived of as purely self-determined. What makes this discussion especially puzzling is that the debate goes far beyond presumed transatlantic differences of upbringing to address fundamental question of novelistic representation. For with *The Portrait* James, for the first time, situates his discourse within the general parameters and traditions of nineteenth-century European fiction and is writing, specifically, under the direct influence of George Eliot's *Middlemarch* and *Daniel Deronda*.

It was at this point that James firmly nailed his colours to the mast and avowed his allegiance to a mode of fiction dedicated to the most searching examination of the processes and circumstances under which character is formed, to the novel of spiritual development that is the *Bildungsroman*. James was subsequently to complain of the thinness and lack of density in the world depicted by Hawthorne, though responsibility for the fault was laid rather at the door of American culture itself, with its lack of historic and venerable institutions, than on the writer who had been forced to work with the available materials. In 'The Art of Fiction' James was to insist on 'the air of reality' achieved through 'solidity of specification'[4] as the supreme achievement of the novel. If the novelist, like the painter, strives 'to catch the colour, the relief, the expression, the surface, the substance of the human spectacle',[5] in such a characterisation substance is quite as important as surface: the novelist must achieve a deeper understanding of life at the same time as he tries to capture a likeness. So the details he introduces will have a symptomatic importance; he will not just be piling them up for their own sake. There must in this tradition of representation be the assumption that an individual's clothing, physical surroundings, reading, acquaintances and friends will be just as indicative as Madame Merle suggests. So James seems to be deploring on one level that which on another he undoubtedly accepts.

A possible way of resolving this contradiction would be to argue that, despite European surfaces. James is still writing within a tradition of American fiction where appearances are to be systematically distrusted, so that the novel offers two alternative methods of reading, where each is supplementary to the other. That is, the reader may accept that Madame Merle plays an agreeable and convivial social role, but may still feel that there is – indeed must be – more to her than this. As James would have it, Madame Merle is 'deep'; the subtler purposes that really animate her existence must be searched for – and, in this light, her hidden relationship with Osmond, if unforeseen, need nevertheless not come as a surprise. In the same way, there can be no doubt that Gilbert Osmond is an aesthete and that he is a man who has found himself an agreeable social niche, as even the most casual perusal of his Tuscan villa would suggest; but these traits offer only the most oblique pointer to the self-centred ruthlessness of the man. The conventions of realistic representation can be simultaneously deployed and yet be subject to their own internal critique.

On the other hand, we could provokingly turn the terms of the equation round and suggest that the truth which lies beyond appearance as barely suspected evil is programmatically determined by the paranoia of the puritan imagination, which refuses to rest on what it deems to be an inherently deceptive surface and thus empties the solidity of specification of any rationale, other than that of constructing a plausible illusion! In other words 'the air of reality' is not the absolute value that James elsewhere claims that it is; for, if it were, the problem of cognitively grasping the the real would not loom up in his fiction as massively and menacingly as it does. The real is there above all to be bracketed. Individual identity is created through an interpretative struggle that, in so far as it always goes beyond appearance, is a refusal of barriers and limits in more than sense. Transcendentalism's rejection of the actual can be recast as a hermeneutics of suspicion, and at the back of an Isabel who is idealistic enough to be taken in lies a novelist who is idealistic enough not to be.

James's whole relationship to the tradition of the European

novel is deeply ambivalent, and this manifests itself as much in his presentation of Isabel's decision to marry Gilbert Osmond as in anything else. Much critical discussion of *The Portrait of a Lady* has focused on the innocence and naïvety of the part of Isabel that leads her to make this catastrophic mistake, which nevertheless has the constructive consequence of forcing her to face the world with greater fortitude and realism. Isabel, in a word, has become wiser. In this way *The Portrait* is assimilated to the *Bildungsroman* model, where the hero or heroine, in Goethe, Jane Austen or George Eliot – or for that matter in Turgenev or Stendhal – develops from a raw, impressionable youth filled with vague and unrealisable ideals into a sadder, wiser person who can now come to terms with personal limitations as much as the objective limits of a real social world. Obviously such a moral trajectory has a great deal of relevance to *The Portrait of a Lady*, but it does need to be emphasised that this is very far from being the whole story, since James quite explicitly disassociates himself from the mood of philosophical resignation so characteristic of the genre. In *The Portrait* it is not Isabel but Osmond whom James identifies with this, who speaks of his determination 'Not to worry – not to strive or struggle. To resign myself. To be content with little' (p. 227). Osmond, of course, is a hypocrite, but he nevertheless accepts the power of limits just as surely as Isabel denies them. Of Isabel James observes, 'Deep in her soul – deeper than any appetite for renunciation – was the sense that life would be her business, for a long time to come' (p. 466).

It might seem that such an ascription is so vague as to be scarcely worth making, but, within the discourse of the novel, something of importance is being said all the same. Isabel will continue to function as a free and *active* moral agent; she will never passively acquiesce in any situation or myopically blunder on in some deep intellectual trance; she will always act strictly in accordance with the dictates of her conscience. Isabel, unlike Osmond, will continue to struggle, so that the novel's refusal of any final closure is also an Emersonian refusal of the limit. Although Isabel's decision to marry Osmond may have involved a serious error of judgement, James wants us to recognise that that decision was expressive of a noble and generous idealism, which is not automatically falsified because it errs. For it was, above all, a free decision in a way that marrying Lord Warburton or Caspar Goodwood never could have been. In either case she would simply have become the ineffectual, unrecognised extension of a more powerful man, without any field of action in which to exert her spirit of independence. She would cease to be a subject in her own right. The decision to marry Osmond involves no truckling to conventional expectations. It is bold, uninhibited, defiant. What devalues that decision is not so much that Osmond is cold, self-centred and rigid, but rather that Isabel comes to recognise that her perception of Osmond was subtly manipulated by Madame Merle, so that it was not genuinely free in the way that she imagined. Isabel's concluding gestures – her decision to return to see Ralph Touchett in London in the face of the outright opposition of her husband, and her subsequent return to Italy – are so balanced against one another as to effect an intricate reconcilement of contrasted cultural traditions. By leaving Osmond in order to proclaim her affection for another man, Isabel acts with extreme indiscretion and thereby demonstrates that their relationship can never be solely on his terms. By returning to him she nevertheless accepts that she must live with the consequences of her actions. But whatever she does Isabel will never passively surrender.

In this, of course, she is completely different from her fictional successor, Verena Tarrant, the inspirational public speaker for the American women's movement, whose fate is at the centre of *The Bostonians* (1886). *The Bostonians* is James's only full-length novel to deal with the American scene, and its sharply critical edge was to ensure its curious omission from Scribner's twenty-six volume New York Edition of James's works. *The Bostonians*, for all its complexity and assured depiction of New England culture, will always be a problem novel simply because, though it is ostensibly about the crusade for women's rights, James's real interests lie elsewhere. The objection to the book here must be not simply that James was clearly lacking in sympathy for this women's movement, but, further, that it represents James's adamant refusal to take any kind of political or ideological activity seriously. With James the political is always a sham, and a public stance always a screen for the 'real' personal and private motives that lie behind them. In thinking this James is merely part of a massive reaction against the hypocrisy and self-righteousness of nineteenth-century culture, in which any ostensible, openly acknowledged motive is one that will automatically be placed in frankly derisory brackets. So it is now necessary to insist, with equal bluntness, that the intellectual and personal energies that go into political activity need to be taken seriously and addressed in equally political terms. The claim that political organisations are nothing more than a context for individuals to make friends, influence people and seek personal advancement is not merely ideological in itself and a shallow device for discrediting view with which one is out of sympathy, but it further constitutes an ostrich-like determination to evade the recognition of anything that is collective, social or institutional. It feeds the myth that individuals are self-generated and self-generating. Christianity as much as communism or Islam, the Jockey Club and Women's Institutes as much as the imperial Chinese bureaucracy, become epiphenomena. But even individual convictions become unreal. In the case of Verena Tarrant it seems altogether implausible, even from a psychological point of view, that a person so heavily involved in the struggle for women's rights should simply succumb to the attractions of a man who is so frankly contemptuous or her views. Could James have written this with the sex roles reversed? Far from giving the narrative plausibility, the fact that Verena is young, impressionable and essentially passive only serves to demonstrate how determined James is to evade the issue. Ideas really do matter, and *The Bostonians* is deeply flawed by James's obstinate determination – worthy of his implacable Southerner, Basil Ransom – simply to brush past them as if they were invisible.

At bottom, *The Bostonians* is Henry James's lament for the passing of the old, innocent, supremely self-confident pre-war America, where it was still possible to act with clarity and vigour in the belief that all would ultimately turn out for the best and that all the good and brave causes would finally prevail. What has gone is not only the sense of the United States as a unified culture, held together by a common sense of purpose, but the belief that New England stands at the centre of it as both voice and conscience of the nation. *The Bostonians* is full of symptoms of malaise, whether it is to be found in the power of the press, the decline of Marmion from active fishing-port to lethargic seaside resort, or in the paradoxical combination of super-refined gentility with what James at least would see as the pretence of political activism. Certainly he would wish to stress the way in which such a genuinely courageous figure as Miss Birdseye, whose dedication has led her to play a real and often dangerous – if slightly dotty – part on the stage of the world in the cause of temperance and black emancipation, has been supplanted by the likes of Olive Chancellor, whose privileged, narcissistic existence is the comfortable base from which she seeks to live vicariously through others. Basil Ransom, and perhaps James also, might want to explain this by some formula about the 'feminisation' of American life, but what Basil calls 'the crazy character of the age' (p. 269) is fundamentally the dispersal of this sense of an on-going, expanding American identity. America in the 1830s and 1840s was the scene of a myriad wild and wonderful schemes, in a way which was still relatively unthreatening, since all this could be seen as reflecting the energy and diversity of the national character. In the aftermath of war, however, it is a different matter. Projects that once seemed merely quaint, humorous or misguided now seem positively threatening. James's own overreaction to feminist activism is prompted not only by masculine fear but also by an anxiety that the United States, already divided in two, is on the point of splintering into hundreds of tiny pieces. The passing of Miss Birdseye represents the final moment of closure for the Transcendental movement, the loss of an authority and self-confidence that can never be recaptured. The Transcendentalists, like Miss Birdseye, were often quirky, but they were never merely quirky; they never ceased to believe that they spoke for America. They would never have accepted minority status, even tacitly. They were fortunate enough to believe in a future in which they would be entirely vindicated.

Although it is offered to the reader as a novel of character and motive, the allegorical thrust of *The Bostonians* is inescapable. The ruthless, unremitting struggle of Olive Chancellor and Basil Ransom over Verena Tarrant, of which James says, 'The situation between them was too grim; it was war to the knife; it was a question of which should pull hardest' (p. 373), is the bitter, long-fought battle between North and South for the future of America. Verena herself, naïve, idealistic, eloquent, relatively unformed, represents the emergent American spirit, which now seems to have no autonomous or self-fulfilling destiny but must be subject to the capture of one set of interests or the other. Although Verena is able to arouse her audiences to enthusiasm, even James suggests by his emphasis on her theatricality that this can never represent anything other than a pleasing illusion, possibilities that are without the possibility of actualisation. Taken in conjunction with the death of Miss Birdseye, Verena's failure to appear on the platform in the final pages of *The Bostonians* is also a sign that the whole early American culture of lyceums and lecture halls, where so many hopes for an American future were once glowingly outlined, has itself become an anachronism. But Venera is also the victim of American excessiveness, caught as she is between Basil Ransom's 'merciless devotion' and the grasp of Olive, 'too clinching, too terrible' (p. 376). Olive is strenuous and she expects her adversary to be strenuous also, which, despite his laid-back and lackadaisical manner, he is. Everything in the world of *The Bostonians* is excessive, exaggerated and inflated, and it is clearly this aspect of American life that James has learned to distrust. If Verena's oratory is over the top, so too is Olive's obsessional custodianship of her and Basil's determination to crush her feminist views. When Mrs Burrage says to Olive, 'Don't attempt the impossible. You have got hold of a good thing; don't spoil it by trying to stretch it too far' (p. 308), we know that this is advice that it is impossible for Olive to accept, just as we know that Basil can never be content just to love Verena for herself, since she is to be the means whereby he will seek to reclaim his own deeply battered and demoralised Southern ego: 'He didn't care for her engagements, her companions, or all the expectancy of her friends; to "squelch" all that, at a stroke, was the dearest wish of his heart. It would represent his own success, it would symbolise his victory' (p. 382).

James sees the Civil War as the product of such fanaticism. Like others before and since, he is ready to lay the responsibility for the loss of this deeply cherished sense of national unity at the abolitionists' door. In his very first conversation with Verena, Basil, with jocular bitterness, suggests that all this feminist talk about women and peace is sheer cant: 'And as for our four fearful years of slaughter, of course, you won't deny that there the ladies were the great motive power. The Abolitionists brought it on, and were not the Abolitionists principally female? Who was that celebrity that was mentioned last night? – Eliza P. Mosely. I regard Eliza as the cause of the biggest war of which history preserves the record' (p. 111). What cannot, of course, be admitted is that the cracks and contradictions in American life were far too jagged to be more than temporarily papered over by Transcendental rhetoric, or that the pure and integral American ideal which the future was supposed to deliver miscarried along the way. *The Bostonians* represents the surfacing of worries and fears about America that James had long tried to suppress.

From the wreckage of *The Bostonians* James was able to salvage many dark insights into the way in which even the most intimate relationships can be invaded by the will to coerce and manipulate, but for the moment the writing of it left him bereft of any consoling faith. Everything that America once seemed to stand for now seemed to be writ in wind and water. In *The Princess Casamassima* (1886) and *The Tragic Muse* (1890) he endeavoured to fill the gap with an aesthetic creed, often reminiscent of Walter Pater.

Hyacinth Robinson, the bookbinding working-class hero of *The Princess Casamassima*, is saved from the simplifications and violent reductions of revolutionary ideology when he is able to avail himself of the generosity of Mr Vetch and embark on that ultimate spiritual crusade, the Grand Tour. Through his powerful aesthetic response to the manifold beauties that he sees he is compelled to acknowledge both the actual misery of the world and, at the same time, a force that can transcend it:

> He saw the immeasurable misery of the people, and yet he saw all that had been as it were, rescued and redeemed from it: the treasures, the felicities, the splendours, the successes of the world. This quality took the form sometimes, to his imagination, of a vast, vague, dazzling presence, an irradiation of light from objects undefined, mixed with the atmosphere of Paris and Rome.[6]

The passage picks up and evokes James's own personal sense of the Sublime when he first stood in the Gallerie d'Apollon in the Louvre; it is deeply autobiographical, but James can scarcely expect the reader to follow him in thinking that the Louvre, the Uffizi and the Vatican somehow cancel out the entire sum of human misery under nineteenth-century capitalism.

In *The Tragic Muse* the religion of art is even more central. Through the interwoven stories of Nick Dormer the painter and Miriam Rooth the actress and 'tragic muse', James insists that, where art is concerned, nothing less than total dedication will do. When Nick tries his hand at politics and endeavours to make his way in the social world he becomes utterly disillusioned:

> I've imperilled my immortal soul, or at least I've bemuddled my intelligence, by all the things I don't care for I've tried to do,

and all the things I detest I've tried to be, and all the things I never can be that I've tried to look as if I were – all the appearances and imitations, the pretences and hypocrisies in which I've steeped myself to the eyes; and at the end of it (it serves me right!) my reward is simply to learn that I'm still not half humbug enough.[7]

At this point James's endorsement of an absolute otherworldliness comes close to being a rapprochement with all that he had once execrated in the figure of Gilbert Osmond, though Osmond, admittedly, was a dilettante.

The writing of *The Princess Casamassima* and *The Tragic Muse* was a dark and tortuous intellectual passage in which James came close to losing touch altogether with the convictions and imaginative energies that had shaped his earlier fiction. In *The Portrait of a Lady* he had achieved a complex reconciliation between his clear sense of the moral value of American idealism and of his equally firm belief in the representational tradition of the European novel, with its painstaking depiction of the individual within a carefully realised and quite specific social context. 'The Art of Fiction', written soon after the publication of *The Portrait* yet often taken all too naïvely as a *vade mecum* to James's fiction as a whole, reflected this newfound confidence, but it was not a mood that would last for long. From *The Bostonians* and its successors it would appear that James was progressively losing his faith in both idealism and social representation. The overweening idealist might not merely be deceived about the world but about his or herself as well. Yet, equally, the mere piling-up of descriptive detail, the preoccupation with social class and social roles, was in danger of becoming an end in itself. The confident presentation by novelist to reader of recognisable yet idiosyncratic stereotypes was in danger of becoming a transaction so automatic that it could no longer attend to the complexities of psychic life. The novel of idealism risked emptiness and hollow assertion; the novel of social representation courted superficiality of another kind. In his later work James endeavours to deepen and intensify the conflict between individual and society, so that it becomes nothing less than a desperate life-and-death struggle, where all is at risk.

A better guide to his later practice than 'The Art of Fiction' is his review of William Dean Howells's *The Story of a Play*. The review, which appeared in 1898, the year after the publication of *What Maisie Knew*, demonstrates just how resistant James could be to the assumptions of a certain kind of literary realism:

> Mr Howells' volume has suggested to me that he has not cut into the subject quite so deep as the intensity of the experience – for I assume his experience – might have made possible. It is a chapter of bewilderments, but they are for the most part cleared up, and the writer's fundamental optimism appears to have, on the whole matter, the last word. . . . In short I think the general opportunity a great one, and am brought back, by the limits of the particular impression Mr Howells has been content to give of it, to that final sense of the predestined beauty of behaviour on the part of everyone concerned – kindness, patience, submission to boredom, and general innocent humanity – which is what most remains with me from almost any picture he produces. It is sure to be, at the worst, a world all lubricated with good nature and the tone of pleasantry. Life, in his pages, is never too hard, too ugly, passions and perversities never too sharp, not to allow, on the part of his people, of such an exercise of friendly wit about each other as may well, when one considers it, minimize shocks and strains. So it muffles and softens, all round, the edges of *The Story of a Play*. The mutual indulgences of the whole thing fairly bathe the prospect in something like a suffusion of that 'romantic' to which the author's theory of the novel offers so little hospitality. And that, for the moment, is an odd consummation.[8]

James's quarrel with Howells surfaces more tangibly in *The Ambassadors*, a novel which germinated in the notebooks from some reported remarks of Howells to Jonathan Sturges in Paris:

> Oh, you are young, you are young, be glad of it: be glad of it and *live*. Live all you can: it's a mistake not to. It doesn't so much matter what you do – but live. This place makes it all come over me. I see it now. I haven't done so – and now I'm old. It's too late. It has gone past me – I've lost it. You have time. You are young. Live![9]

Not merely is Strether a Howells-like figure; James is insistent that this portrayal of the American in Paris will *not* be bathed in geniality but will, on the contrary, force him through experiences that will shake him to the very depths of his being. 'Living' may even be correlated with the ability to feel pain. In James's later critical writings and especially in the prefaces to the New York Edition 'intensity' is a word that constantly recurs, and it may serve to remind us how the later James, in his concern for emotional effect, reveals an unexpected kinship with Poe.

The Turn of the Screw, of course, is the classic instance of James's virtuosity in writing the tale of terror, yet there is still the disposition to regard it as an isolated though brilliant *tour de force* and to lay more stress on its interpretative convolutions than on its ability to shock. Yet it is striking that James, in a parenthetical reference to *Arthur Gordon Pym*, criticises the conclusion not for its absurdity, but because, in his view, it fails to achieve its effect. James's later writing is not content to rest in the literally representational. Many details are intentionally left vague. James makes no attempt to describe Maisie in *What Maisie Knew*, deliberately creates a mystery about the sources of the Newsome fortune in *The Ambassadors*, and never describes either Densher's last meeting with Milly in *The Wings of The Dove* or the contents of Milly's final letter. The circumstantial and the contingent are subordinated to a narrative organised around certain privileged moments of consciousness, to certain carefully prepared and elaborately staged effects. He had not worked for the theatre for nothing. James is quite capable of being as ornate and melodramatic as either 'The Masque of the Red Death' or 'The Fall of the House of Usher'. The massive, richly elaborated sentences, encrusted with glittering, strangely disturbing metaphors, move tentatively yet relentlessly towards disclosure, like heavy, velvet theatrical curtains as they vibrate before opening on the final act. Unlike Howells, James is not afraid to be 'too' anything. Excessiveness is the sign of truth.

The excessiveness has a strange, symbiotic relationship with James's later predilection for the small subject. With evident satisfaction, James placed *The Awkward Age* within a group of his productions which, through an 'unforeseen principle of growth', had developed quite as astonishingly as Jack's beanstalk: 'They were projected as small things, yet had finally to be provided for as comparative monsters' (*Art of the Novel*, p. 98). There is certainly something odd about this, for we might rather have expected that James would insist on the seriousness and profundity of his theme, the inevitability with which it enforces its imperious claims on the reader's attention. Certainly the James of *Roderick Hudson*, though permitting himself to be somewhat ironic at the expense of Roderick's grandiose pretensions, nevertheless felt that in the modern period the artist owed it to himself to embark on great projects, to set himself high heroic goals. With the later James the Sublime must find its entry by some other way, through a manifest disproportion between the artistic germ and its subsequent realisation. As Bernard Richards suggests 'What distinguishes James from many authors . . . is his particular pride is being able to point to very slight and trivial sources for his novels.'[10]

The issue itself is by no means trivial. For James the growth of such literary oaks from anecdotal acorns was testimony to the power of the creative imagination. Moreover, if this transformative force of the imagination is what matters, then conventional distinctions between the subject and its treatment break down, for the *donnée* itself is subjected to expansion and ramification without limit: 'Once "out", like a house-dog of a temper above confinement, it defies the mere whistle, it roams, it hunts, it seeks out and "sees" life; it can be brought back but by hand and then only to take its futile thrashing' (*Art of the Novel*, p. 144). By this metaphor James suggests, somewhat unexpectedly for a writer often taken to be an arch-formalist, that what really matters is to give the subject its head. Moreover, if the work is actually consituted through this imaginative pulling and stretching, then it follows that there can never come a time when the work truly is monstrous in any pejorative sense, for such a word rather serves to point to the sublimity and power of the transformatory elaboration. The very notion of the monstrous brings out the hidden homology with the tale of terror, whether practised by Poe or by James himself, which is that it aspires to envelop and overwhelm the reader in a narrative so finely focused as to achieve the maximum of intensity.

In his Preface to *The Awkward Age* James himself quite deliberately raises the question of whether it is actually possible for a subject to suffer (if that be the word) by over-treatment. He answers in the negative. A work can never be called to account in this way, since there is no fixed or stable standard by which we could possibly assess its superfluity. Just as Blake damned braces and blessed relaxes, so James finds all imaginative energy self-validating:

The thing carries itself to any maturer and gratified sense as with every symptom of soundness, an insolence of health and joy. And from this precisely I deduce my moral; which is to the effect that, since our only way, in general, of knowing that we have had too much of anything is by *feeling* that too much: so, by the same token, when we don't feel the excess (and I am contending, mind, that in 'The Awkward Age' the multiplicity yields to the order) how do we know that the measure not recorded, the notch not reached, does represent adequacy or satiety?   (*Art of the Novel*, pp. 117–18)

James, at this point, covers himself with a self-justificatory parenthesis in which the customary axiom that multiplicity must yield to order is invoked even though the whole thrust of his argument is precisely to put the very possibility of such a discrimination in question and to reverse the conventional hierarchisation of terms. It would involve assumptions about stability and measurement which James explicitly denies: 'If our art has certainly, for the impression it produces, to defer to the rise and fall, in the critical temperature of the telltale mercury, it still hasn't to reckon with the engraved thermometer-face.' (p. 118). What James is arguing here is that aetheticised discussion of art in the eighteenth-century manner, in terms of beauty, form and proportion, completely miss the point. Fiction has, above all, to make an impact and it can scarcely do this unless the writer gives it everything he has got. Deep down, James was more than ever the unabashed Romantic.

An important reason for what F. R. Leavis, speaking of *The Ambassadors*, called 'an effect of disporportionate "doing"'[11] is James's concern to render fully the difficulty of interpretation, to show the mind itself at work in its struggle to grasp shifting and various appearances. If James turns aside from the procedures of the 'objective novel', this is both because he feels that this all-seeing, all-foreseeing narrativity reduces the complexity of experience, and because he believes that it also reduces events to a common level, so that the reader is more concerned with how they slot into a narrative sequence than with their subjective meaning or importance. Thus, to present the world from within the horizons of a particular consciousness necessarily amplifies it in more than one sense. For when the future is unknown the world again becomes a dangerous place. Less becomes more in a desperate game of decipherment, where the mood of the player is quite as crucial as his ability to read the signs or even the signs themselves. We are plunged back into the agonies of a puritan consciousness, where nothing can ever be taken on trust and where the excess of meaning over event is the inescapable starting-point.

So there are epistemological grounds for the Jamesian disproportion. The novel has come to forget its Richardsonian beginnings, and has endeavoured both to suppress interpretation and to offer narratives that will assure truth by the very clarity and straightforwardness with which they are presented. James utterly undermines this equation. For human behaviour will always be projective. Of any occurrence people will ask not only what it *was* – problematic as that may be in itself – but also what it *means*: that is, how it is to be understood by the various parties involved as an expression of interests, motives and future intentions. Every event creates its own scenarios and is already implicated in such scenarios. The novel has been a game of cards without active players, built out of sequences rather than active play, and hence it has been more like snap or knock-out whist than either bridge or poker. By restoring the interpretative, James thereby also restores the subjective as well. In his discussion of the ghost story, which I do not hestitate to extend to his later fiction in general, James insists that what matters is not the phenomena themselves so much as the way in which they are handled by consciousness (with *The Turn of the Screw* as an obvious case in point):

> With the preference I have noted for the 'neat' evocation – the image, of any sort, with fewest loose ends dangling and fewest features missing, the image kept in fine the most susceptible of intensity – with this predilection, I say, the safest arena for the play of moving accidents and mighty mutations and strange encounters, or whatever odd matters is the field, as I may call it, rather of their second than of their first exhibition. By which, to avoid obscurity, I mean nothing more cryptic than I feel myself show them best by showing almost exclusively the way they are felt, by recognising as their main interest some impression strongly made by them and intensely received. We but too probably break down, I have ever reasoned, when we attempt the prodigy, the appeal to mystification, in itself; with its 'objective' side too emphasized the report (it is ten to one) will

practically run thin. We want it clear, goodness knows, but we also want it thick, and we get the thickness in the human consciousness that entertains and records, that amplifies and interprets it. (*Art of the Novel*, p. 256)

Whereas the European novel in its classic form seeks to create an illusion of reality through the accumulation of detail and circumstance, James strives for a phenomenological density, achieved through attention to the very processes by which we build up a picture of the world and endeavour to interpret it. But this world is not so much the physical world of railings, stucco façades, brass doorknobs and rolled umbrellas as the elusive, wavering movement of human relationships, which change not merely 'in themselves' but in the fitful and flickering perception we have of them. Yet James's language seems paradoxical, since he seems to ascribe material substance to a mode of writing which might seem rather to dematerialise experience, by locating it so unequivocally in the activity of the perceiving subject. But as James sees it, the traditional narrative style is a highly compressed shorthand that contrives to omit almost everything that matters. If the fictional world seems to overflow when the interpretative is restored to it, this plenitude of impressions makes it evocative of life itself, which can never be fixed or stabilised in the ways that the novel presumes. Temporality itself becomes plastic.

Another aspect of the small subject that needs to be considered is James's use of characters who lack significant pretensions and who seem to have no important claims on our attention. Maisie and Nanda Brookenham of *The Awkward Age* are 'only' children. Lambert Strether is just a run-of-the-mill, middle-aged American, a man to whom nothing very much has ever happened. Why does James not only choose to write about such recessive characters but seem positively to glory in it? James raised the question himself in his Preface to *The Spoils of Poynton*, with reference to his heroine, Fleda Vetch, whom he had named after one of the shyest and most retiring of wild flowers: 'It is easy to object of course "Why the deuce then Fleda Vetch, why a mere little flurried bundle of petticoats, why not Hamlet or Milton's Satan at once, if you're going in for a superior display of mind"' (*Art of the Novel*, p. 129). To which he immediately answers,

The 'things' are radiant, shedding afar, with a merciless monotony, all their light, exerting their ravage without remorse; and Fleda almost demoniacally both sees and feels, while the others but feel without seeing. Thus we get perhaps a vivid enough little example, in the concrete of the general truth, for the spectator of life, that the fixed constituents of almost any reproducible action are the fools who minister, at a particular crisis, to the intensity of the free spirit engaged with them. The fools are interesting by contrast, by the saliency they acquire, and by a hundred other of their advantages; and the free spirit, always much tormented, and by no means always triumphant, is heroic, ironic, pathetic or whatever, and as exemplified in the record of Fleda Vetch, for instance, 'successful', only through having remained free.   (pp. 129–30)

But we must not therefore assume that James himself is being equally humble, since the general terms in which he presents his much put-upon heroine precisely reproduce his analysis, in the Preface to *The Princess Casamassima*, of the deeper significance of Hamlet and Lear:

> Their being finely aware – as Hamlet and Lear, say, are finely aware – *makes* absolutely the intensity of their adventure, gives the maximum of sense to what befalls them. . . . Hamlet and Lear are surrounded, amid their complications, by the stupid and the blind, who minister in all sort of ways to their recorded fate.   (*Art of the Novel*, p. 62)

The argument is doubtless elitist in that James believes that only those who think and feel deeply are capable of the tragic, and it casts a rather strange light on Lear in particular as a kind of Dark Age Lambert Strether, but it is also unexpectedly democratic! For James wishes to revivify his readers' sense of the absolute value for the individual of retaining the spirit of freedom, together with the sensitivity and openness that should go with it, by divorcing it completely from any conventional overtones of 'greatness'. At the back of James's faith in such independent spirits lies the Transcendental faith in the common man and Emerson's conviction that, seen through the eye of a democratic faith, even the humblest details of ordinary life can be spiritually transfigured, can acquire a profound significance and worth. So James, like the sage of Concord, embraces the commonplace and, like Whitman, he finds potentiality and beauty in the most unlooked-for places. Against this will rise the almost instantaneous objection that, while Fleda Vetch indisputably belongs with the humble, the same can hardly be said of Milly Theale or Maggie Verver, his fabulously wealthy American princesses. But there is an answer to this too, whether or not we are prepared to accept it, when in the Preface to *The Portrait of a Lady*, in support of his contention that in *The Merchant of Venice* 'Portia matters to *us*' James argues,

> That she does so, at any rate, and that almost everything comes round to it again, supports my contention as to this fine example of the value recognised in the mere young thing. (I say 'mere' young thing because I guess that even Shakespeare, preoccupied mainly though he may have been with the passions of princes, would scarcely have pretended to found the best of his appeal for her on her high social position.)
>
> (*Art of the Novel*, p. 50)

Though Millie and Maggie figure in powerful mythological narrative where their wealth and status cannot be regarded as merely contingent or accidental, at least part of James's strategy in those novels is to invite us to think of them as being nevertheless mere young things, who are as vulnerable to passion, pain and anxiety as anyone else.

The puzzle of James's development as a novelist after *The Portrait of a Lady* is in the last analysis attributable to the fact that he came to recognise that the spirit of the European novel, to which he had come as an eager acolyte, was one which went against the grain of his own intellectual convictions. When it came right down to it James simply could not accept that the path of wisdom lay in reconciling oneself with the world even if that meant abandoning all the hopes and aspirations that it seemed to resist. As one raised in the high Transcendental tradition, he could not accept that an attempt on the part of the individual to bring himself into harmony with the world could be construed as anything other than a betrayal. *The Tragic Muse* is an uneasy book because James is unable to come up with a satisfactory rebuttal to the arguments of Gabriel Nash, which, as Quentin Anderson has persuasively suggested,[12] are strongly reminiscent of those of his father, William James Senior. James's father believed that it was possible to be an artist in life without actually being an artist in the conventional sense – as Nash says in the novel: 'One is one's self a fine consequence. That's the most important one we have to do with. . . . Merely to be is such a métier; to live is such an art; to feel is such a career.'[13] Henry James could not accept this implicit devaluation of the arts, but he did share both in the New England conviction that the self is the most powerful and potent thing in the universe, and, equally, that its value could not be measured or accounted for solely in terms of the part it played on the stage of the world. As Emerson writes, 'Nor can you, if I am true, excite me to the least uneasiness by saying "He acted and thou sittest still." I see action to be good when the need is, and sitting still to be also good.'[14]

Action is only one of the many moods of the soul. It cannot be privileged over any of the others. Indeed, it is not in the glare of public acclaim that the soul knows its own worth, but in the inwardness of private meditation. In his later fiction James strives to recover this sense of the soul as a transcendent power that will always remain true to itself and which will continually struggle to free itself from the toils of social existence. For James, as for Emerson, the world continually erodes the individual's sense of personal worth and deflects him from the realisation of his deepest impulses. To forget oneself is the greatest of sins. To recover this sense of self even in the face of the most formidable obstacles can be the greatest of blessings. The words with which Emerson concludes 'Illusions', the final essay of *The Conduct of Life*, have a particular appositeness to late James:

> Every god is there sitting in his sphere. The young mortal enters the hall of the firmament: there is he alone with them alone, they pouring on him benedictions and gifts, and beckoning him up to their thrones. On the instant, and incessantly, fall snow-storms of illusions. He fancies himself in a vast crowd which sways this way and that, and whose movement and doings he must obey: he fancies himself poor, orphaned, insignificant. The mad crowd drives hither and thither, now furiously commanding this thing to be done, now that. What is he that he should resist their will, and think or act for himself? Every moment new changes, and new showers of deceptions, to

baffle and distract him. And when, by and by, for an instant, the air clears, and the cloud lifts a little, there are the gods still sitting around him on their thrones, – they alone with him alone.[15]

For the later James the bedrock of personal identity is this illimitable, almost intuitive, spirit of resistance.

No Jamesian protagonist has greater need of such a principle of resistance than Maisie, the young child at the centre of *What Maisie Knew*. Maisie is the child of Beale and Ida Farange, and will, it is agreed, spend six months with each parent alternately after their divorce. In practice she finds herself shifting between the charge of two governesses: at her mother's the formidably moralistic, middle-aged Mrs Wix, in shabby black dress and steel-rimmed spectacles; at her father's the young and attractive Miss Overmore. Neither parent remains unattached for long. Her father marries Miss Overmore, while her mother marries the charming Sir Claude, a man who is also some years her junior and who takes a special interest in the welfare of Maisie, in part for personal reasons of his own. This arrangement also proves temporary. As Ida pursues a variety of men, who flit in and out of the novel largely as names that cannot be attributed to anyone with any degree of confidence, Sir Claude takes up with the new Mrs Beale Farange, an affair for which his concern for Maisie provides a convenient cover. To begin with Maisie is the passive and largely uncomprehending spectator of mysterious adult events, of a game, played by complex rules, in which it appears that the principals are always in danger of being compromised or exerting a certain pressure to be squared. Maisie plays an ambiguous part in all this since she is a subject who cannot be a subject, and her own presence is used to justify morally ambiguous goings-on and lend them an air of innocence, however incongruous. Maisie is the equivocal signifier of 'an excess of the queer thing which seemed to waver so widely between innocence and guilt' (p. 232).

Maisie is initially 'a mite of a half-scared infant in a great dim theatre' (p. 9), but, simply because she has to concern herself with her own destiny – the sub-sub-plot to countless other sub-plots – she is compelled, through fear and uncertainty, to try to decipher the language and behaviour of adults, which only reaches her in the form of a complex and elusive code. Maisie is the most dramatic instance in late James of the asymmetry between behaviour and discourse, of the way in which language can often seem a desperately rickety, swaying rope bridge flung across unspoken chasms in human relations. Maisie must make her way across this bridge without ever knowing where she is going or what is at stake. James multiplies the interpretative difficulties in the novel, since we have not only to interpret the significance of what is happening but must further attempt to decipher just what Maisie is making of it all. For James, the creativity of the free spirit and the excessiveness of interpretation are one. The ability to speculate, to hypothesise and to question is absolutely crucial to personal development. It is through Maisie's 'sense of freedom to make things out for herself' (p. 99) that she ceases to be placed in the position of the child.

In her predicament Maisie gets very little in the way of help or useful guidance from her principal guardian, Mrs Wix. In *Maisie*, *The Awkward Age* and *The Ambassadors* James views the custodians of moral rectitude with the greatest possible scepticism. He believes that those who seek to impose their moral categories on the world not only fail to grasp the complexities of human experience, which will always resist such simple formulae, but, far more significantly, will always remain blind to their own motives for imposing them. Morality is an instrument of domination, as James, with the long cultural history of New England behind him, was well placed to grasp. So Maisie's education is best precisely because it is a mis-education that lacks the stability, continuity and coherence of a conventional education. If Maisie is never completely brainwashed by the fantasy world of Mrs Wix, it is because she is well aware of what has been left out, because she is conscious that Mrs Wix's 'subjects' are simply a way of avoiding other subjects:

> She had not the spirit of adventure – the child could perfectly see how many subjects she was afraid of. She took refuge on the firm ground of fiction, through which indeed there curled the blue river of truth. She knew swarms of stories, mostly those of novels she had read; relating them with a memory that never faltered and a wealth of detail that was Maisie's delight. They were all about love and beauty and countesses and wickedness. Her conversation was practically an endless narrative, a great garden of romance, with sudden vistas into her own life and gushing fountains of homeliness. (p. 27)

Needless to say, Mrs Wix cannot avoid giving these tales a personal gloss. She necessarily filters everything in relation to her own perception of things. For her these commonplace stereotypes seem as true and eternal as the Platonic forms. But, since Maisie, in order to understand, is compelled to look at events from diverse points of view, she is forced to go beyond such a single-minded, simple-minded view of things. Mrs Wix cannot even grasp her own motives – above all her grotesque passion for Sir Claude.

In the latter part of the novel, when the cast of Sir Claude, Mrs Wix, Maisie, Mrs Beale and Susan Ash are transported *en masse* to France, James develops an antithesis between such presumed stable moral values and the expanding universe of moral relativity – very reminiscent of Henry Adams's distinction between the Virgin and the Dynamo, but with negative and positive polarities reversed. Mrs Wix remains attached to the Virgin and likes nothing better in Boulogne (a new cultural experience let us not forget) than to sit on a bench contemplating a gilt Madonna. Maisie, on the contrary, is exhilarated by the sense of release that she experiences. Here, all the old familiar boundaries have been erased. It seems that anything is possible:

> The place and the people were all a picture together, a picture that, when they went down to the wide sands, shimmered in a thousand tints, with the pretty organisation of the *plage*, with the gaiety of spectators and bathers, with that of the language and the weather, and above all with our young lady's unprecedented situation. For it appeared to her that no one since the beginning of time could have had such an adventure or, in an hour, so much experience; as a sequel to which she only needed, in order to feel with conscious wonder how the past was changed, to hear Susan, inscrutably aggravated, express a preference for the Edgware Road. The past was so changed and the circle it formed so overstepped that on the very afternoon, in the course of another walk, she found herself inquiring of Sir Claude – and without a single scruple – if he was prepared as yet to name the moment at which they should start for Paris.
>
> (pp. 232–3)

Needless to say, Sir Claude is *not* ready for Maisie's initiative, any more than he is for any of the others'; he is demonstrably disconcerted by her attempt to step out of the childish role, yet for that very reason it marks a crucial stage in her development. For James, in these later novels, the individual finds himself or herself trapped by the expectations of others, so that the realisation of freedom always involves a certain spirit of excessiveness that will refuse all compromise and set these restrictions aside. Maisie is as jealous of Mrs Beale as Mrs Wix, and in asking Sir Claude to give Mrs Beale up she is playing for high stakes; but by this gesture she asks to be taken on her own terms and refuses the dependent position. Maisie's gamble fails and she is thrown back on the guardianship of Mrs Wix. But this does not mean that her education has been in vain. On the contrary, Maisie sees *more* and this is a power that can never be taken from her – when James talks about Maisie wanting to know 'all', he is not altogether joking. The miracle of Maisie, the thing that makes Maisie so amazing, is that she is able to develop instinctively across all the barriers that are placed in her path. She transcends the actual. James actualises in this novel the confidence of Emerson, who writes,

> As the traveller throws his reins on his horse's neck and trusts to the instinct of the animal to find his road, so much we do with the divine animal who carries us through this world. For if in any manner we can simulate this instinct, new passages are opened for us into nature; the mind flows into and through things hardest and highest, and metamorphosis is possible.[16]

It has been Mrs Wix's endeavour to keep Maisie in an ignorant and subordinate position: a determination epitomised by the struggle over the letter from Maisie's father to Mrs Beale, which Mrs Wix insists is unsuitable for the eyes of an innocent child, but which Sir Claude believes it will be beneficial for her to see: 'You think it too bad, eh? But it's precisely because its bad that it seemed to me it would have a lesson and virtue for her' (p. 255). It is now impossible for Maisie to remain the spiritual prisoner of Mrs Wix, because she has developed a freedom of consciousness that can never be restricted and which has the power to look 'bad' things in the face. If what Maisie knows exceeds any possibility of specification, then Maisie will always remains supremely free. For James, paradoxical and idealist as this may seem, the ability of the mind to handle the information that enters consciousness is the first and greatest freedom. And for this reason Maisie will always keep on bobbing up again, like a cork on a surface disrupted by violent waves.

Of all the fictional characters in American literature, Lambert Strether, the narrative focus of *The Ambassadors* (1903), is the most unlikely candidate for the role of excessive hero; yet this is the part he plays, despite his own intense devotion to the household gods of Woollett, Massachusetts. Strether is a lean, bespectacled, middle-aged American, the editor of a literary journal. Life has rolled him along customary grooves almost without his recognising it. Late in life he comes to realise that he has never ever enjoyed any independence or had any fun. Like Mencken's stereotypical puritan, Strether has been tormented by the thought that somebody somewhere has actually been having that fun, but in his case the final turn of the screw is the revelation that that somebody could have been him. The task allotted to Strether by his intended, the wealthy Mrs Newcome of Woollett, that he should bring home her wayward son Chad to run the family business and extract him from the fleshpots of Paris, is one that perfectly symbolises his predicament. Strether functions by remote control, turned this way and that by signals from farthest Massachusetts, deeply programmed to respond to everything he encounters in a semi-automatic fashion.

Initially the world presents itself to Strether as a gallery of stereotypes, or, to put it another way, he has in his possession a series of rubber stamps which can impose an identificatory mark on all human goods to show that they have been checked and registered. In this task Strether is actually less adept than Miss Gostrey, whom he meets in the opening pages of the novel, who is 'the mistress of a hundred cases or categories, receptacles of the mind, subdivisions for convenience, in which, from a full experience, she pigeon-holed her fellow mortals with a hand as free as that of a compositor scattering type' (p. 21). Strether would miss most of these nuances, which is only to say that he works with a more restricted scheme of classification, the more likely to break down at the first hint of possible falsification. Strether's is a deeply split and deeply inhibited personality. He is always so concerned about what Woollett (a kind of shorthand for the puritan mind in general) is likely to think on any particular topic that he is unable to respond without anxiety to the experiences of the moment. As he confesses to Miss Gostrey, 'I'm always considering something else; something else, I mean, than the thing of the moment. The obsession of the other thing is the terror. I'm considering at present for instance something else than *you*' (p. 26) – that something being his *alter ego*, Mrs Newsome. Strether has actually surrendered all power to think and feel for himself; indeed any attempt on his part to do so would seem outrageous and excessive. For, though dear old Woollett is certainly excessive in the extent and power of its anathemas, it is nevertheless defined through its ability to find almost anything excessive. Even the slightest infraction of the code invokes the crackle of eternal bonfires. Confronted with the 'vast bright Babylon' of Paris as 'some huge iridescent object, a jewel brilliant and hard', Strether reflects, 'It all depended of course – which was a gleam of light – on how the "too much" was measured. . . . Was it possible to like Paris enough without liking it too much?' (pp. 64–5); but even this formulation indicates some faint stirrings of resistance, for in Woollett Paris is 'too much' by definition. To attempt to exclude the excessive is to lose touch with everything that Woollett represents.

In the first half of *The Ambassadors* Strether begins to relax and unwind amid the casual and essentially genial surroundings of Paris. He is still acutely conscious of the multiple interdictions and moral reservations that Woollett would be disposed to make, but at this distance, for him if not for his fellow exile Waymarsh, the letter of the law no longer seems quite so important. Strether is certainly willing to be strict and censorious when the occasion suits, but for the moment he is prepared to suspend judgement, not because he doubts that judgement is needed or because he is already beginning to waver, but because, like any good puritan, he would like it to be final and conclusive. Yet at the same time he finds this alien world strangely alluring, as when he takes to 'sudden flights of fancy in Louvre galleries, hungry gazes through clear plates behind which lemon-coloured volumes were as fresh as fruit on the tree' (p. 63).

Pleasure is suddenly tantalising close in a way that it never was in Woollett, and Strether finds himself like a man stiffly rising after a long period on his knees, as he feels the warmth and pulse of circulation returning. Little details of existence begin to impinge on his consciousness that would formerly have slipped past almost without his noticing them, from the bare-headed girls in the street, carrying their oblong boxes by a buckled strap, to the texture of his napkin and the crispness of a baguette. He suddenly seems to have all the time in the world to observe and savour such things. Yet even here he is conscious of danger: from his first walks, which appear in the guise of 'a finely lurid intimation of what one might find at the end of the process' (p. 37), to his almost flagrant confession of corruption to Madame de Vionnet – a significant choice of confessor in itself – when he admits to buying a complete set of the works of Victor Hugo, bound in red and gold. Strether feels bound to admit to 'the exorbitance of his purchase, the seventy blazing volumes that were so out of proportion'; and when Madame de Vionnet queries, 'Out of proportion to what?', he responds 'Well, to any other plunge' (p. 174). James comments, 'Yet he felt as he spoke how at that instant he was plunging' (ibid.).

Strether, having dipped his toe in the water, suddenly finds the water coming up to his neck, not so much because of anything that he has actually done as because he is now conscious of himself as a oddly unpredictable element in the proceedings. Even with this slight relaxation of his self-discipline he has the feeling that things are slipping out of his control. He is a man applying the brake and the accelerator at one and the same time. At some point along the way Strether will have burned his bridges once and for all, but his predicament is that he now has no way of quite knowing when he has passed beyond the pale, since the internal moral clock that should advise him is becoming increasingly wilful and erratic. If there is any one such moment it is probably in this very scene as he sits at his ease opposite Madame de Vionnet over an *omelette aux tomates*, for in Woollett's eyes his proposal to have breakfast with such a fatally compromised woman compromises him even more and compounds his already serious delay. From being in mortal jeopardy of damnation Strether is now in the jaws of hell itself. He has insensibly crossed over clearly marked boundaries, and precisely what will condemn him in Woollett is that they have become so blurred and faded in his own mind as almost to cease to exist. There is hope for the sinner who will repent and acknowledge his own sin, but Strether has actually begun to question the categories. He is nevertheless acutely conscious of impending disaster. He has the sense that things are running away from him and looming up is 'the smash in which a regular runaway probably ends' (p. 177). Yet, despite his anxiety, the iron has entered into Strether's soul – in James's reiterated metaphor, 'It *was* clearly better to suffer as a sheep than as a lamb. One might as well perish by the sword as by famine' (ibid.).

Since virtually anything that Strether does will be interpreted as straying from the path of righteousness as laid down in Woollett, we have this sense that Strether was actually doomed from the very outset, from the moment, after disembarking in Liverpool, when he sat opposite Miss Gostrey in her low-cut evening dress. It is Strether's fate to be excessive through possessing a small chink in his armour-plated puritan conscience through which the external world can reach him. He must play his part out to the bitter end – not an easy thing for a middle-aged man to do when that means cutting himself off from everything to which he once belonged. Too late in the day Strether realises the importance of living to the limit. In thus advising Little Bilham, he employs a suitably flamboyant figure:

> The affair – I mean the affair of life – couldn't, no doubt, have been different for me; for it's at the best a tin mould, either fluted and embossed, with ornamental excrescences, or else smooth and dreadfully plain, into which, a helpless jelly, one's consciousness is poured – so that one 'takes' the form, as the great cook says, and is more or less compactly held by it; one lives in fine as one can. (p. 132)

Here James comes closer than he had ever done to acknowledging the formative powers of culture – we have only to compare this with the discussion between Isabel and Madame Merle to be conscious of the altered emphasis. The characteristic New England upbringing is seen by James as peculiarly disabling precisely because it can make no allowance for pleasure, which is seen not only as immoral, but as introducing unnecessary complications into an otherwise simple and orderly puritan scheme of things. The rigour of Woollett is such that almost anything can be 'harmful', yet the harmfulness of that system is something that can never be spoken. Pleasure is the rococo, always and everywhere over the top.

Although *The Ambassadors* in its odd, oblique way is as much a breviary of modern hedonism as any product of the French symbolist movement or the lemon-coloured volumes that Strether gazed at, this is not itself to be conceived of in those puritan terms, but rather to put them in question. James was acutely conscious of the possibilities for cliché in the theme of an American in Paris, but he took that risk because he wished to refocus the terms of the opposition. Jim Pocock, Waymarsh and Sarah are all, in their different ways, prepared to take advantage of the possibilities for enjoyment that Paris offers, but they do so in bad faith and in the spirit of holiday. They will flirt with the forbidden and obtain pleasure from their acute sense of being, for the moment, positively wicked, but in a spirit that can never question the assumption that what they are doing is thoroughly immoral. Far from unsettling their ideas, the visit to Paris positively reinforces them. They will sin in order to be guilty. They will return to Woollett and Melrose even more convinced of the righteousness of their familiar ways and of the corruptness of alien manners. They are not prepared to change, revise or even slightly modify the attitudes of a lifetime. If they cannot admit that Chad could have in any way been 'improved' by his relationship with Madame de Vionnet, an attractive married woman considerably older than himself, this is for a whole ensemble of complexly interwoven reasons. Chad's 'improvement' is of a sort that Woollett lacks the terms to recognise, but it is unthinkable that such an improper relationship could improve anyway. It calls for the abandonment of moral stereotypes that form the basis of confident and unreflecting action, the opening-up of the nightmare of interpretation, the jettisoning of the compass into dark and menacing waters, the attempt to sail by instinct and dead-reckoning and a postive willingness to listen to siren voices. No wonder Woollett is worried!

On his European journey Strether discovers both the pleasures and the risks of interpretation. In the United States, without being aware of it, his whole relationship to the world was shortcircuited and aborted because he had never been allowed to be spontaneous. Strether has never speculated, never mused or wondered. He has never been at a loss. He has never doubted or been surprised. So what comes upon Strether, with the violent force of a revelation, is that even the tiniest fragment of consciousness, the smallest observation, the most minuscule inference, is positively saturated with the spirit of freedom. Through the act of interpretation we begin to discover ourselves as well as others. So Strether, in pondering the case of Chad, finds his own long-buried sense of self slowly but irresistibly resurfacing. He feels, with an acuteness bordering upon exhilaration, that at bottom he is not simply an ambassador but an independent person, whose thoughts and feelings really do count – if not in Woollett, Massachusetts. He realises that Mrs Newsome's behaviour towards him has been not merely patronising, but deeply insulting, since implicit in it all has been a refusal to acknowledge him as a person. She has simply allotted him the role of acting for her at a distance. The despatching of the Pococks and the cessation of her correspondence are potent indications that Strether has failed in his mission; but Strether now sees that he has simply been used and discarded, that he himself never mattered for a moment. With immense courage for such a habitual, timorous person, Strether grasps the fact that freedom is an all-or-nothing matter. Either he is to construct his own interpretation of events and rely on his own judgement, or else he must collapse back into the abject role of ambassador. In deciding to be free Strether has everything to lose, and, on the face of it, precious little to gain, since he thereby cuts himself off both from his own past and from the financial and moral security that Woollett so equivocally represents. In Strether's desperate gamble all he can achieve is the right to make a fool of himself: which is, of course, precisely what happens when, by the river at the Cheval Blanc, he discovers that Chad's relationship with Madame de Vionnet is not as innocent as he had imagined, but rather morally compromising in just the way Woollett had envisaged from the outset. Such are the risks of interpretation.

For James interpretation is necessarily excessive. It necessitates the admission of a multiplicity of possibilities that are not merely fascinating in themselves but create freedom through the very gesture of hypothesising. In the interpretative Sublime there can be no law or limit. A plethora of alternatives is inescapable. In the enraptured distinction that James makes between Strether and Little Bilham in the second part of the novel, he seeks to celebrate the glory and the excess of the freely interpretating consciousness:

> Little Bilham, taking his course back to the music, only shook his good-natured ears an instant, in the manner of a terrier who has got wet; while Strether relapsed into the sense – which had for him in these days most of comfort – that he was free to believe in anything that from hour to hour kept him going. He had positively motions and flutters of this conscious hour-to-hour kind, temporary surrenders to irony, to fancy, frequent instinctive snatches at the growing rose of observation, constantly stronger for him, as he felt, in scent and colour, and in which he could bury his nose even to wantonness.
>
> (pp. 261–2)

Strether's very being is now grounded in the imagination. James surely intends him as an unexpected and involuntary poet, who through the most unforeseen circumstances is forced to break with the complacency and materialism of American life in a belated, but not vain, attempt to find his own identity.

Just as in *What Maisie Knew* James ironically contrasted the limitations of the schematicised knowledge offered at the lectures Maisie attends – 'where the fountain of knowledge, in the form usually of a high voice that she took at first to be angry, plashed in the stillness of the rows of faces thrust out like empty jugs' (p. 164) – with the interpretative oceans to be traversed by Maisie herself, simply in the course of growing up, so in *The Ambassadors* he stresses the alteration in Strether that comes from not being solely dependent on Mrs Newsome for his perceptions of the world: 'the time seemed already far off when he had held out his small thirsty cup to the spout of her pail was scarce touched now and other fountains had flowed for him; she fell into her place as but one of his tributaries' (p. 196). Strether comes to take his place in a gallery of American hermeneutic heroes, alongside Pierre and Huck Finn, who recklessly hurl themselves into the abyss of interpretation, no matter what the consequences may be for themselves or for others, convinced that those who rest on the surface of appearances have never lived. Not for nothing, not altogether ironically, is Strether named after Balzac's questing, visionary hero Louis Lambert. His 'belated, uncanny clutches at the unusual, the ideal' (p. 232) are not the aberrant symptoms of a mid-life crisis, but signs of personal authenticity. Strether has every opportunity to disclaim them, and such disclaimers would have the force of redeeming him in the eyes of Woollett, but he deliberately chooses not to do so. His experience will only have meant something, will have an incontestable force, if he pays a price for it. Hence what he calls 'my fantastic need of making my dose stiff' (p. 259). Strether seeks to empty himself of worldliness in order to re-experience his own plenitude of being the more intensely. *That* is reward enough.

I have discussed *The Ambassadors* out of chronological sequence because it seems the natural successor to *What Maisie Knew* in its concern with interpretative freedom and because it is relatively optimistic. Although the world of *The Ambassadors* does have its shadows, it nevertheless seems positively tranquil when compared with the sense of menace and oppression that hovers over *The Wings of the Dove* (1902) and *The Golden Bowl* (1904). In these novels the very idea of freedom, though no less central to James's concerns as a writer, begins to appear distinctly paradoxical. His characters now seem fated from the outset. They struggle desperately in webs of their own fabrication, and the challenge they face is no longer that of whatever it is that they should or should not do, as with Isabel Archer, but rather how they can conceivably hope to undo whatever it is that has wittingly or unwittingly already been done. James no longer poses the problem of freedom in the abstract. Freedom is whatever can be salvaged from the wreckage. At the same time it has become a zero-sum concept – more for one person means less for somebody else. As James put it later, in the Preface to *What Maisie Knew*,

> No themes are so human as those which reflect for us, out of the confusion of life, the close connexion of bliss and bale, of the things that help with the things that hurt, so dangling before us for ever that hard bright metal, of so strange an alloy, one face of which is somebody's right and ease and the other somebody's pain and wrong.   (*Art of the Novel*, p. 143)

Freedom itself has become excessive. In *The Wings of the Dove* Milly Theale, the fabulously wealthy American heiress, often seems less like a dove than a gigantic roc, who possesses the terrifying power to transport those she encounters into new and immensely forbidding moral regions. With Milly any sense of the normal is suspended.

The Wings of the Dove was, of course, James's final act of homage to his cousin Minnie Temple, in which her early death from tuberculosis became an integral part of a large and more complex theme. Yet, with the passage of time, James's whole perception of her as typifying the American heroine had subtly, but significantly, changed. Just as in Borges's story 'Pierre Menard' the narrative of *Don Quixote* is altered by the very attempt to repeat it verbatim several hundred years later, so for James, a mere twenty years later, the significance of the American heroine as symbolising a sense of boundless possibility, the Emersonian refusal of limits, is no longer as unequivocal as it might once have seemed – or, rather, the possibility of such hopeful repetition has itself faded since *The Portrait of a Lady*. The once clear and untroubled surface of the Transcendental lake has been thrown into turbulence by the Civil War – still worse, it is no longer the sublime object it once seemed, but begins more and more to look like a village duck pond! That distinctive American idealism that projected before it a luminous and always more beautiful future becomes itself subject to historical closure. So it is in a spirit of melancholy that James returns to his theme. The problem in his mind is now whether it is still possible to think of America as representing a peculiar moral force, or whether, alarmingly, it is simply a force, whose significance is economically condensed into the dollar sign. James's more complex awareness of the polycentricity of the world of human action itself made such allegorisation more doubtful; for allegory pulls the significance of the action in a certain direction as a master discourse that will suppress all others. So both *The Wings of the Dove* and *The Golden Bowl* are equivocal, partial allegories, where a powerful sense of America's redemptive mission to the world never quite manages to suppress our suspicion that the right of Milly and Maggie is never quite as clear as it seems, and that their triumphant apotheoses may indeed produce someone else's 'pain and wrong'.

The melancholy resonances in *The Wings of the Dove* attain their maximum reverberation in the chilling, decaying, demoralising setting of Venice in winter, where Milly is to die. In James's earlier fiction such an event would take on the character of an oxymoron – so that, when Daisy Miller succumbs to the miasmas of the Colosseum, the event articulates the dissimilarity between the Old World and the New. But here there is a certain aptness, since James now sees that idealism as doomed. If Milly is still a symbol of American hopes, they have become vanishing hopes, and, if Milly is to be 'the princess' (p. 85), 'heiress of all the ages' (p. 79), we nevertheless have the feeling that she has come into her inheritance at the Last Chance saloon. If Milly is to be the light of the world to a hopelessly fallen and spiritually benighted Europe, this is because America's promise to herself to be such an inspiriting beacon cannot be forgotten. And here one cannot avoid thinking of the Statue of Liberty itself, as representing just such a reaffirmation of the meaning of America. Milly says of herself, 'I'm a survivor – a survivor of a general wreck' (p. 149), and, although this literally refers to the fact that she is all that remains of a family of six, including her mother and her father, this self-description has far larger implications. For to James's sense the old New England culture he was brought up in went down in the general wreck of the Civil War quite as much as did the old South. The optimism and hopefulness about human nature that had once prevailed was the war's first casualty. So, to be faithful to America it is necessary to be faithful not only to the America that once was, but to the further vision that it had of what it could one day be. Milly will incarnate this dream in all its purity and its excessiveness, so that it can never be sullied by the hand of time; she is to be 'the final flower, the immense, extravagant, unregulated cluster' (p. 79). Milly's death in Venice is the swansong of young America.

The Wings of the Dove, like *The Golden Bowl*, is inescapably a symbolist artwork; but, uniquely in James's mature fiction, it is the site of style wars. At the beginning of the novel James carefully establishes a Dickensian world of seediness, sordidness and remorseless circumstantial pressure as Kate Croy is ground between the upper and lower millstones of her brutal and overbearing Aunt Maud and her unscrupulous father, Lionel Croy; but this world is then stylistically interrupted and disrupted by the appearance in Europe of Milly Theale. Naturalism, with its elaborate marshalling of the circumstantial, gives way to a symbolic mode in which Milly, who seems to transcend all possible circumstances, is theatrically constituted through a string of hyperbolic figures which nevertheless mark her out as a locus of contradiction, gentle, all-powerful, yet the passive target for a collective violence. Milly's fate, marked by her impossible yet inescapable terminal illness, is to be too good for the world, to be a victim who victimises both herself and others, whose vividness is already under erasure like the Bronzino portrait, 'a face almost livid in hue, yet handsome in sadness', magnificent in 'brocaded and wasted reds' that is 'dead, dead, dead' (p. 137). It is as if London simply actualises and mobilises all the meanings that have been implicit in Milly from the first, as if James turns the cards face upwards at the outset and then insists on playing through the hand to the bitter end.

The symbolist influence in *The Wings of the Dove* derives especially from Maurice Maeterlinck's play *Pelléas et Mélisande*. Maeterlinck's move away from theatrical naturalism towards a highly stylised, almost ritualistic, form is overtly registered in the novel when James describes an encounter between Kate Croy and Milly as follows:

> Certain aspects of the connection of these young women show for us, such is the twilight that gathers about them, in the likeness of some dim scene in a Maeterlinck play; we have positively the image, in the delicate dusk, of the figures so associated yet so opposed, so mutually watchful: that of the angular, pale princess, ostrich-plumed, black robed, hung about with amulets, reminders, relics, mainly seated, mainly still, and that of the upright, restless, slow-circling lady of her court, who exchanges with her, across the black water streaked with evening gleams, fitful questions and answers. The upright lady, with thick, dark braids down her back, drawing over the grass a more embroidered train, makes the whole circuit, and makes it again, and the broken talk, brief and sparingly allusive, seems more to cover than to free their sense. This is because, when it fairly comes to not having others to consider, they meet in an air that appears rather anxiously to wait for their words. Such an impression as that was in fact grave, and might be tragic.... (p. 262)

Maeterlinck's dramas are suffused by an atmosphere of almost inexplicable menace. Silence counts for more than speech. Nothing is ever overtly stated. The feelings of the characters are signalled through symbolic gestures. In *Pelléas* Mélisande's love for Pelléas is suggested when she leans out of a window and her long, blonde hair spills over him; her lack of love for her husband, Golaud, is intimated in the scene when with Pelléas she absent-mindedly toys with her wedding-ring and loses it down a well. Passion and jealousy become the more powerful because they can never be spoken, because the emotional vibrations which feed that passion are never in the public domain. The characters torture themselves and each other as the violence of their feelings batters against the delicacy of their collective predicament. The mutual love of Pelléas and Mélisande is as innocent as it is guilty, guilty as it is innocent, for it is just the fact that their love seems so innocent that strikes Golaud like a savage, unexpected blow. Likewise in *The Wings of the Dove* James sought to show how the love of Kate and Densher, which they keep hidden from Milly so that she will think that Densher is really 'available', is at once tender and cruel. The circling movement that James describes in the above passage becomes a dominant figure in his own late fiction, as the narrative seeks not only to expose the situation from different viewpoints, but to intensify the power of that situation by the very obsessiveness with which it is held in focus. It is through this intense pressure of observation itself that the drama unfolds. The events are structured by the very perspective from which they are viewed. Yet the most crucial moments in the novel – the meeting between Milly and Lord Mark in Venice, her final interview with Densher, the letter she writes to him – remain enigmatic and are not overtly described. The narrative is governed by a perverse law of being always elliptical and oblique. Maeterlinckian twilight is all that our perception can hope to attain. Complete disclosure is never a possibility.

Milly, in her extraordinary combination of innocence, wealth and power, is inescapably excessive. She enters a London society where everyone is already implicated in some complex relationship with every other socially appropriate person and where each person is subtly beholden – as Lord Mark observes, and who better than he to observe it, 'no one ever did anything for nothing' (p. 106). In this world of mutual interdependence Milly is simply a phenomenon. She becomes the centre even when on the periphery. Stirring the stream 'like a leviathan' (p. 81) with her fabulous wealth, she is in a position to be uniquely powerful. Her will is her law: 'Milly's range was thus immense: she had to ask nobody for anything, to refer nothing to any one; her freedom and her fancy were her law; an obsequious world surrounded her, she could sniff up at every step its fumes' (p. 114).

Milly's power is mythical in its absoluteness but it acquires weight and body when contrasted with the plight of Kate Croy and Densher, who know all too well how their sense of possibility is strictly determined by the sum of their fixed assets. In London people are assessed, counted and assayed in the most precise fashion – that is, if they wish to be considered part of polite society. Their very identity, their most secret wishes and desires count for little in a social marketplace where it is their destiny to be commodities that are bought and sold. This they must come to terms with as the absolute law of their existence. Milly makes their situation even more intolerable than it already is, just because she is able 'to enjoy boundless freedom, the freedom of the wind in the desert' (p. 79).

While they are known quantities, pegs to be screwed into holes, Millie 'exceeded, escaped measure' (p. 83). The money is crucial to this but, as always for James, it is more than just money; for the money is the way in which the excessive claims of American freedom can actually be made palpable. That freedom is the ability to negate and live beyond the artificial constraints of society, so that, in theory, it should be possible to live without either using others or being used in turn. The novel hinges on this notional possibility. Yet Milly, in this most extravagant of fairytales, both uses and is used, so that the purity she ideally represents seems increasingly ephemeral – and James himself is aware of this.

The daunting enigma of the novel stems from the fatality that binds the characters together with the labyrinthine loops of a Gordian knot. That Merton Densher should have an affair with Milly in Venice before she finally dies is something that they all desire, from Mrs Lowder to Milly, from Kate to Densher himself. Only Lord Mark is against it, because he wishes to marry Milly himself, for his own selfish reasons. But then they all have their selfish reasons. The paradox that James presents us with is that all the characters are motivated by self-interest, yet at the same time we are asked to make intricate, perhaps impossible, moral distinctions between them. Perhaps James's oddest characterisation of the book occurs in his Preface to the New York Edition, where he presents Milly as a Lorelei, the Rhine maiden who lured people to their death:

> If her impulse to wrest from her shrinking hour still as much of the fruit of life as possible, if this longing can take effect only by the aid of others, their participation (appealed to, entangled and coerced as they find themselves) becomes their drama too – that of their promoting her illusion, under her importunity, for reasons, for interests and advantages, from motives and points of view, of their own. . . . Somehow, too, at such a rate, one would see the persons subject to them drawn in as by some pool of a Lorelei – see them terrified and tempted and charmed; bribed away, it may even be, from more prescribed and natural orbits, inheriting from their connexion with her strange difficulties and still stranger opportunities, confronted with rare questions and called upon for new discriminations.
> (*Art of the Novel*, p. 201)

Such a description mobilises forcefully many of the subterranean implications of the novel and shocks by the way it presents Milly in quite a sinister light. Yet it is undoubtedly the case that Milly is a principle of fate for others, just as they, collectively, are a principle of fate for her. As Densher, obscurely caught in a web of his own making and of other's, reflects, 'Mrs Lowder wanted, by so odd an evolution of her exuberance, exactly what each of the others did; and he was between them all, he was in the midst' (p. 299).

It is now hard to know whether America is the victim of Europe or whether it is not America that leads Europe in chains. The recurrent fear in *The Wings of the Dove* is that the ideal of freedom to which James has been committed is nothing more than a tantalising illusion and that it may simply be a coin that has bondage inscribed on the obverse face; that personal relationships must necessarily be worked out through a whole series of oblique and implicit commitments in the course of which that hypothetical clarity of motivation and freedom of action is somehow, but indisputably, lost. Freedom, it seems, can only exist as a form of collective will (the will that we find once again in the compacts of *The Golden Bowl*) where all must concur in thinking that a relationship between Densher and Milly is a good thing and that somehow thinking it must make it so. Yet the relationship for all concerned is a massive gamble, and the fortuitousness of the possible outcome only muddies the waters still further. For, if they do not know what they are getting into, how can they possibly know what good it will be?

Milly's affair with Densher is simultaneously innocent and corrupt. It is innocent because she clutches so desperately at this last chance for happiness and because Densher has rashly entered into unknown regions, where calculation and measurement have no real purchase. But it is corrupt all the same, because, as Kate says to Densher, 'She never wanted the truth. . . . She wanted you' (p. 361). Perhaps Milly did not know, though she must have had more than an inkling of it. Even if she did not know the details of the secret engagement, this could not have been known by definition and it only becomes germane when we have a clear sense – as we do not – of just who is taking advantage. Happiness has become the cover for a variety of amoralities. The proprieties scarcely seem to matter, only the good faith of the participants, but they have constructed a context in which good faith is scarcely a meaningful concept – it is certainly a perspectival one. Densher in his visits to Milly's disintegrating Venetian palace is made uncomfortably aware of Eugenio as his double, as he becomes more and more of a gigolo, and that Lord Mark on his mercenary, unscrupulous errands is his *Doppelgänger* also. Yet Densher needs to salvage his pride, to believe that, despite appearances, despite his sense of being 'perpetually bent' (p. 281) to Kate Croy's will, despite being manipulated at a distance (like Lambert Strether), he nevertheless retains the freedom to think and feel. He will have to betray someone even as he tries to betray no one.

When Densher finally acknowledges, after Milly's death, that he had come truly to love her, and when he simultaneously renounces the vast fortune she has left him as a sign of good faith, it seems that he has, at a stroke, broken the chains of self-interest and circumstance, and is for once able to act in a way that is truly free. Perhaps it is just this opportunity that Milly has given him. Yet only Densher can do this. He seems unfairly privileged, as does Milly, since he was after all a willing partner in Kate's scheme, and the offer he now makes Kate, though noble from his point of view, is from hers positively insulting. Kate has had to trust Densher over long, anxious months in giving him the total commitment he asked of her; yet now he feels free to treat her with contempt, to ask that she give up the money as proof of her sincerity while simultaneously asking her to accept that he is in love with the memory of a dead woman. Densher's demands are excessive. Judgement can certainly be passed on Kate, and many a reader will feel this a fine come-uppance, but the fact remains that Densher himself has dirty hands, perhaps the dirtiest of all. The ambiguity of Densher's remark, 'We shall never again be as we were' (p. 403), is that it invokes their once natural and spontaneous relationship before Milly came along, but was it Milly who destroyed it or they? The notion of Densher's redemption by Milly is more equivocal than it seems because it only leaves behind it an awful spiritual vacancy. Even as James asks us to applaud Densher's action, he seems to acknowledge that it is intolerable – as if the whole guilt of moral confusion can be swept away by a single stern puritan gesture, by yet one more radical simplification.

In *The Wings of the Dove* James was conscious of an asymmetry between the characters, but he nevertheless could not help keeping his finger pressed down on Milly's side of the scale. There is a distinct unfairness in *The Golden Bowl*, but on this occasion James is much more forthcoming about it. Once more James takes his characters into an unknown region, where they seek desperately to get their bearings although the terrain has no landmarks and the compass is frantically spinning. *The Golden Bowl* is the strange, seemingly inevitable, yet almost ironic, culmination of the grand Transcendental refusal to acknowledge limits to human conduct, but the Americans who take the stage here are hardly such as might have stopped insouciantly out of the pages of Whitman's 'A Song of Myself'. The redefinition of the United States in the post-Civil War era in terms of industrial power and technological progress coincides with a loss of certainty about what the American, this new man, can be taken to represent. In *The Golden Bowl* the American pretension to redeem Europe is as equivocal as it has ever been: the alarming prospect that opens up is of an America that is not so much a moral force as a force – perhaps even claiming, as force, a self-validating moral authority. By the opening of the twentieth century, American *ressentiment* and feelings of inferiority *vis-à-vis* Europe are beginning to seem slightly absurd, and it is scarcely possible to continue to view the United States as an innocent abroad in the world of international politics. For the United States is now an imperialist power, with an ever increasing 'presence' in the Caribbean, the Pacific and South America. American identity was itself predicated on an eternal opposition between Europe and America, and on a mythic distinction between nature and culture, that was becoming harder and harder to sustain. The contradictions in *The Golden Bowl* are located not so much in the international theme as in the image of America itself. James cannot evade the recognition that what the United States represents is as deeply flawed and fissured as the golden bowl itself.

In *The Golden Bowl* James not only presents the situation in which the various actors are involved from their multiple perspectives, but he draws radical conclusions from it. For he compels us to recognise that what is at stake is not simply subjective perception but moral judgement as well. With these shifts of point of view we have an altered perception of what is at stake, of the nature of the characters' motives, and we are led to modify our view of the characters themselves. The diachronic progression of the novel is simultaneously circling and unfolding, yet it cannot really be both at once, since the former resists closure as much as the latter seeks to impose it. The difficulty is that, if morality looks differently *here* from *there*, then it becomes rather hard to decide what morality itself could be: the whole Kantian system by which we predicate that to be moral our actions must be universalisable is thrown into confusion. Of course, we know in practice that people do have different standards of moral behaviour, which are not just a matter of higher or lower, and that they might also be disposed to reinterpret their principles to coincide with their sense of what would be most fitting in a particular context. They might believe that it was hypothetically right to do *x*, but nevertheless feel that that would be wrong if it involved breaking the law. Nevertheless we have the feeling that we cannot abrogate the demand that principles be universalisable and morally binding, for it would then seem that they were no longer truly moral principles. In *The Golden Bowl* James implies that, where personal relationships are concerned, our notion of how things should turn out will always and necessarily be egocentric. In some sense the world already acknowledges this by granting that there is a *de facto* legitimacy to going off with one's best friend's partner, and that the ensuing sense of betrayal is simply something that all the participants will have to live with. Where James goes further is to suggest that love is always unruly, always spilling over boundaries, and that it can never be reconciled with anything else, even personal freedom. Love is never reasonable, never fair, never tolerant, never moral. Love is always excessive. In the saturnalia of the spirit you always get more – and less – than you bargained for.

The Golden Bowl is an essay in rewriting, on the one hand of *The Wings of the Dove*, on the other of Hawthorne's *The Marble Faun*. It is as if the challenge which Hawthorne threw down, that of re-examining our notions of good and evil, for so long ignored, is finally taken up by James nearly half a century later. Of such oblique, belated and elusive dialogues is American cultural history made. Both novels are meditations on themes of sin, guilt and possible redemption; both, in their own fashion, play with 'forbidden' and heretical ideas. Like Donatello in *The Marble Faun*, Amerigo is an Italian nobleman of fabulous pedigree, a figure essentially virtuous and innocent, but one who, through the love of a woman, is drawn into unforeseen complexities to become the sharer in an unspeakable, secret guilt. In both novels a relatively sinful pair – Miriam–Donatello, Charlotte–Amerigo – is contrasted with a relatively virtuous pair: Hilda–Kenyon,

Maggie–Adam Verver. Just as Hilda seems almost unnaturally virtuous, to the point where it seems that she cannot even be exposed to the idea of evil, so Fanny Assingham says of Maggie, 'She wasn't born to know evil. She must never know it' (*The Golden Bowl*, p. 59).

Yet, like Hawthorne, James indicates that the consciousness of sin may have a positive value, since it can lead to a greater recognition of human complexity and thus become an instrument of intellectual and moral growth. In so far as we are able to view the ending of *The Golden Bowl* as positive and affirmatory (a very big 'if' indeed), with Amerigo restored to Maggie and apparently now totally dedicated to her, this figures as a reworking of *The Marble Faun*. The Hawthorne argument appears in the lengthy discussion that takes place between Fanny Assingham and her husband at the end of book I of *The Golden Bowl*. Fanny argues that, in the long run, the affair between Amerigo and Charlotte will have productive consequences for Maggie: 'The way it comes to me is that she *will* live. The way it comes to me is that she'll triumph' (p. 281).

Maggie's life has hitherto been too easy. Nothing has ever really happened to her. She has never ever had to struggle. At bottom she has never had a fulfilling and complete relationship with Amerigo, since they are still separated both by her close ties with her father and by the invisible barrier of the former attachment between Amerigo and Charlotte, of which Maggie at this point knows nothing. So, when Colonel Assingham talks of Maggie getting her husband back, Fanny says,

> 'It isn't a question of recovery. It won't be a question of any vulgar struggle. To "get him back" she must have lost him, and to have lost him she must have had him.' With which Fanny shook her head. 'What I take her to be waking up to is the truth that, all the while, she really hasn't had him. Never.' (Ibid.)

Just as Hilda is brought to a consciousness of evil by involuntarily witnessing Donatello's murder of the mysterious stranger, so too with Maggie. Fanny says that her 'sense will have to open':

> 'To what's called Evil – with a very big E: for the first time in her life. To the discovery of it, to the knowledge of it, to the crude

experience of it.' And she gave, for the possibility, the largest measure. 'To the harsh, bewildering brush, the daily chilling breath of it.' (p. 282)

The discoveries, by their very shock value, will have a salutary, energising effect upon her: 'They'll have to be disagreeable to make her sit up. They'll have to be disagreeable to make her decide to live' (p. 283). On this reading of the novel its conclusion is triumphant: Maggie and Amerigo truly possess one another for the very first time, transcending simultaneously their innocence as much as their guilt. They now love without obstacle or barrier.

However, what makes Maggie's restorative action problematic is that the relationships established at the outset of the novel were inherently false, and that the bowl does not so much symbolise an ideal of perfect love between all four characters, Maggie, Adam, Charlotte and Amerigo, that Charlotte and Amerigo were incapable of living up to, as suggest that the idea of itself was cracked and flawed from the start. What makes the harmony improbable is that it must embrace so many asymmetries. Since Maggie loves her father deeply and wishes to spend as much time as possible with him, it is convenient for her that he should match and complement her marriage to Amerigo by a similar arrangement with Charlotte. In this way he both absolves her of guilt and creates a situation where the separation will be less acute. Maggie and her father believe in the marriage with Charlotte for what they take to be altruistic reasons, but this 'altruism' hardly benefits Charlote and Amerigo, who, in their different ways, become the victims of the Ververs' convenience. James sets things up in such a way as to suggest that there never *can* be a harmony of interests; that such 'harmony' would always be for some and against others, that someone will necessarily be shortchanged in the arrangement. The second asymmetry is between Maggie and Adam on the one hand, and Charlotte and Amerigo on the other. Amerigo and Charlotte are so beholden to the Ververs for their financial rescue that they forfeit their independence by the very fact of their marriage in a way that the Ververs do not. The fabulous wealth of the Ververs gives them a very definite edge. In trading their pedigree and social skills for financial security, Amerigo and Charlotte become simply possessions, which is part of the bargain. For them life comes to a stop. The one thing that they must never do is disrupt the harmony. In *The Golden Bowl* James subtly reworks the myth of the Fall and suggests that in Paradise life would have been intolerable precisely because of the way in which it was hedged around with prohibitions. The Garden of Eden can never be truly a paradise because it is a paradise on God's terms not man's; the restriction he places on man negate the dream of freedom and gratification that Paradise should imply. Order and freedom can only be reconciled with deceitful formulas in which subordination is legitimised. The situation constructed by Maggie and Adam will always be one that benefits them, and Maggie most of all. As Fanny Assingham says, the forms of conduct that are imposed are '*Their* forms' – '"Maggie's and Mr Verver's – those they *impose* on Charlotte and the Prince. Those", she developed, "that, so perversely, as I say, have succeeded in setting themselves up as the right ones"' (p. 287).

The evidence suggests that Amerigo and Charlotte might actually have been prepared to abide by the 'rules' – really nothing more than an informal understanding, by the way, of what the Ververs can expect for their money – and it is only because of the deep collusion between Maggie and her father that they are virtually forced into renewing their former relationship. Yet, because the relationship between Amerigo and Charlotte is asymmetrical with its ostensible counterpart, it follows that any contact between them will necessarily be guilty, furtive and manipulative, while the Ververs will always be clear, open, honest and above-board. The paradoxical way in which James sets up this situation forces us to question the habitual assumptions we might be disposed to make about what is good or bad, natural or unnatural. Why, specifically, should we assume that it is morally wrong for Amerigo and Charlotte to become lovers, yet perfectly in order for Maggie and Adam to neglect their spouses and expect to be able to manipulate them in support of their semi-incestuous relationship? The advantage of the innocence of both Maggie and her father is that it is the mechanism by which they can preserve their 'innocence' – in other words, secure in their own good faith in a way that the Prince and Charlotte can never be, remain blind to the selfish and self-centred dimension to their behaviour. They have erected a myth of harmony and now expect others to live by it, yet the bad faith involved must always be that of others – never their own. Adam Verver's decision to marry Charlotte is excessive because it attempts to schematicise human relationships and subordinate them to a symbolic order. The other three becomes the victims of his transcendental ideas. As Maggie herself comes to recognise, this was the crucial mistake:

> She groaned to herself, while the vain imagination lasted, '*Why* did he marry? ah, why *did* he?' and then it came up to her more than ever that nothing could have been more beautiful than the way in which, till Charlotte came so much more into their life, Amerigo hadn't interfered. What she had gone on owing him for this mounted up again, to her eyes, like a column of figures – or call it even, if one would, a house of cards; it was her father's wonderful act that had tipped the house down and made the sum wrong. (p. 357)

The excessive generates further excesses.

The golden bowl is a hyperbolic figure that sets in motion a chain of anti-figures that undermine it. The Prince's intense consciousness of his own freedom in cancelling the figure by spending time illicitly with Charlotte itself takes the form of an extravagant image 'as perfect and rounded as some lustrous pearl' (p. 263), while the consequence of that affair for Maggie becomes yet another excessive figure – the pagoda that introduces book II. The pagoda figure actualises the nightmare that was always illicit in the bowl itself: that, instead of being a figure that will repress subjectivity, it actually intensifies it, by forcing on the participants an awareness of the actual deformity of the ideal, it represents. Maggie experiences the pagoda as a threatening alien power, precisely because it announces not a simple figure but the possibility of a multiplicity of points of view, and because it is apparently impenetrable, an emblem of the problem of interpretation itself:

> This situation had been occupying for months and months, the very centre of the garden of her life, but it had reared itself there like some strange, tall tower of ivory, or perhaps rather some wonderful, beautiful but outlandish pagoda, coloured and figured and adorned, at the overhanging eaves, with silver bells that tinkled, ever so charmingly, when stirred by chance airs. She walked round and round it – that was what she felt; she had carried on her existence in the space left her for circulation, a space that sometimes seemed ample and sometimes narrow;

looking up, all the while, at the fair structure that spread itself so amply and rose so high, but never quite making out, as yet, where she might have entered had she wished. (p. 299)

Maggie, as innocent, has never had to look beyond the surface, but the existence of hidden flaws in the golden bowl suggests that she will inevitably be forced to do so. Now she is abruptly faced with the enigma and the nightmare of decipherment. What the pagoda signifies is that the relationships between the characters are shaped and constituted by interpretation, so that a recognition of this is like the sudden interposing of a veil, where once was transparency. When James writes, 'The great decorated surface had remained consistently impenetrable and inscrutable' (ibid.), this cannot but evoke the frustrations of Melville's Ahab and his compulsive desire to strike through the mask. The excessiveness of the pagoda is itself the excessiveness of interpretation, its inexorable tendency to proliferate, multiply and to get completely out of all proportion. The pagoda, once acknowledged, becomes awe-inspiring and positively intimidating, because it seems to present a challenge to mastery yet to be always already beyond the possibility of such mastery. For the early American puritans, man's struggle with recalcitrant, impenetrable signs seemed but one of the many disturbing consequences of the Fall – so, here, the pagod signifies above all a disastrous loss of certainty, a world without guarantees. What makes Maggie's disorientation doubly disturbing is that she is unable to put her finger on any one tangible thing that could have given rise to it. The very tranquillity of the situation is menacing – like the pagoda – in that this itself is something that calls for decipherment, so that a starting-point for analysis is endlessly deferred. As Adam Verver says to Maggie, 'Everything is remarkably pleasant isn't it? – but *where*, for it, after all, are we? up in a balloon and whirling through space, or down in the depths of the earth, in the glimmering passages of a goldmine' (p. 351). The intimations of Jules Verne here point to the dizzying dimensions of the problem; for, if they are to get their bearings, just what are they going to take their bearings from?

Book II of *The Golden Bowl* is acted out under the aegis of the sign and bears witness to the power of the sign. It is at once a struggle to interpret and a struggle over *who* is to do that interpreting. For Maggie recognises that, so long as she is the one who is struggling to decipher, she is placed on the defensive. The translucency she faces can never be rendered totally transparent. What the pagoda represents can never be entirely cancelled: '"There are many things", said Mrs Assingham, "that we shall never know." Maggie took it with a long reflection, "Never"' (p. 427). So it is part of Maggie's task to throw the burden of interpretation back onto Amerigo and Charlotte, by symbolically disrupting the tranquillity that ostensibly reigns, and so doing in such a way as to render inscrutable her own perceptions and intentions. Their present sense of mastery is grounded in their confidence both that they best know what the situation is, and that the discrepancy between appearance and what lies behind that appearance is a can of worms that no one can afford to open up. At least one way of looking at *The Golden Bowl* is to see it as a game of trading hermeneutic places, in which Amerigo and Charlotte turn the tables on the Ververs and Maggie turns the tables back again, by placing Amerigo and Charlotte in the paralysing uncertainty of not quite knowing where they stand. As Maggie puts it,

> 'Their least danger, they know, is in going on with all the things that I've seemed to accept and that I've given no indication, at any moment, of not accepting. Everything that has come up for them has come up in an extraordinary manner, without my having by a sound or a sign given myself away – so that it's all wonderful as you may conceive. They move at any rate among the dangers I speak of – between that of their doing too much and that of not having any longer the confidence, or the nerve, or whatever you may call it, to do enough.' Her tone, by this time, might have shown a strangeness to match her smile; which was still more marked as she wound up 'And that's how I make them do what I like!'   (p. 383)

It is an index of Maggie's growing self-confidence that she now feels able to move freely through the forest of signs, which in the pagoda episode she found so demoralising; that she now feels that she has become a 'mistress of shades' (p. 403), Maggie's manipulative art is to make excessive gestures that seem to call for interpretation but which are insufficiently contextualisable to be open to any kind of confident reading. The result for Amerigo and Charlotte is the same semiotic panic that once gripped Maggie. Enlisting the Assinghams into her scheme, she deliberately puzzles Amerigo by the 'extravagance of her affability' to the Assinghams (p. 409). By dressing in an unusually florid manner she at once signals her emotional distress and, at the same time, presents her husband with an enigma as oppressive as ever the pagoda was for her:

> Her maid had already left her, and she presented herself, in the large, clear room, where everything was admirable, but where nothing was out of place, as, for the first time in her life, rather 'bedizened'. Was it that she had put on too many things, overcharged herself with jewels, wore in particular more of them than usual, and bigger ones, in her hair? – a question her visitor presently answered by attributing this appearance largely to the bright red spot, red as some monstrous ruby, that burned in either of her cheeks. These two items of her aspect had, promptly enough, their own light for Mrs Assingham, who made out by it that nothing more pathetic could be imagined than the refuge and disguise her agitation had instinctively asked of the arts of dress, multiplied to extravagance, almost to incoherence.   (pp. 410–11)

In this intricate description James intricately interweaves differential signifying possibilities: on the one hand Maggie is a kind of Ophelia whose emotion is completely legible, but, on the other, the overcharged semiotic statement is always bordering on being unreadable, because it draws so much attention to itself as to make it an event without a specifiable cause.

Of all these disruptive signals, the most crucial is that of the shattering of the golden bowl by Fanny Assingham. The bowl apparently is the key to the signifying-system of the novel, which makes Maggie the more vulnerable because of her ignorance of its existence. So long as she does not know it exists, she cannot know what it means, so that this shared secret between Charlotte and Amerigo is the basis of their interpretative mastery. So by bringing the bowl out into the open Maggie can render visible all that has invisibly been oppressing her. But the bowl never ceases to function as a sign. Fanny Assingham believes that she can destroy the bowl's signifying potential by smashing it: '"Whatever you meant by it – and I don't want to know *now* – has ceased to exist", Mrs Assingham said' (p. 430).

But interpretation goes on, even invading the action that was supposed to cancel it, as Amerigo unexpectedly enters and witnesses her action, thereby altering the meaning of her gesture. It now, more radically, becomes a sign that the mythical harmony between them has been irrevocably shattered, and marks a point from which there can be no turning back. Yet it is not a moment of transparency, for the bowl represents different things to different people and its destruction raises as many questions as it seems to resolve – for Amerigo the question of just how much Maggie knows, for Maggie the question of what Amerigo will understand by it. Everything about this pivotal moment is excessive – especially since Maggie's actual discovery of the bowl flouts all ordinary notions of probability: as Amerigo says, 'I agree with you the coincidence is extraordinary – the sort of thing that happens mainly in novels and plays' (p. 442). James here foregrounds the symbolic and allegorical nature of his narrative yet at the same time renders it problematic, since the symbol is not fixed to whatever the author may have 'meant' by it but becomes a counter in the relationships between the characters. Yet to acknowledge this is also to destroy the connection between the bowl and a trascendent vision of love and harmony, for the bowl thus conceived precludes any relativistic interpretation. The smashing of the bowl thus also signifies the failure of this symbolic mastery. It is relatively itself that splits apart all that the bowl would represent.

This sense of relativity is complexly represented in the card-playing scene at Fawns, perhaps the most virtuoso piece of writing in James's entire literary career. For, although the episode is vividly presented from Maggie's deeply emotional point of view, where her sense of being the betrayed wife is sharply intensified by her indignation that her beloved father is thereby betrayed also, it is nevertheless stereoscopically presented so that we can perceive how it could be constructed from other vantage-points also. Indeed, it is essential that we do so. By being excluded from the game Maggie is actually placed in a position of power, since she is free to disregard the rules that others are bound by. Her absence marks the fact that it is no longer the same game and that for play to continue everything must be mediated through her. The imaginary unity of the group is now exposed as a sham, but it is a sham she can compel the others to give substance to, so long as it is a fiction that they dare not disclaim. Yet to Maggie's eyes they are still seemingly united against her, in a common vision that it is she who has become the problem. So there is a powerful pressure on her to deny her consciousness of a yawning gap between the actual and the ideal:

> It all left her, as she wandered off, with the strangest of impressions – the sense forced upon her as never yet, of an appeal, a positive confidence, from the four pairs of eyes, that was deeper than any negation, and that seemed to speak on the part of each, of some relation to be contrived by her, a relation with herself, which would spare the individual the danger, the actual present strain, of the relation with the others. They thus tacitly put it upon her to be disposed of, the whole complexity of their peril, and she promptly saw why: because she was there, and there just *as* she was, to lift it off them and take it; to charge herself with it as the scapegoat of old, of whom she had once seen a terrible picture, had been charged with the sins of the people and had gone forth into the desert to sink under his burden and die. (p. 469)

As free, Maggie is powerful as Charlotte once was, but her freedom can only be disruptive of the prevailing 'harmony' and have the effect of excluding her from an apparently peaceful scene of sociability and consensus. Freedom is always potentially disruptive, and harmonious appearances may be just the way in which its unpredictable consequences can be controlled. At all events, the situation is one of the most intense psychological pressure on all sides – a game of 'chicken' in which someone will be forced to capitulate. As Maggie sees it, and sees them seeing it, there is a certain inevitability about that person being herself. She has come to figure as the flaw in the bowl that has to be covered and smoothed over. It is her consciousness that is the problem: 'It was only the golden bowl as Maggie herself knew it that had been broken. The breakage stood not for any wrought discomposure among the triumphant three – it stood merely for the dire deformity of her attitude toward them' (p. 473).

Thus, though presenting everything through Maggie's eyes, James brings us strangely to the point of recognising that there can be no truth of the situation, since that truth itself is intersubjectively constructed, so that a collective perception is a truth that truth vainly tries to contradict. The struggle for 'truth' is a struggle for power, which Maggie or Charlotte must win. As Charlotte, disconcerted by Maggie's free-floating position, gets up from the card-table to follow her – 'The splendid shining supple creature was out of the cage, was at large' (ibid.) – the scene becomes a battle as to how the actions of the scene itself are to be interpreted. Charlotte, conscious of Maggie's bid for mastery, endeavours both to impose her own perception on Maggie and to act out a scene from her own script of mutual harmony, so that Maggie will become a character in her play rather than *vice versa*. Meaning changes according to one's point of view:

> They presently went back the way she had come, but she stopped Maggie again within range of the smoking-room window and made her stand where the party at cards would be before her. Side by side, for three minutes, they fixed this picture of quiet harmonies, the positive charm of it and, as might have been said, the full significance – which, as it was now brought home to Maggie, could be no more after all, than a matter of interpretation, differing always for a different interpreter. As she herself had hovered in sight of it a quarter of an hour before, it would have been a thing for her to show Charlotte, to show in righteous irony, in reproach too stern for anything but silence. But now it was she who was being shown it, and shown it by Charlotte, and she saw quickly enough that, as Charlotte showed it, so she must presently seem to take it. (p. 476)

However, these meanings do not peacefully coexist but seek to dominate. What has for Maggie been a scene of horror, of seeing 'evil seated, all at ease' (p. 471), she is now asked, under Charlotte's psychological pressure, to re-view as a 'picture of quiet harmonies' – though the scene is significantly altered by the absence of the scarlet woman, of Charlotte herself. This, quite explicitly, is a temptation scene in which Maggie is invited to acquiesce in something that she knows to be false, in the belief that in this way harmony can be restored. To do otherwise would be to deny the value that the bowl represents. The bowl can be restored by the saving collective myth that it has never been broken. But Charlotte overplays her hand. She first tries to exert from Maggie an admission that she has no complaint against her, thus making Maggie both a liar and an accomplice and placing her in a position of subordination. The tables are seemingly turned once more. But Charlotte's extravagant public gesture of kissing

Maggie as a sign that the compact is sealed backfires. When Maggie does not reciprocate, 'the prodigious kiss' (p. 482) betrays by its very prodigiousness that it is a persuasive rhetorical gesture. The kiss is a self-destructive figure which exposes the crack by the very fact of trying to conceal it.

So, after trailing by many points and after only hanging on by the skin of her teeth, Maggie comes back from the dead to win game, set and match. The scenario has a gratifying symmetry. Maggie has got her husband back. Charlotte, the bad one, the true scapegoat, is punished by being exiled to American City. An impossible dream of love and perfect harmony is supplanted by a genuine, powerful, possessive love that can and must admit to jealousy, because it is the real thing. Maggie's eyes have been opened and she is better and wiser for it. Amerigo is purged of the bad faith that has corrupted his relationship with Maggie from the outset. So, although there is loss on all sides, there is a greater gain. For the love of Amerigo and Maggie can now be a love without constraint or limit, that is continually spilling over. The novel seems positively to incite the reader to be captured and captivated by the power of its rhetoric. At last the long nightmare of interpretation is over. But, while acknowledging the forcefulness with which an exploding relativity is once more brought under the sign of allegory, I nevertheless find it hard to follow other critics in their sense of relief and euphoria – to acquiesce in John Bayley's suggestion that Maggie protects 'their higher selves',[17] or Dorothea Krook's celebration of 'Maggie's triumphant work of redemption',[18] or Naomi Lebowitz's 'expansion of innocence open to life, into wisdom and love'.[19] By the excessiveness of its conclusion *The Golden Bowl* enforces a recognition of the perspective from which it is articulated, and quite crucial to it is the fact that Maggie cannot bring herself to look into her husband's eyes. For to do so would be not merely to see his submission but to reopen the multiplying vantage points that she has been so desperately trying to close down. The dream of the bowl is a dream of immediacy in which there could never be a gap between experience and the perception of it, and where happiness would abolish interpretation since there would be nothing left to interpret. But the reader, while acknowledging the compelling power and beauty of the dream, can no more liquidate the complexities the book has traversed than can the novel itself. We are left contemplating one side of the coin, but we know there is another. The time for unclouded consummations is past.

Notes

CHAPTER 1. INTRODUCTION: AFTER THE CIVIL WAR

1. William Dean Howells, *A Foregone Conclusion* (Edinburgh, 1882) p. 61.
2. Ibid., p. 273.
3. Ibid., p. 294.
4. Ibid., p. 296.
5. Ibid., p. 54.
6. Ibid., p. 313.
7. Octavius Brooks Frothingham, *Transcendentalism in New England* (Philadelphia, 1972) p. 143.
8. Ibid., pp. 182–3.
9. Oliver Wendell Holmes, *Works*, vol. xi (Boston and New York, 1892) *Emerson*, p. 306.
10. Richard Hofstadter, *The American Political Tradition* (London, 1967) p. 92.
11. *Herndon's Life of Lincoln*, ed. P. M. Angle (Cleveland and New York, 1965) pp. 475–6.
12. Ibid., p. 490.
13. Herman Melville, *The Confidence-Man*, ed. H. Cohen (New York, 1964) p. 54.

CHAPTER 2. HERMAN MELVILLE: 'SCAFFOLDINGS SCALING HEAVEN'

Unless otherwise indicated, page references to Melville's works are given in the text. For *Typee*, *Mardi* and *Pierre* the texts cited are those edited by H. Hayford, H. Parker and G. T. Tanselle (Evanston, Ill., 1968, 1970 and 1971, respectively). Other editions cited are as follows: *Piazza Tales*, ed. E. S. Oliver (New York, 1962); *Billy Budd Sailor*, ed. H. Hayford and M. M. Seatts, Jr (Chicago, 1962); *Moby-Dick*, ed. H. Hayford and H. Parker (New York, 1967).

1. *Melville: The Critical Heritage*, ed. W. G. Branch (London, 1974) p. 54.
2. Ibid., pp. 54–5.
3. Ibid., p. 55.
4. Ibid., pp. 64–5.
5. Ibid., pp. 78–9.
6. Ibid., p. 56.

7. Ibid., p. 60.
8. Ibid., p. 82.
9. Ibid., p. 83.
10. Ibid., p. 81.
11. Ibid., p. 77.
12. Herman Melville, *Letters*, ed. M. R. Davis and W. H. Gilman (New Haven, Conn., 1960) p. 26.
13. Samuel Johnson, *The History of Rasselas*, ed. G. Tillotson and B. Jenkins (London, 1971) p. 6.
14. Melville, *Letters*, p. 70.
15. There is also a mocking allusion here to Emerson's 'Nature', ch. 6, where Emerson writes, 'Turn the eyes upside down, by looking at the landscape through your legs, and how agreeable is the picture, though you have seen it any time these twenty years!'
16. Arthur Hobson Quinn, in *Moby-Dick as Doubloon*, ed. H. Parker and H. Hayford (New York, 1970) p. 178.
17. Melville, *Letters*, pp. 91–2.
18. Newton Arvin, *Herman Melville* (New York, 1950) p. 151.
19. Ibid., p. 159.
20. Ibid., p. 157.
21. *Melville: The Critical Heritage*, p. 255.
22. Quinn, *Moby-Dick as Doubloon*, p. 13.
23. Ibid.
24. *Melville: The Critical Heritage*, p. 284.
25. Ibid., p., 286
26. Ibid., p. 288.
27. Ibid., p. 260.
28. Ibid., p. 253.
29. Ibid., p. 265.
30. Ralph Waldo Emerson, *Collected Works*, II, ed. J. Slater, A. R. Ferguson and J. F. Carr (Cambridge, Mass., 1979) p. 182.
31. Ralph Waldo Emerson, *Collected Works*, I, ed. R. E. Spiller and A. R. Ferguson (Cambridge, Mass., 1971) p. 10.
32. Arvin, *Melville*, pp. 192–3.
33. Marius Bewley, *The Eccentric Design* (New York, 1963) pp. 201–5.
34. Spinoza, *Ethics*, tr. A. Boyle (London, 1979) pp. 74–5.
35. Ibid., p. 197.
36. Ibid., p. 176.
37. Edward Bulwer-Lytton, *Ernest Maltravers* (London, 1840) Dedication, p. v.
38. Ibid., p. 31.
39. Ibid.
40. Edward Bulwer-Lytton, *Alice or the Mysteries* (London, 1840) p. 302.
41. Ibid., p. 315.
42. Thomas de Quincey, *Confessions of an English Opium Eater*, ed. A. Hayter (London, 1971) pp. 107–8.
43. Herman Melville, *Israel Potter* (London, 1925) p. 297.
44. Herman Melville, *The Confidence Man*, ed. H. Cohen (New York, 1964) p. 205.

45. Ibid.
46. Emerson, *Works*, I, 207.

CHAPTER 3. MARK TWAIN: THE TORTURE OF EXCESS

Unless otherwise indicated, page references to Twain's works are given in the text. The editions cited are as follows: *Sketches New and Old*, Author's National Edition (New York and London, 1903); *The Innocents Abroad*, Author's National Edition (New York and London, 1911) 2 vols; *Roughing It*, ed. F. R. Rogers and P. Baender (Berkeley, Calif., and London, 1972); *A Connecticut Yankee in King Arthur's Court*, ed. B. L. Stein (Berkeley, Calif., and London, 1979); *Mississippi Writings* (New York, 1982). *Mississippi Writings* includes *Tom Sawyer*, *Huckleberry Finn* and *Life on the Mississippi*.

1. *Mark Twain: The Critical Heritage*, ed. F. Anderson with K. M. Sanderson (London, 1971) p. 26.
2. Ibid.
3. Ibid., p. 21.
4. Ibid., p. 24.
5. Ibid.
6. Ibid., p. 37.
7. Ibid.
8. Ibid., pp. 33–4.
9. Ibid., p. 34.
10. Mark Twain, *The Gilded Age*, ed. H. van Thal (London, 1967) p. 292.
11. *Twain: The Critical Heritage*, p. 51.
12. Ibid., p. 48.
13. See David Morse, *Romanticism: A Structural Analysis* (London, 1982) pp. 166–72.
14. *Twain: The Critical Heritage*, p. 154.
15. Ibid.
16. Ibid., pp. 269–70.
17. Henry Nash Smith, *Mark Twain's Fable of Progress* (New Brunswick, NJ, 1964) p. 39.

CHAPTER 4. HENRY JAMES: REFUSING THE LIMIT

For the more frequently cited of%James's writings, page reference are given in the text. The editions used are as follows: *What Maisie Knew*, New York Edition (London, 1908); *Roderick Hudson*, Intro. L. Edel (New York, 1960); *The Art of the Novel*, ed. R. P. Blackmur (New York, 1962); *The Ambassadors*, ed. S. P. Rosenbaum (New York, 1964); *The Portrait of a Lady*, ed. R. D. Bamberg (New York, 1975); *The American*, ed. J. W. Tuttleton (New York, 1978); *The Wings of the Dove*, ed. J. D. Crowley and R. A. Hocks (New York, 1978); *The Golden Bowl*, ed.

V. Llewellyn Smith (Oxford and New York, 1983); *The Bostonians*, ed. C. R. Anderson (London, 1984).

1. Fyodor Dostoevsky, *The Brothers Karamazov*, tr. D. Magarshack (London, 1982) p. 269.
2. Henry James, *Complete Tales*, IV, ed. L. Edel (New York, 1962) p. 191.
3. Ibid., pp. 197–8.
4. Henry James, *The Future of the Novel*, ed. L. Edel (New York, 1956) p. 14.
5. Ibid.
6. Henry James, *The Princess Casamassima*, New York Edition (London, 1908) II, 217–18.
7. Henry James, *The Tragic Muse*, New York Edition (London, 1908) II, 9.
8. Henry James, *The American Essays*, ed. L. Edel (New York, 1956) pp. 256–7.
9. Henry James, *The Notebooks*, ed. F. O. Matthiessen and K. B. Murdock (New York, 1961) p. 226.
10. Bernard Richards, '*The Ambassadors* and the Sacred Fount: The Artist Manqué', in *The Air of Reality*, ed. J. Goode (London, 1972) p. 220.
11. F. R. Leavis, *The Great Tradition* (New York, 1963) p. 161.
12. See Quentin Anderson, *The American Henry James* (London, 1958) pp. 98–123.
13. James, *The Tragic Muse*, p. 33.
14. Ralph Waldo Emerson, *Collected Works*, II, ed. A. R. Ferguson, J. F. Carr and J. Slater (Cambridge, Mass., 1979) p. 94.
15. Ralph Waldo Emerson, *Essays and Lectures* (New York, 1983) pp. 1123–4.
16. *The Portable Emerson*, ed. C. Bode with M. Cowley (New York, 1981) pp. 255–6.
17. John Bayley, *The Characters of Love* (London, 1960) p. 240.
18. Dorothea Krook, *The Ordeal of Consciousness in Henry James* (Cambridge, 1963) pp. 321–2.
19. Naomi Lebowitz, *The Imagination of Loving* (Detroit, 1965) p. 141.

Index

Adams, Henry, 154
Anderson, Henrik, 121
Anderson, Quentin, 150–1
Arvin, Newton, 37, 49–50
Astor, J. J., 74–5
Austen, Jane, 136

Balzac, Honoré de, 162
Bayle, Pierre, 28
Bewley, Marius, 50–1
Borges, Jorge Luis, 163
Borrow, George, 16
Brady, Matthew, 9
Brown, John, 8, 114
Bulwer-Lytton, Edward, Lord Lytton, 63–4, 66
    Alice, or the Mysteries, 63–4
    Ernest Maltravers, 63–4
    Zanoni, 63
Byron, George Gordon, Lord, 74

Calvin, John, 34
Carlyle, Thomas, 64
    Sartor Resartus, 42
Chace, Owin, 42
Church, Frederick Edwin, 21
Coleridge, Samuel Taylor, 68
Cooper, James Fenimore
    The Monikins, 30
Crèvecoeur, Michel-Guillaume Jean de, 117

Dante Alighieri, 51, 66
De Quincey, Thomas, 66, 68–9
Dostoevsky, Fyodor
    The Brothers Karamazov, 126–7
Duyckinck, Evert, 41–2

Edison, Thomas Alva, 2
Eliot, George, 134
    Daniel Deronda, 134
    Middlemarch, 134
Emersen, Ralph Walde, 7, 12, 48, 72–3, 84, 133, 136, 149–50, 151–2, 155

Fitzgerald, F. Scott
    The Great Gatsby, 10
Franklin, Benjamin, 72–3
Franch, Warren Chester, 9
Frothingham, Octavius Brooks
    Transcendentalism in New England, 6–7

Goethe, Johann Wolfgang von, 63, 136
Gould, Jay, 110

Harte, Bret, 89
Hawthorne, Nathaniel, 134
    The Marble Faun, 172–3
Heller, Joseph
    Catch 22, 10
Herndon, William Henry, 8
Hofstadter, Richard, 7
Holmes, Oliver Wendell, 7
Howard, Leon, 63
Howells, William Dean, 6, 95, 110–11, 142–4
    A Foregone Conclusion. 2–5
    The Story of a Play, 142–3

Jackson, Andrew, 8
James, Henry, 2, 9–10, 115–83
    The Ambassadors, 144, 153, 156–63
    The American, 122–7, 128
    The Awkward Age, 144–6, 148, 153
    The Bostonians, 137–41, 142
    Daisy Miller, 128–9
    The Golden Bowl, 9–10, 163, 164, 169, 170–83
    The Portrait of a Lady, 127–37, 142, 149, 150, 163
    The Princess Casamassima, 141–2
    Roderick Hudson, 115–22, 123, 145
    The Spoils of Poynton, 148–9
    The Tragic Muse, 141–2, 150–1
    The Turn of the Screw, 144
    What Maisie Knew, 143, 144, 152, 163–4
    The Wings of the Dove, 144, 163–70
James, William, Sr, 151

Index

Johnson, Samuel, 12
   Rasselas, 16, 17

Kant, Immanuel, 34, 45, 172
Kerouac, Jack
   On the Road, 10
Krook, Dorothea, 183

Leavis, F. R., 146
Lebowitz, Naomi, 183
Lincoln, Abraham, 7–9

Maeterlinck, Maurice
   Pelléas et Mélisande, 165–7
Melville Herman, 9–10, 11–79
   Bartleby, 73–7
   Billy Budd, 77–9
   The Confidence Man, 9–10, 72–3, 107
   Israel Potter, 72–3
   Mardi, 11, 26–36, 115
   Moby-Dick, 36–63, 177
   Omoo, 25–6, 40, 44
   Pierre, 63–72
   Redburn, 36–7, 42
   Typee, 12–25, 40, 44, 71, 77
   White-Jacket, 36–7, 42, 70
Mencken, H. L., 156
Milton, John, 17, 55
Montaigne, Michel de, 28
Morris, William, 111
Murray, John, 26

Nietzsche, Friedrich, 126

Parker, Hershel, 63
Pater, Walter, 141
Phelps, William Lyon, 112
Plato, 34, 51
Poe, Edgar Allan, 144
Pound, Ezra, 71

Quinn, Arthur Hobson, 28

Rabelais, François, 28

Rousseau, Jean-Jacques, 12

Saint-Gaudens, Augustus, 9
Schiller, Friedrich, 45
Scott, Sir Walter, 99–101
   Waverley, 17, 99
Shakespeare, William, 51
   Hamlet, 66, 149
   King Lear, 55, 149
   The Merchant of Venice, 150
Shaw, Lemuel, 16, 37
Shelley, Percy Bysshe
   'Alaster', 30
   Prometheus Unbound, 45
Smith, Henry Nash, 113
Sophocles, 51
Spinoza, Benedictus de, 34–5, 50–62
Stendhal, 136
Sturges, Jonathan, 143
Swift, Jonathan
   Gulliver's Travels, 30

Taine, Hippolyte, 129
Thoreau, Henry David, 70
Turgenev, Ivan, 136
Twain, Mark, 2, 9–10, 80–114
   'The Celebrated Jumping Frog of Calaveras County', 80–1
   A Connecticut Yankee in King Arthur's Court, 110–14
   The Gilded Age, 90–1
   Huckleberry Finn, 98–110, 111, 113
   The Innocents Abroad, 82–90, 102–3, 112, 123
   Life on the Mississippi, 103–4
   Pudd'nhead Wilson, 107
   Roughin' It, 90–5, 105
   Tom Sawyer, 95–8, 105

Washington, George, 8
Whitman, Walt, 7, 117, 124, 131, 150, 171
William of Ockham, 34